READERS' GUIDES TO ESSENTIAL CRITICISM

CONSULTANT EDITOR: NICOLAS TREDELL

Published

Lucie Armitt   George Eliot: *Adam Bede – The Mill on the Floss – Middlemarch*
Simon Avery   Thomas Hardy: *The Mayor of Casterbridge – Jude the Obscure*
Paul Baines   Daniel Defoe: *Robinson Crusoe – Moll Flanders*
Annika Bautz   Jane Austen: *Sense and Sensibility – Pride and Prejudice – Emma*
Matthew Beedham   The Novels of Kazuo Ishiguro
Richard Beynon   D. H. Lawrence: *The Rainbow – Women in Love*
Peter Boxall   Samuel Beckett: *Waiting for Godot – Endgame*
Claire Brennan   The Poetry of Sylvia Plath
Susan Bruce   Shakespeare: *King Lear*
Sandie Byrne   Jane Austen: *Mansfield Park*
Alison Chapman   Elizabeth Gaskell: *Mary Barton – North and South*
Peter Childs   The Fiction of Ian McEwan
Christine Clegg   Vladimir Nabokov: *Lolita*
John Coyle   James Joyce: *Ulysses – A Portrait of the Artist as a Young Man*
Martin Coyle   Shakespeare: *Richard II*
Justin D. Edwards   Postcolonial Literature
Michael Faherty   The Poetry of W. B. Yeats
Sarah Gamble   The Fiction of Angela Carter
Jodi-Anne George   Beowulf
Jodi-Anne George   Chaucer: *The General Prologue to The Canterbury Tales*
Jane Goldman   Virginia Woolf: *To the Lighthouse – The Waves*
Huw Griffiths   Shakespeare: *Hamlet*
Vanessa Guignery   The Fiction of Julian Barnes
Louisa Hadley   The Fiction of A. S. Byatt
Geoffrey Harvey   Thomas Hardy: *Tess of the d'Urbervilles*
Paul Hendon   The Poetry of W. H. Auden
Terry Hodgson   The Plays of Tom Stoppard for Stage, Radio, TV and Film
William Hughes   Bram Stoker: *Dracula*
Stuart Hutchinson   Mark Twain: *Tom Sawyer-Huckleberry Finn*
Stuart Hutchinson   Edith Wharton: *The House of Mirth – The Custom of the Country*
Betty Jay   E. M. Forster: *A Passage to India*
Aaron Kelly   Twentieth-Century Irish Literature
Elmer Kennedy-   The Poetry of Seamus Heaney
  Andrews
Elmer Kennedy-   Nathaniel Hawthorne: *The Scarlet Letter*
  Andrews
Daniel Lea   George Orwell: *Animal Farm – Nineteen Eighty-Four*
Rachel Lister   Alice Walker: *The Color Purple*
Sara Lodge   Charlotte Brontë: *Jane Eyre*
Philippa Lyon   Twentieth-Century War Poetry
Merja Makinen   The Novels of Jeanette Winterson
Matt McGuire   Contemporary Scottish Literature
Timothy Milnes   Wordsworth: *The Prelude*
Jago Morrison   The Fiction of Chinua Achebe

Carl Plasa	Tony Morrison: *Beloved*
Carl Plasa	Jean Rhys: *Wide Sargasso Sea*
Nicholas Potter	Shakespeare: *Antony and Cleopatra*
Nicholas Potter	Shakespeare: *Othello*
Nicholas Potter	Shakespeare's Late Plays: *Pericles, Cymbeline, The Winter's Tale, The Tempest*
Steven Price	The Plays, Screenplays and Films of David Mamet
Andrew Radford	Victorian Sensation Fiction
Berthold Schoene-Harwood	Mary Shelley: *Frankenstein*
Nick Selby	T. S. Eliot: *The Waste Land*
Nick Selby	Herman Melville: *Moby Dick*
Nick Selby	The Poetry of Walt Whitman
David Smale	Salman Rushdie: *Midnight's Chidren – The Satanic Verses*
Patsy Stoneman	Emily Brontë: *Wuthering Heights*
Susie Thomas	Hanif Kureishi
Nicolas Tredell	F. Scott Fitzgerald: *The Great Gatsby*
Nicolas Tredell	Joseph Conrad: *Heart of Darkness*
Nicolas Tredell	Charles Dickens: *Great Expectations*
Nicolas Tredell	William Faulkner: *The Sound and the Fury – As I Lay Dying*
Nicolas Tredell	Shakespeare: *A Midsummer Night's Dream*
Nicolas Tredell	Shakespeare: *Macbeth*
Nicolas Tredell	The Fiction of Martin Amis
Matthew Woodcock	Shakespeare: *Henry V*
Angela Wright	Gothic Fiction

Forthcoming

Thomas P. Adler	Tennessee Williams: *A Streetcar Named Desire – Cat on a Hot Tin Roof*
Pascale Aebischer	Jacobean Drama
Brian Baker	Science Fiction
Stephen J. Burn	Postmodern American Fiction
Sarah Haggarty & Jon Mee	Willam Blake: *Songs of Innocence and Experience*
Michael Meyer	John Steinbeck: *Of Mice and Men – The Grapes of Wrath*
Michael Whitworth	Virginia Woolf: *Mrs Dalloway*
Gina Wisker	The Fiction of Margaret Atwood
Gillian Woods	Shakespeare: *Romeo and Juliet*

Palgrave Readers' Guides to Essential Criticism
Series Standing Order
ISBN 1–4039–0108–2
(outside North America only)

You can receive future titles in this series as they are published by placing a standing order. Please contact your bookseller or, in the case of difficulty, write to us at the address below with your name and address, the title of the series and the ISBN quoted above.

Customer Services Department, Macmillan Distribution Ltd, Houndmills, Basingstoke, Hampshire RG21 6XS, England

Alice Walker
The Color Purple

RACHEL LISTER

Consultant editor: Nicolas Tredell

palgrave
macmillan

No portion of this publication may be reproduced, copied or transmitted
save with written permission or in accordance with the provisions of the
Copyright, Designs and Patents Act 1988, or under the terms of any licence
permitting limited copying issued by the Copyright Licensing Agency,
Saffron House, 6-10 Kirby Street, London EC1N 8TS.

Any person who does any unauthorized act in relation to this publication
may be liable to criminal prosecution and civil claims for damages.

The author has asserted her right to be identified
as the author of this work in accordance with the Copyright,
Designs and Patents Act 1988.

First published 2010 by
PALGRAVE MACMILLAN

Palgrave Macmillan in the UK is an imprint of Macmillan Publishers Limited,
registered in England, company number 785998, of Houndmills, Basingstoke,
Hampshire RG21 6XS.

Palgrave Macmillan in the US is a division of St Martin's Press LLC,
175 Fifth Avenue, New York, NY 10010.

Palgrave Macmillan is the global academic imprint of the above companies
and has companies and representatives throughout the world.

Palgrave® and Macmillan® are registered trademarks in the United States,
the United Kingdom, Europe and other countries.

ISBN-13: 978–0–230–20185–9 hardback
ISBN-13: 978–0–230–20186–6 paperback

This book is printed on paper suitable for recycling and made from fully
managed and sustained forest sources. Logging, pulping and manufacturing
processes are expected to conform to the environmental regulations of the
country of origin.

A catalogue record for this book is available from the British Library.

A catalog record for this book is available from the Library of Congress.

10   9   8   7   6   5   4   3   2   1
19 18 17 16 15 14 13 12 11 10

Printed in China

Contents

Author's Note   x

Acknowledgements   xi

Introduction: *The Color Purple*   1

The introduction to this Guide offers a summary of Alice Walker's life and her major professional achievements as well as an overview of the Guide's content and lines of enquiry.

CHAPTER ONE   7

The Conception and Reception of *The Color Purple*

The opening chapter of this Guide examines the conception and reception of *The Color Purple* and its adaptations. The first section considers Alice Walker's commentary on the novel's conception, drawing on her essay 'Writing *The Color Purple*' and various interviews. The chapter then examines a range of reviews of the novel. It includes the influential responses of Gloria Steinem and Trudier Harris, both of whom established viewpoints taken up in later readings of the novel. This section places a particular focus on those reviews that engaged the issues that would fuel subsequent debate: the novel's generic identity; its treatment of black masculinity; its representation of Africa; its 'utopian' ending. The section ends by looking at Steven C. Weisenburger's detailed assessment of the novel's reception and canonization. The final sections of the chapter outline responses to Steven Spielberg's controversial cinematic reworking of *The Color Purple* and the musical theatre adaptation of the novel.

CHAPTER TWO   27

Defining *The Color Purple*: The Question of Genre

Chapter Two focuses on the much-contested generic identity of *The Color Purple*. Some critics have chosen to investigate Walker's engagement with the epistolary tradition, while others have considered the novel's credentials as a postmodern slave narrative or folk tale. Some early reviews confidently placed the novel within a particular tradition and critics responded by examining the novel's resistance to generic boundaries. The chapter offers a cross-section of readings by Keith Byerman, Margaret Walsh, bell hooks, Calvin C. Hernton, Linda S. Kauffman and Molly Hite, who opens up a new avenue of exploration in her interpretation of *The Color Purple's* engagement with romance.

CHAPTER THREE 48

Language and Narrative Poetics in *The Color Purple*

Chapter Three focuses on Walker's manipulation of language and narrative poetics in *The Color Purple*. The first section presents readings of the novel's engagement with the politics of orality and literacy. Celie's letters, written in black folk speech, have prompted critics to explore possible tensions between speech and writing in the novel and to debate the level of agency exercised by Celie both as writer and narrator. Readings in this section also consider the impact of the shift to Standard English with the arrival of sister Nettie's letters. This chapter concludes with Henry Louis Gates, Jr.'s, seminal reading of narrative poetics and identity politics in *The Color Purple*, 'Color Me Zora,' which examines the 'doubly voiced discourse' of *The Color Purple* through analysis of Walker's use of free indirect discourse.

CHAPTER FOUR 61

Language and Subjectivity in *The Color Purple*

The readings in Chapter Four focus on the heroine's journey toward autonomy and empowerment. The first section looks at interpretations that chart and explore significant shifts in Celie's apprehension of reality, her environment, her relationships and her body. In 'Lettered Bodies and Corporeal Texts' (1988), Wendy Wall shows us the close relationship between form and theme in *The Color Purple* by exploring how Celie's letters embody the tension between unity and fragmentation that is central to her self-conception. In '"Nothing can be sole or whole that has not been rent": Fragmentation in the Quilt and *The Color Purple*' (1992), Judy Elsley pursues these issues with close analysis of the novel's imagery. The second section deals with innovative psychoanalytical readings by Charles Proudfit and Daniel W. Ross. Although these readings approach Celie's development from different psychoanalytical perspectives, both scrutinize the novel's back story and illuminate its significance to Celie's sense of identity.

CHAPTER FIVE 74

Reading Race in *The Color Purple*

The much-debated racial politics of *The Color Purple* are the focus of Chapter Five. Readers and critics have disagreed widely on the extent to which the novel engages issues of race. Critics such as Melissa Walker have argued that Walker's focus is too narrow: she tells the story of the development of an impoverished black woman, divorcing her from her context and denying her political awareness. Other critics have read the novel as a vivid dramatization of the impact of racist ideology on black communities in America and Africa. This chapter presents readings that explore the novel's representation of race relations through detailed analysis of the novel. Readings in the first section of the chapter scrutinize Walker's approach to race relations in rural Georgia, focusing particularly on the impact of her characters' encounters with racist whites. The content of Nettie's letters is the focus of the second section of the chapter. It looks at critical responses to Walker's representation of African culture and of the impact of Western colonialism. Lauren Berlant's highly influential reading 'Race, Gender, and Nation in *The Color Purple*' (1988) explores the novel's embattled engagement with nationalist discourse and offers a number of ways of reading its much-debated final scene. Linda Selzer's sensitive reading of the novel's various cultural encounters, 'Race and Domesticity in *The Color Purple*' (1995), delivers valuable insight into the relationship between the novel's domestic and political discourses.

CHAPTER SIX 89

Class and Consumerism in *The Color Purple*

Chapter Six explores Walker's treatment of class in *The Color Purple*. It examines opposing understandings of the novel's socio-economic politics and different interpretations of Celie's economic prosperity and entrepreneurial success. While critics such as Cynthia Hamilton and Melissa Walker draw links between the novel's social ideology and 1980s capitalism, others such as Maroula Joannou provide a defence of Celie's business by stressing its relational ethos. The chapter also considers Carl Dix's review of the novel for *The Revolutionary Worker* and Walker's response to his observation that 'the inheritance of private property is not a viable solution in terms of the masses of poor people.' The chapter closes with Peter Kerry Powers's reading '"Pa Is Not Our Pa": Sacred History and Political Imagination in *The Color Purple*' (1995), which explores the relationship between Celie's economic progress and the novel's theological discourse.

CHAPTER SEVEN 104

The Color Purple: Feminist Text?

Chapter Seven addresses issues arising from Walker's self-designated status as a 'womanist' and the novel's current status as feminist Ur-text. The chapter begins by considering readings that explore the appeal of the novel to women from a range of cultural matrices and their embracing of Celie as a feminist heroine. Trudier Harris questions this categorization of Celie, arguing that she is too passive to qualify as a feminist heroine. Gina Michelle Collins's reading of Celie's survival strategies, elaborated in '*The Color Purple*: What Feminism Can Learn from a Southern Tradition' (1990), is at variance with Harris's views. This first section of the chapter concludes with the highly influential reading of Christine Froula, which investigates Walker's engagement with representations of women in Western literature. The second section of this chapter is concerned with Walker's place in the African-American women's literary canon. In particular, it explores Walker's relationship with 'literary foremother' Zora Neale Hurston, considering comparative readings of *The Color Purple* and Hurston's most famous novel, *Their Eyes Were Watching God*. The chapter looks at essays by James C. Hall, Diane F. Sadoff and Molly Hite, who take a close look at the politics of Walker's intertextual relationship with Hurston.

CHAPTER EIGHT 123

Gender and Sexuality in *The Color Purple*

The final chapter of this Guide engages with the wealth of critical interest in the sexual and gender politics of *The Color Purple*. The first section, 'Black Masculinity in *The Color Purple*,' charts opposing responses to Walker's depiction of black men in the novel. Ralph D. Story and George Stade argue that Walker relies upon stereotypes in her representation of male characters, criticize her handling of Albert's 'redemption' and object to the sidelining of male/female relationships in the novel. As well as examining evaluations of her male characters, this section also considers responses to the hostility generated by Walker's gender politics. Anita Jones and King-Kok Cheung counter criticism of Walker by suggesting that she leaves us with a tantalizing glimpse of a world where hegemonic gender and sexual politics have lost their currency. This section closes with a twenty-first century reading that sheds new light on some of these issues, Candice Marie Jenkins's 'Queering Black Patriarchy: The Salvific Wish and Masculine Possibility in Alice Walker's *The Color Purple*' (2002). The second section of this chapter focuses on responses to the novel's sexual politics, with particular emphasis on queer readings. It considers the reaction to Celie and Shug's relationship in early reviews and explores more detailed readings by Linda Abbandonato, bell hooks and Renée C. Hoogland.

Conclusion   141

This book concludes by reflecting on the breadth of academic research on *The Color Purple* while also highlighting those neglected dimensions of the novel which might inspire new readings. The conclusion gives further consideration to the enduring popularity of Celie's story in the twenty-first century, looking at responses to the novel and its adaptations which have been recorded online. It also discusses the long-term impact of the novel on Walker's literary reputation and the reception of her later work.

NOTES   146

SELECT BIBLIOGRAPHY   165

INDEX   173

Author's Note

All page references to *The Color Purple* come from the Women's Press (1983) paperback edition, which will be referred to herein as *CP*. Where possible dates have been provided for all authors and other significant figures and their works when they are first mentioned in the Guide. In some cases dates were unavailable.

Acknowledgements

My thanks go to Nicolas Tredell and Sonya Barker for their careful reading and invaluable guidance. I would also like to thank Felicity Noble and Priya Venkat for their assistance and considerable patience. I am deeply grateful to Pam Knights for her support over the years and to Diana Collecott for introducing me to Alice Walker. I would also like to thank the staff, especially Judith Walton, at Durham University Library. I would not have been able to write this book without their assistance and efficiency. Special thanks go to Brian, Mum, Dad and Sarah for their generous support and encouragement.

Introduction: *The Color Purple*

The Color Purple is Alice Walker's third and most famous novel. It has been hailed as 'an American novel of permanent importance,'[1] a 'significant cultural intervention,'[2] a 'book of the people'[3] and 'the perfect emancipation novel.'[4] First published in America in 1982, the novel immediately attracted critical attention and polarized both reviewers and readers. It would stimulate ongoing political debate and inspire a wealth of critical interpretations. With *The Color Purple,* Alice Walker became the first black woman to receive the Pulitzer Prize and the National Book Award. The reputation of the novel precedes it to such an extent that critics have claimed the right to comment on it at length while admitting in the same breath that they have not read it. David Bradley, an admirer of Walker's early work, reveals that he was so familiar with debates about *The Color Purple* that he resisted it for a time: 'I had read enough about the book to want to avoid it like the plague.'[5]

Set in America's rural South, *The Color Purple* charts the development of heroine-narrator Celie toward spiritual, sexual and emotional fulfilment. When the novel opens, Celie is a young girl, oppressed and abused by the man whom she believes to be her father. She has two children by 'Pa' but they are taken from her as babies. At the age of nineteen, Celie is handed over in marriage to an abusive man initially known to her and the reader only as 'Mr.—.' One day Celie sees her baby girl in town with a lady. She approaches the lady and asks her what the baby is called. The lady tells her that the baby is called Pauline but that she calls her Olivia. Celie had embroidered the name Olivia on her baby's nappy before she had been forced to give her away. The lady with Olivia is married to a reverend. Celie's beloved sister Nettie runs away from home and goes to stay with Celie and Mr.— and when Nettie refuses Mr.—'s advances he tells Celie that her sister will have to leave. Celie gives Nettie the name of the reverend and tells her sister to ask to speak to his wife.

It is through her encounters with women that Celie begins to apprehend the possibility of empowerment and self-fulfilment. She strikes up a friendship with Sofia, the wife of Mr.—'s son Harpo. It is with Mr.—'s lover, the blues singer Shug Avery, that Celie experiences sexual pleasure for the first time.

Composed entirely of letters, *The Color Purple* has been identified as the first African-American epistolary novel.[6] Celie records her experience in letters that are initially addressed to God. One day she and Shug discover that Mr.— has been hiding letters from Nettie since her departure. Twenty-one of the novel's ninety letters are written by Nettie and document her experiences in Africa with missionaries Samuel and Corrine and their adopted children, Olivia and Adam. Nettie's letters also transport Celie and the reader to the past, revealing that the man who raped Celie was in fact their stepfather. Their real father, a successful businessman, had been lynched by racist white men. Nettie eventually discovers that Olivia and Adam are the children whom Celie was forced to give away. Having become reacquainted with Nettie, Celie stops writing to God and addresses her subsequent letters to her sister.

With the support of Shug, Celie breaks free from her marriage. In one of the novel's most celebrated and quoted scenes, she curses Mr.— and asserts her right to freedom and fulfilment. She and Shug move to Memphis where Celie becomes a successful seamstress. She returns to Georgia to attend the funeral of Sofia's mother and finds that 'Pa' has also died and that she has inherited her real father's property and land. In her childhood home she sets up a successful business producing and selling unisex trousers, 'Folkspants, Unlimited,' but is devastated when Shug leaves her for a young man. Nettie writes to tell her that she is returning to America, but Celie receives news that her ship has sunk. Mr.— hands Celie a telegram; as Celie notes, this is the first time that he has done this. The telegram tells her that the ship that Nettie, Samuel, and the children left Africa on has sunk. All of the letters that Celie has written Nettie since her departure return unopened. However, at the end of the novel Nettie returns to Georgia, now married to Samuel. Celie is reunited with her two children. Mr.—, whose name is revealed as Albert, accepts Celie's rejection of heterosexuality and they build a friendship on new terms. Celie's final letter captures the contentment of her community as they participate in their own celebration of American Independence Day. God heads a list of addressees as Celie offers thanks for her friends, prosperity and fulfilment.

Alice Malsenior Walker was born on February 9, 1944, in the rural town of Eatonton, Georgia. Walker kept her maiden name in recognition of her debt to her female ancestors, in particular her great-great-great-grandmother, Mary Poole, who was a slave and who walked from Virginia to Eatonton while carrying two babies. Walker recognizes the influence of her own mother in her storytelling methodology. She writes: 'through years of listening to my mother's stories of her life, I have absorbed not only the stories themselves, but something of the manner in which she spoke, something of the urgency that involves the knowledge that her stories – like her life – must be recorded.'[7]

At the age of 8, Walker was shot and blinded in her right eye by her brother's BB gun. She has identified the accident as a pivotal moment in her life. From this point she assumed the 'solitary, lonely position [...] of an outcast' from which she 'began to really see people and things, to really notice relationships and to learn to be patient enough to care about how they turned out.'[8] She gave expression to this shift in vision by writing poetry. However, the incident also threatened her credentials as a future writer: 'I couldn't look at people directly because I thought I was ugly. Flannery O'Connor [1925–1964] says that a writer has to be able to stare, to see everything that's going on. I never looked up.'[9]

After earning a scholarship, Walker attended Spelman College in Atlanta and went on to study at Sarah Lawrence College, where her poetry teacher, Muriel Rukeyser (1913–80), introduced her work to the poet Langston Hughes (1902–67). Hughes read Walker's short story, 'To Hell with Dying,' and published it in an anthology of black writers. In 1964, she travelled to Africa, an experience that informed her depiction of Nettie's experiences in *The Color Purple*. Upon her return, Walker discovered that she was pregnant and considered committing suicide. She had an abortion and again found refuge in the act of writing. Her first volume of poetry, *Once*, was published in 1965.

During breaks from university, Walker became involved in the civil rights movement. During the sixties she worked for Head Start programs and voter registration drives. The civil rights movement fostered in Walker both '[a] deep cynicism about the possibility of some people to change,' and 'a kind of optimism.'[10] Walker's involvement in the movement also helped her to consolidate her sense of vocation. When asked if it prevented her from writing, she replies that 'the writing had to become the involvement': 'I used to go to demonstrations and always feel that I was not even there, in a way, that I was really just eyes viewing it. I finally realized that it was because I knew that I should be writing and so I did.'[11]

It was in 1970 that Walker experienced her most crucial literary encounter when she discovered the works of Harlem Renaissance writer Zora Neale Hurston (1903–60). Walker is now largely credited with securing Hurston's place in the African-American literary canon. In 1973, Walker travelled to Florida to find Hurston's grave, an experience she recorded in the essay 'Looking for Zora.' Six years later she edited an anthology of Hurston's work, *I Love Myself When I Am Laughing ... and Then Again When I Am Looking Mean and Impressive*. Walker's intertextual dialogue with Hurston forms the basis of several essays featured in this Guide.

Throughout her career Walker has asserted her commitment to representing and 'exploring the oppressions, the insanities, the loyalties, and the triumphs of black women.'[12] Her first novel evolved from memories of her childhood. Although the hero lends his name to its title, *The Third Life of Grange Copeland* (1970) centres on his relationships with women, in particular his granddaughter Ruth. Described by Walker as a 'very realistic novel,' it was her 'one-time shot' at a 'chronological structure.'[13] The novel was generally well received, but some critics raised questions about its treatment of black masculinity: a concern that would resurface continually in readings of Walker's later work and reached fever pitch with the publication of *The Color Purple*.

In *Meridian* (1976), Walker eschews linearity and experiments with a more pliable form: 'I wanted to do something like a crazy quilt, or like *Cane* [(1923), [by Jean Toomer] (1894–1967)] – if you want to be literary – something that works on the mind in different patterns.'[14] *Meridian* explores the experience of a young woman from the South who leaves her husband and child to help her community during the civil rights movement. The novel raises questions about the pull of private and public roles, which has become central to Walker's fiction. The critical response to *Meridian* frustrated Walker. In 1983, she told Claudia Tate (1947–2002) that she had yet to encounter a critic 'who could do it justice' by 'treating it in its entirety.'[15]

The 1970s was a particularly rich period for literature by black American women writers. The decade witnessed the critical and commercial success of Maya Angelou (b. 1928), Toni Morrison (b. 1931), Paule Marshall (b. 1929), Toni Cade Bambara (1939–95) and, of course, Alice Walker. Although known primarily as a novelist, Walker has continued to write short stories and poetry throughout her career. Volumes of poetry include *Revolutionary Petunias* (1973), for which Walker won the Lillian Smith Award and earned a National Book Award nomination. *In Love and Trouble* (1973), a collection of short stories, includes the much-admired and anthologized story 'Everyday Use,' in which Walker employs one of the dominant metaphors of her oeuvre, the quilt, to figure black women's creative energy. Walker was awarded the Rosenthal Award of the National Institute of Arts and Letters for *In Love and Trouble*. A further collection of stories, *You Can't Keep a Good Woman Down*, appeared in 1981.

Following the publication of *The Color Purple*, Walker published a collection of autobiographical and critical essays, *In Search of Our Mothers' Gardens: Womanist Prose* (1984). In the foreword to the collection she draws on the titular metaphor of her most famous work to declare herself a 'womanist,' stating: 'Womanist is to feminist as purple is to lavender.' Walker's womanism has formed the cornerstone of many readings of her novels and it is worth establishing its meaning here. Walker defines a *womanist* as a 'black feminist or feminist of color,' and traces the term back to 'the black folk expression of mothers to female children, "You acting womanish," i.e. like a woman.' The term is '[i]nterchangeable with another black folk expression: "You trying to be grown." Responsible. In charge. *Serious*' (Walker's italics). A woman-ist is someone who 'loves other women, sexually and/or nonsexually. Appreciates and prefers women's culture, women's emotional flexibil-ity (values tears as natural counterbalance of laughter), and women's strength,' but is 'traditionally universalist' and '[c]ommitted to the survival and wholeness of entire people. Male *and* female' (Walker's italics).[16]

Later novels by Walker include *The Temple of My Familiar* (1989), which takes up the story of Tashi, a woman who first appears in Nettie's letters in *The Color Purple*. Female circumcision is the theme of Walker's novel *Possessing the Secret of Joy* (1992) and nonfiction work *Warrior Marks* (1993). In 2001, Walker published a collection of autobiographi-cal stories about love, *The Way Forward Is with a Broken Heart*. In the same year she produced a collection of essays entitled *Sent by Earth: A Message from the Grandmother Spirit After the Bombing of the World Trade Center*. The essays deliver Walker's thoughts on a range of contemporary issues such as the Iraq War, the prevalence of racism and misogyny in America and the effects of the terrorist attacks of September 11, 2001. Walker's latest novel, *Now Is the Time to Open Your Heart* appeared in 2004. Her most recent ventures include a children's book in verse, *There Is a Flower at the Tip of My Nose Smelling Me* (2006) and a collection of essays in prose and verse, *We Are the Ones We Have Been Waiting For* (2006). In 2006, Walker was inducted into the California Hall of Fame. While her work continues to sell, it has not achieved the commercial success or criti-cal acclaim of *The Color Purple*. Some reviews identify didacticism as a recurring characteristic of her work.

Upon reading *The Color Purple*, feminist critic and writer Gloria Steinem (b. 1934) predicted correctly that it would 'be the kind of literary event that transforms a small and intense reputation into a pop-ular one.'[17] The novel spent over twenty-five weeks on the *New York Times* bestsellers list and, in the words of Maria Lauret, 'bec[a]me – with [Toni Morrison's] *Beloved* [1987] – *the* teaching novel of choice in the (still emerging) canon of African-American women's writing' (Lauret's italics).[18] As critic Molly Hite observes, the novel's 'publication [...] transformed Alice Walker from an indubitably serious black writer whose fiction belonged to a tradition of gritty, if occasionally "magical," realism into a popular novelist, with all the perquisites and drawbacks attendant on that position.'[19]

Walker has repeatedly expressed her surprise at the 'astounding' suc-cess of the novel, which sold six million copies worldwide in its first five years.[20] That number doubled over the next decade and it would become '*one of the five most re-read books in America*.'[21] The novel has been reissued twice to mark its tenth and twenty-fifth anniversaries.

Celie's story has become an industry of its own, retaining cross-cultural appeal and taking on new forms, most notably in the controversial film directed by Steven Spielberg (b. 1946), for which Walker served as a consultant, and a musical version adapted for the stage by writer Marsha Norman (b. 1947). The release and reception of Spielberg's cinematic reworking generated a wealth of comparative readings between the novel and the film and prompted many literary critics to return to the novel and assess its place in America's cultural landscape.

This Guide will chart the critical history of *The Color Purple*, stretching from the initial reviews to the latest, twenty-first-century readings. It moves from consideration of the novel's conception and early reception through its formal and linguistic properties to its much-scrutinized identity politics. While the main focus of this Guide is *The Color Purple*, chapters make reference to Walker's social and literary criticism where appropriate, engaging with essays and articles that pertain to the novel's conception, reception and politics. Many critics have drawn on Spielberg's film and its reception to sustain or develop their readings. This Guide engages with interpretations of his cinematic adaptation where fitting.

Celie's story shows no sign of losing its appeal and will undoubtedly continue to delight and antagonize readers in the twenty-first century. This Guide aims to engage with the most innovative critical explorations of *The Color Purple*, thereby illuminating the most productive ways of reading this demanding novel.

CHAPTER ONE

The Conception and Reception of *The Color Purple*

CONCEPTION OF THE NOVEL

In her essay 'Writing *The Color Purple*,' Alice Walker describes the moment when she discovered the key to the new narrative that she was preparing to write:

■ I was hiking through the woods with my sister, Ruth, talking about a lovers' triangle of which we both knew. She said: 'And you know, one day The Wife asked The Other Woman for a pair of her drawers.' Instantly the missing piece of the story I was mentally writing – about two women who felt married to the same man – fell into place. And for months – through illnesses, divorce, several moves, travel abroad, all kinds of heartaches and revelations – I carried my sister's comment delicately balanced in the center of the novel's construction I was building in my head.'[1] □

Walker conceived *The Color Purple* as a historical novel that would engage a 'womanist' vision of history – a history that 'starts not with the taking of lands, or the births, battles, and deaths of Great Men, but with one woman asking another for her underwear.'[2]

In her accounts of how she came to write *The Color Purple*, Walker has cast herself in the role of medium – channelling the characters and their story – rather than all-knowing author. According to Walker, the novel's major characters presented themselves to her and asserted their needs immediately. They 'refused to visit' her while she lived in New York, so Walker moved to a rural California town resembling the characters' home in Georgia. They instructed her to give up all other work in order to write their story. As she prepared to write, she worked on a quilt – her favourite metaphor for her narrative methodology – while the characters became acquainted with one another. In the dedication for the tenth-anniversary edition of the book, Walker again referred to herself as a conduit for the creative, transcendental force embodied by her characters: she thanks '*the Spirit*: Without whose assistance/Neither this book/Nor I/Would have been/Written.' She closes the book by thanking 'everybody in this book for coming' and signs off as 'A.W., author and medium.'[3]

Much of the inspiration for Walker's most celebrated characters sprang from her family history. In a 1986 television documentary for the BBC's *Omnibus* program, Walker explained that it was the experience of her step-grandmother, Rachel, who was 'battered down,' that most informed the conception of Celie. The character of Albert was based on Walker's grandfather. The influence of Walker's aunts asserted itself in the conception of Shug Avery. These were the women who were 'interesting' to Walker as a girl because they represented a different narrative from the one that her mother was locked into.[4]

It was another black American writer, Sojourner Truth (1797–1883), who inspired the use of the epistolary form and the choice of God as the addressee: when Truth 'cried out' having lost her children to slave-owners, 'none but God heard her.' Truth's cry is, for Walker, 'the precursor of a letter to God.' In a conversation with Sharon Wilson and guest readers of *Kalliope* magazine in 1984, Walker stated: 'I can imagine Sojourner Truth saying, "God, what can I do – they've sold my children." Celie is able to write, "Dear God, this has happened to me and I have to tell somebody and so I write to you."'[5]

Since the book's publication, Walker has continued to participate in the critical dialogue surrounding *The Color Purple*, adding and updating her own commentary on the novel through a variety of interviews and essays. New editions of the novel have given her the opportunity to comment on its reception and to reassert her original vision of what has become her most celebrated work. When *The Color Purple* was reissued in a tenth-anniversary edition in 1992, Walker added lyrics from the song *Do Like You* by Stevie Wonder (b. 1950) as an epigraph in order to illuminate the ways in which the characters learn from one another and to signal the pedagogical potential of the novel.

RECEPTION OF THE NOVEL

The Color Purple has provided fertile ground for an array of interpretations, many of which emerged from early reviews of the novel. The following accounts capture the diversity of initial responses, engaging issues that would later become the central focus of more comprehensive critical readings: the generic identity of the novel; its representation of black men; the portrayal of Africa in Nettie's letters; the dramatization of lesbian love; the 'utopian' ending.

Some critics seized immediately upon the potential of *The Color Purple* to transcend cultural barriers. One of the earliest reviews came from feminist, political activist and editor of *Ms.* magazine, Gloria Steinem. Walker was working for *Ms.* when she conceived *The Color Purple*.

It would be difficult to find a more persistently positive review of the book than Steinem's. Walker herself has recognized Steinem as 'a real champion' of the novel.[6] Several critics, however, have taken issue with Steinem's unqualified praise and have used her review as a springboard for their counter-readings. Steinem notes that unlike many 'books about the poor and powerless,' *The Color Purple* 'is not written *about* one group but *for* another, *about* the poor but *for* the middle class' (Steinem's italics). This novel, she writes, 'is populist, in the best sense.' Steinem asserts that readers who recognize themselves in the characters 'will read and enjoy' *The Color Purple*, and she goes so far as to state that 'it's hard to imagine anyone in this country this novel couldn't reach.'[7]

Steinem takes pleasure in the novel's expansiveness *and* its economy, and is one of the very few critics to congratulate Walker on her astute handling of plot, claiming that '[n]o Russian novel could outdo [*The Color Purple*] for complicated family relationships, wide scope, and human coincidence.' However, the novel also offers 'succinct discussions about the existence of God, the politics of religion, and what's going on in the daily news, all of which are pure Alice. (There are also many surprises that, as in life, seem inevitable in retrospect.)' Walker achieves all of this with an 'economy of words that follows Picasso's rule of art. Every line is necessary. Nothing could be deleted without changing everything.'[8]

Steinem's parenthetical reminder that life can dish up surprises seems to pre-empt doubts about the realist credentials of the novel. Writing for the *New York Review of Books*, Robert Towers (1923–95) has difficulty locating *The Color Purple* within the realist tradition, which he presumes was its desired place. He writes: 'Alice Walker still has a lot to learn about plotting and structuring what is clearly intended to be a realistic novel. The revelations involving the fate of Celie's lost babies and the identity of her real father seem crudely contrived – the stuff of melodrama or fairy tales.'[9] (Issues arising from Walker's engagement with various literary traditions and generic conventions are addressed in more detail in Chapter 2 of this Guide.)

For many reviewers, concerns about plot manipulation and generic identity were outweighed by the novel's undeniable linguistic power. Most reviewers recognized *The Color Purple* as a turning point for Walker, seeing in its poetry the fulfilment of potential only hinted at in previous novels. For Steinem, Celie's voice is the 'successful culmination of Alice Walker's longer and longer trips outside the safety of standard English and into the speech of her characters.' Through Celie's use of black folk speech, Walker 'takes the leap completely.'[10] Steinem also alerts reviewers to the political implications of Celie's 'irresistible' unmediated narration:

■ there are no self-conscious apostrophes and contractions to assure us that the writer really knows what the proper spelling or grammar should be, and no quotation marks to keep us at our distance. Celie just puts words down the way they sound and feel. She literally writes her heart out. Pretty soon, the reader can't imagine why anyone would bother to write any other way.[11] □

Writing for *The Nation* in 1982, Dinitia Smith hailed the novel as a 'major advance for Walker's art,' identifying its 'pithy, direct black folk idiom' as its 'greatest strength, reminding us that if Walker is sometimes ideologue, she is also a poet.'[12] Towers also identifies Celie's voice as the novel's greatest strength; he is unable to 'imagine Celie apart from her language,' which evokes 'not only a memorable and infinitely touching character but a whole submerged world.'[13]

It was the introduction of a different voice, that of Celie's sister Nettie, that posed a problem for many reviewers. Steinem is one of the few who praised the shift in narrative perspective and geographical location, which transports the reader to Africa, where Nettie has been recording her experiences with the Olinka tribe and the missionaries Samuel and Corrine. Steinem champions the realism of this account, going so far as to suggest that this 'chapter' deserves a place in 'international economics courses': '[Nettie's] personal, blow-by-blow account of what happens when a British rubber plantation buys the village where she lives as a missionary explains more about the intimate workings of colonialism than many academic tomes have accomplished.'[14]

Most critics, however, took the opposing view. Towers argues that the representation of Africa 'lacks authenticity': this is, he stresses, 'not because Miss Walker is ignorant of Africa [...] but because she has failed to endow Nettie with her own distinctive voice.' He continues: 'the fact that Nettie is better educated than Celie – and a great reader – should not have drained her epistolary style of all personal flavor, leaving her essentially uncharacterized, a mere reporter of events.'[15]

In her review of the novel, Smith sees Nettie's letters as little more than a vehicle for Walker's 'didacticism':[16] 'when Nettie declares that "the world is changing. . . . It is no longer a world just for boys and men" [*CP* 136] [...] we wince at the ponderousness, the obviousness of the message.' However, at times the message of Nettie's letters becomes clouded: Smith notes that the white people who 'disrupt Olinka society also destroy the old (and presumably bad) tribal patriarchy.' Smith wonders: 'Does this mean the white man's coming is a good thing? I doubt it, but I was puzzled.'[17]

Smith praises Walker for her powerful depiction of the damage caused by racism in America through the narrative of Sofia, Celie's step-daughter-in-law. In a much-quoted scene, Sofia is in town with her children when the mayor's wife praises their cleanliness and offers Sofia a job as her maid. When Sofia replies, 'Hell no,' she is slapped by the mayor.[18] Sofia retaliates and is sent to prison. She is released only to be sent to work as a maid at the mayor's house. The mayor's wife allows Sofia to go home to visit her children, whom she has not seen for five years, but decides after fifteen minutes that she can no longer cope without Sofia's full attention and so she ends the visit. 'No writer,' Smith claims, 'has made the intimate hurt of racism more palpable than Walker.'[19]

Tempering this enthusiasm, however, have been concerns about the novel's portrayal of black men and the seemingly implausible transformation of Albert. According to Smith, Walker presents 'relationships between women' as the 'chief agency of redemption in the novel.' Smith detects 'a note of tendentiousness' in Walker's gender politics, however:

■ The men in this book change *only* when their women join together and rebel – and then, the change is so complete as to be unrealistic. It was hard for me to believe that a person as violent, brooding and just plain nasty as Mr. ___ could ever become that sweet, quiet man smoking and chatting on the porch (Smith's italics). □

In a predominantly positive review, Mel Watkins (b. 1940) rates *The Color Purple* higher than Walker's previous works of fiction, praising its lyricism and restraint. In a review for the *New York Times Book Review*, 'Some Letters Went to God' (1982), Watkins identifies gender politics as the novel's central theme and attributes the credibility and emotional power of the novel to the 'authenticity' of Celie's 'folk voice' which 'forces intimate identification with the heroine.'[20] Nettie's voice fades in comparison: 'While Nettie's letters broaden and reinforce the theme of female oppression by describing customs of the Olinka tribe that parallel some found in the American South, they are often mere monologues on African history. Appearing, as they do, after Celie's intensely subjective voice has been established, they seem lackluster and intrusive.'[21]

In a review for the journal *Freedomways*, Maryemma Graham declares *The Color Purple* to be an 'outstanding novel.' Writing one year after the novel's publication, she applauds its flawless synthesis of 'stylistic innovations and an authentic folk voice,' before going on to question its realist credentials.[22] Graham has no difficulty with the novel's structure, which she declares to be 'masterful';[23] for her, the novel's authenticity is compromised instead by its sidelining of historical circumstance and simplification of gender politics. She objects to the way in which the novel's handling of gender politics ignores the interaction of a range of social factors:

■ While there is no denying that male supremacy and sexist oppression pervade our society, an analysis that identifies men as the sole source of female oppression and professes that mere personality change in individuals is the remedy is misguided. Gender oppression cannot be separated from racial and economic oppression that Black people experience, and that Black women face in a very special way.[24] □

Graham feels that Walker missed an opportunity to explore this 'three-way connection,' especially given the context of the novel where 'the conditions of land tenancy made Black women easy targets for triple exploitation.' For Graham, only Sofia's story approached 'this broader view of Black women's oppression.' However, Graham finds Walker's characterization of this 'defiant victim [...] somewhat strange, her radical honesty being viewed as atypical for working class Black women.' Moreover, Graham expresses doubt over the credibility of Celie's sudden change of fortune: 'For the majority of black women, in Celie's time and place as well as today, such a whirlwind shift in fortunes was/is not hardly possible since the causes of their oppression are much more systemic.'[25]

Many early reviews expressed uncertainty regarding the novel's focus. Some reviewers perceived a tension between the novel's exploration of one woman's personal struggle and its engagement of wider political implications. This observation would also be echoed in other detailed critical readings of the novel. Gerald L. Early (b. 1952), in his review-essay '*The Color Purple*: Everybody's Protest Art' (1986), comments on both the novel and its cinematic adaptation. He argues that most of the flaws of both the novel and Spielberg's adaptation stem from their 'alienation from history,' which is betrayed by the utopian ending.[26] He finds 'a great deal of history within the novel itself' through 'references to Harlem, [the blues singer] Bessie Smith (1894–1937), African emigration, [the historian] J. A. Rodgers [*sic*.] (1833–1966), and European imperialism.' Nevertheless, the 'historicity' of *The Color Purple* 'seems false and unconvincing, a kind of obvious scaffolding.'[27] Like Graham, Early feels that Walker does not do enough to dramatize the lasting impact of social change:

■ The bits of history seem undigested and set in the text like lumps. Like the film, Walker's novel, despite its historical references, really wishes to deny history by refusing to show what change and passage of time mean in a society. This is why the social-protest aspects of the novel, some nicely worked up bits of grim naturalism, are inchoate and why the utopian ending must exist. Walker decided that her heroine has no real way to work out her problems within the context of history. And salvation history becomes the utter supersession of oppression-history through the assertion of an unoppressed self. The problem this presents for the reader is that Celie does not find a convincing way to reclaim her humanity and to reassemble the values of her world.[28] □

As *The Color Purple*'s popularity amongst readers became ever more apparent, critics began to place the issues of reception and canonicity at the centre of their readings. There can be little doubt that the enduring popularity of the novel has provoked much of the vitriol that has been directed toward it. In a conversation with Sharon Wilson, Walker expressed her own surprise at the novel's popularity, attributing it to winning the Pulitzer Prize:

■ I think that made a lot of people notice [the novel] who wouldn't have. The media wouldn't have noticed it particularly had it not won the prize, and to tell you the truth, I'm still rather astonished that it did. It's not the kind of book that I would have thought anyone in this country – except a very, very few people – would have given a prize to.[29] □

Trudier Harris addresses the issue of canonization in her provocative review-essay, 'On *The Color Purple*, Stereotypes and Silence' (1984), published two years after the novel's release. One of Walker's harshest critics, Harris launches a protest against the novel's canonization, challenging its elevation to the status of Ur-text for black women. She provides direct responses to some of the claims that Steinem made for the novel in 1982. Like Steinem's rapturous praise, Harris's disparagement has generated many other critical readings of the book.

Individual chapters in this Guide will explore various aspects of Harris's essay, but the following exploration presents her 'basic contentions' with the novel: the depiction of Celie is 'unrealistic for' the novel's context; 'Nettie and the letters from Africa were really extraneous to the central concerns of the novel'; the sexual relationship between Shug and Celie 'represents the height of silly romanticism'; and 'the epistolary form of the novel ultimately makes Celie a much more sophisticated character than we are initially led to believe.'[30] In particular, Harris challenges the representative status that *The Color Purple* has acquired, arguing that this betrays the narrowness of the media's conception of black writers. She attributes the novel's success to fortuitous timing:

■ *The Color Purple* has been canonized. I don't think it should have been. The tale of the novel's popularity is the tale of the media's ability, once again, to dictate the tastes of the reading public, and to attempt to shape what is acceptable creation by black American writers. Sadly, a book that might have been ignored if it had been published ten years earlier or later has now become *the* classic novel by a black woman. That happened in great part because the pendulum determining focus on black writers had swung in their favor again, and Alice Walker had been waiting in the wings of the feminist movement and the power it had generated long enough for her curtain call to come [...] for the media, by its very racist nature, seems to be able to focus on only one black writer at a time. While it is not certain how long Alice Walker will be in the limelight for *The Color Purple*, it is certain that the damaging effects reaped by the excessive media attention given to the novel will plague us as scholars and teachers for many years to come (Harris's italics).[31] □

Harris objects to the way that the novel has been 'touted as a work representative of black communities in this country.' She claims that the reception of the novel 'has created a cadre of spectator readers' who 'do not identify with the characters and who do not feel the intensity of their pain, stand back and view the events of the novel as a circus of black human interactions.' Such readers 'show what damage the novel can have; for them, the book reinforces racist stereotypes they may have been heir to and others of which they may have only dreamed.' A further, 'detrimental effect' of the novel's reception, according to Harris, manifests itself in the reticence of black female critics who, stymied by the media's reverence for the novel, 'have seemingly been reluctant to offer detailed, carefully considered criticisms of it.'

Harris blames this reluctance in part on the effect of Gloria Steinem's review, which she contends inhibited other critics from querying the novel's merits. Despite taking exception to what she perceives as the often 'condescending' tone of Steinem's review, Harris agrees with Steinem's evaluation of Celie's voice as expressed in Walker's writing, recognizing it as 'powerful, engaging, subtly humorous, and incisively analytic at the basic level of human interactions.' However, when Harris divorces this admired voice from its narrative, troubling tensions and contradictions arise. She recalls how she felt listening to Walker read an excerpt from the novel at Radcliffe College in 1982: 'all of my objections to Celie disappeared momentarily as Walker wove an audible spell over the audience.' Afterward, though, Harris realized that '[t]he reading epitomized one of the central issues in the novel – the war between form and content.' She finds it particularly difficult to account for Celie's proficiency as a writer and complains that 'the degradation, abuse, dehumanization' documented by Celie 'invites spectator readers to generalize about black people in the same negative ways that have gone on for centuries.' Harris dismisses the plausibility of the development of Celie and those around her. She especially casts doubt on the 'years and years of Celie's acquiescence,' which, 'extreme in their individuality, have been used too readily to affirm what the uninformed or the ill-informed believe is a general pattern of violence and abuse for black women.' The very voice that 'makes Celie articulate [...] has simultaneously encouraged silence from black women, who need to be vocal in voicing their objections to, as well as their praises for, the novel.'[32]

Harris also objects to Steinem's applause for the novel's moral agenda. In her review, Steinem wrote that in *The Color Purple*: 'morality is not a set of external dictates. It doesn't matter if you love the people society says you shouldn't love, or do or don't have children with more than one of them.' Instead, the novel emphasizes that we must not be 'cruel or wasteful,' and must not 'keep the truth from those who need it, suppress someone's will or talent, take more than you need from nature, or fail to use your own talent and will. It's an organic morality of dignity, autonomy, and balance.'[33]

Harris responds with incredulity:

■ What kind of morality is it that espouses that all human degradation is justified if the individual somehow survives all the tortures and uglinesses heaped upon her? Where is the dignity, autonomy, or balance in that? I am not opposed to triumph, but I do have objections to the unrealistic presentation of the path, the *process* that leads to such a triumph, especially when it is used to create a new archetype or to resurrect old myths about black women (Harris's italics).[34] □

Concerns about the novel's elevation to black feminist Ur-text resurface in later readings. Five years after the publication of Harris's review, Tamar Katz compared Celie's transformation in the novel to Walker's trajectory as a writer. In ' "Show Me How to Do Like You": Didacticism and Epistolary Form in *The Color Purple*' (1989), Katz notes that while Walker manoeuvres Celie from the position of 'example' to 'author,' the media has manoeuvred Walker, as it did Zora Neale Hurston, from the position of 'author' to the precarious position of 'example.' Katz notes that Walker, during the 1980s, was 'treated as exemplary' by the 'mass media': she became '*the* black feminist writer' (Katz's italics).[35]

In her essay 'Writing the Subject: Reading *The Color Purple*' (1988), bell hooks (b. 1952) writes that while the novel 'broadens the scope of literary discourse,' the many 'meanings' that it generates for its various readers are '[o]ften' limiting because they are 'contained [...] within a critical discourse that does not resist the urge to simplify, to overshadow, to make this work by a contemporary African-American writer mere sociological treatise on black life or radical feminist tract.'[36] Further extracts from this reading appear later in this Guide.

This section ends with Steven C. Weisenburger's innovative analysis of the novel's reception. 'Errant Narrative and *The Color Purple*' (1989) scrutinizes the political implications of the novel's reception in the light of its inconsistencies, and delivers insight into the common reactions of reviewers of the novel. Noting that these inconsistencies may in fact constitute 'parts of an authorial design,' Weisenburger asks 'what happens when the elemental techniques of narration go astray,' what these errors can reveal 'about the socio-cultural horizon of a narrative fiction' and what the reader's oversight of these errors can tell us about the politics of reception.[37] Weisenburger demonstrates how '[e]rrors' can serve as 'windows on narrative techniques, on the "laws of genre," on political and cultural stresses thematized in the text, and [...] on the ways that stresses can be taken as influencing the production and reception of a narrative fiction.'

According to Weisenburger, Walker's novel 'commits errors of artifice,' which 'themselves point[] to other business – Walker's social work, or "errand."'[38] Initially, he approaches the novel as an exercise in mimesis, identifying those textual errors that undermine its realist credentials: there is in this novel, he claims, an 'erroneous network of internal determinants such as births' and 'the given ages of characters': for example, if we trace Sofia's narrative we see that she gives birth to four children over a period of 'nine or ten months.'[39]

Nettie's letters complicate Sofia's narrative even further. Her references to Sofia's appearances do not tally with Celie's: only months after she left her sister, Nettie sees Sofia working as a maid when she would have been only nine or ten. Moreover, by constantly referring to Olivia and Adam as 'children,' the letters deny their maturation. As Weisenburger notes, Walker herself has registered some of these problems: she wanted to bring 'Celie's own children back to her' but in doing so experienced the 'largest single problem in writing the exact novel [she] wanted to write.'[40]

In the light of these errors, Weisenburger concedes that Harris perhaps has a point about the novel's hasty canonization and goes on to explore the implications of the collective oversight of the novel's inconsistencies. For Weisenburger, Walker's choice of form makes this oversight all the more remarkable. Unlike most first-person narrations that create the 'illusion of continuity' and divert us from 'temporal ellipses or gaps,' the epistolary novel 'calls attention to' the gaps between the constituent letters. However, readers of *The Color Purple* simply did not notice these gaps: 'Countless very sophisticated readers have taken Walker's letters to be just as they appear – as the spontaneous overflow of powerful feelings, a steady stream of emotions recollected in tranquillity.'[41] They have 'opted to maintain the mimetic image of an unedited, continuous, documentary text.'[42] The reception of *The Color Purple* may therefore be viewed as 'a cautionary tale about the tenacity of the metaphysics of presence among quite well-educated people.'

Weisenburger attributes most of the novel's errors to Walker's 'consciousness-raising' agenda: 'as *The Color Purple* neared its close, the author's felt needs – to win her reader's complicity with, and good opinion of her, consciousness-raising work – had overridden the intradiegetic requirements for mimetic verisimilitude.' Ultimately, Weisenburger argues, 'Walker's "womanist" errand had taken priority over the elements of narrative art.'[43] Additional reviews testified that Walker had succeeded in winning the reader's complicity:

■ One ecstatic reader claims that by undertaking wholesale cultural reform Walker's novel becomes 'a masterpiece that exceeds its limits as a work of fiction' (Parker-Smith 483). This was a fairly common refrain of Walker's more ardent supporters, though the novel's status as a 'masterpiece' is not only arguable but even beside the point, which is that in evaluative readings of *Purple* such claims to greatness are always linked with ideas about the novel's cultural work.[44,45] □

Weisenburger goes on to compare Walker's novel to *Pamela* [(1740–41) by Samuel Richardson (1689–1761)] and *Uncle Tom's Cabin* [(1851–52) by Harriet Beecher Stowe (1811–96)]. Like these works, *The Color Purple* 'not only sacrifices mimetic fidelity to the discursive demands of genre, but further sacrifices discursive precision to broader didactic goals.' Weisenburger reflects that *The Color Purple* 'was immensely *popular*, even *effective*,' noting that 'the record of the book reviewers and scholarly essayists is rife with reader-witnesses who testify to the novel's didactic power in resituating, clarifying and solidifying people's lives' (Weisenburger's italics).

Taking his cue from Jane Tompkins's thesis in her exploration of popular nineteenth-century novels, *Sensational Designs: The Cultural Work of American Fiction 1790–1860* (1986), Weisenburger proposes a new way of approaching Walker's novel: 'to put aside questions about what makes *The Color Purple* a work of "art" and ask instead what accounts for its mass-cultural popularity.' He suggests that 'everything Walker's detractors have received negatively – her stock devices of melodrama, sensational turns of plot, preachy dialogue, women-in-distress and stereotyped villains – might be apprehended not only as conventions of genre but as instruments of a cultural project.' The central question of his reading becomes: 'What gave the text that semblance of monumental solidity in its culture?'

In order to answer this question, Weisenburger turns to the novel's theological dimension. The 'issues of femininity and racism' that dominated reviews are, according to Weisenburger, 'just facets of a larger project.'[46] 'Walker's strategy was to reinscribe problems of gender and race in the context of contemporary theology.'[47] Weisenburger aligns Walker's theological project with the humanist ideology published in the 'Humanist Manifesto II' (1973), which placed the rights of the individual at its centre and condemned all forms of racism, sexism and homophobia.

Many critics have read *The Color Purple* through the lens of liberal humanism, arguing that it is concerned first and foremost with delivering essential truths about the human condition and transcending social and cultural divisions.[48] Weisenburger applies the terminology of researchers such as sociologist Robert N. Bellah to place the novel's 'contemporary secularism' at the root of much of its harshest criticism. This secularism, along with 'the counterculture which so popularly endorsed it in the Sixties,' was an 'expression[] of a privileged, hegemonic white society.'

According to Weisenburger, this was the context of 'many of the more virulent attacks on *The Color Purple*, condemned as it was for pandering to white stereotypes of the black male, for being soft on the violent realities of racism in America, for blurring history, and finally for achieving sentimental popularity among a predominantly white reading public.'[49] While Walker 'may well have been attracted [...] to the subversive dialogism of the epistolary form' as a way of disconcerting 'patriarchal codes,' ultimately she 'wound up writing an essentially centrist, *familiar* fiction' (Weisenburger's italics).

Thus, Weisenburger identifies the novel's primary audience as the 'great American mass of humanist, new age believers – secular or church-going.' In Celie's voice they find verification of their feeling that 'the grey-bearded old white God has passed away,' and '[w]ith Shug,' who outlines a pantheistic philosophy to Celie, 'they easily assent to a contemporary naturalist theology.' It was therefore 'inevitabl[e]' that the novel would pose problems for 'fundamentalists who decry the apparent moral relativism of such sentiments,' for 'leftist readers who decry the book's lack of any "realistic" historicity capable of translating her fiction into something politically useful,' and for 'Afro-American critics.'[50]

Weisenburger's research sheds an interesting light on the critical reception and cross-cultural appeal of *The Color Purple*. Many of the issues he raises will resurface in readings explored throughout this Guide.

ADAPTATIONS OF THE NOVEL

Steven Spielberg's *The Color Purple*

This subchapter surveys the critical reception of Steven Spielberg's cinematic adaptation of *The Color Purple*. In commercial terms the film was a huge success, but it provoked some of the most hostile responses from critics and viewers in the history of cinema. In her essay, 'From Walker to Spielberg: Transformations of *The Color Purple*' (1993), Joan Digby writes that 'the film grossed over $94 million on its first run, which boosted paperback sales' of the novel.[51] It premiered in New York in December 1985 and in the United Kingdom in August of the following year. It was nominated for eleven Academy Awards, but won none. In *The Same River Twice: Honoring the Difficult* (1996), Walker was 'relie[ved]' that those involved with the film went home empty-handed, being 'aware of the kind of black characters who had been anointed before. Maids and other white family retainers.'[52] She writes that the lack of awards 'felt very clean,' especially considering that the Academy opted to applaud *Out of Africa* (1985), a 'reactionary and racist' film.[53]

The idea for adapting Walker's most beloved novel was suggested by Steven Spielberg, the director of blockbusters such as *Jaws* (1975) and *E.T.* (1982), and music producer Quincy Jones (b. 1933). Walker originally had many reservations about the project, but after speaking with Jones and Spielberg over the course of several months she approved the film and agreed to participate as a consultant. Ultimately, she gave her consent after conversations with various family members and trusted friends about the paucity of full and realistic representations of black life in American cinema. The consensus was that American film-makers 'just never know what to do with black people. They're used to getting what they know about black life from *Gone with the Wind*' (1939).[54] However, literary critic and friend Barbara Christian (1943–2000) wondered if this might 'change' if the film industry was given the opportunity to dramatize Walker's material. Walker considered all of the people who might not read the book but who might attend a screening of a film.[55]

When she had agreed to the project she set about writing a script, but she did not take well to the adaptation process. Contrary to popular belief, she completed her screenplay but it was never used and she gave her whole-hearted approval to the final script written by Menno Meyjes (b. 1954).[56]

Much of the criticism of the film focused on departures from its source material. Film critic Pauline Kael, while noting these departures – Spielberg 'soft-pedals the lesbian side of the Celie and Shug romance' and presents the men as 'less threatening' – argues that it is in fact the attempt to 'be faithful to Walker' that harms the film most. She compares 'the people on the screen' to 'characters operated by Frank Oz,' but adds that 'they're not much phonier than the people in the book.' The difficulty for Spielberg is, Kael claims, that he is unable to 'give the material the emotional push of that earthy folk style of Walker's': ultimately, he lacks Walker's 'conviction.'[57]

The release of the film reignited earlier debates about the novel to such a degree that, in the words of critic Jacqueline Bobo, 'the two works have become almost interchangeable in many people's minds.'[58] Digby notes the disparity between the largely positive response of cinemagoers to the film and the negative reaction of the critics, some of whom regarded it as 'a sanitized white version of a black text.'[59]

The simple fact of Spielberg being the director had given rise to early concerns in many observers. The *Omnibus* documentary devoted to Walker includes an interview with Spielberg in which he explains why he was initially attracted to the project. His remarks are telling: he emphasizes the universality of the novel and states that he would not have adapted it if 'racial questions' had been at its centre. Indeed, he senses that the novel 'leaps over any sort of [...] racial questions.' Spielberg's interpretation was reflected in the movie's much-derided tagline: 'It's about life, it's about love, it's about us.'

Others waited until they had seen the film before denouncing the choice of Spielberg. Writing for the *New York Times* in 1986, Vincent Canby (1924–2000) drew from Spielberg's commentary on the novel to sustain his criticism of the film:

■ The film's publicity notes quote Mr. Spielberg as having called the book 'a very strong emotional read.' A read? It's a tour de force, but what Mr Spielberg has made of it is a cinema equivalent to a 'read.' His 'Color Purple' is a 'see.' It is physically elaborate, prettily photographed, essentially sunny natured, and not very threatening even in its most doom-filled moments.[60] □

While negative reviews of the novel were often tempered by admiration for Walker's linguistic prowess, critics of the film found little to praise and much to condemn. Many felt that Spielberg had presented the worst dimensions of the novel in visual form, justifying initial reservations about Walker's representation of the black community and, in particular, black men.

Writing for the *Carolina Peacemaker* in 1986, journalist Tony Brown (b. 1933) drew from negative responses to the film to offer his own evaluation of it, despite admitting that he had not seen it and had no intention of doing so. In the article 'Blacks Need to Love One Another,' Brown confirms that he has encountered people who have seen the film and declares: '[they] have lived what I'm sure my reaction would be.' Just as Harris had worried that the media's racist reception of black writers conditioned the positioning of Walker's novel as *the* novel about black female experience, Brown expresses concern that, owing to the scarcity of films dealing with 'black themes,' Spielberg's *The Color Purple* 'becomes the only statement on black men.'[61]

The same issue of the *Carolina Peacemaker* featured a 'rebuttal' to Brown's article by Anita Jones. She expresses incredulity that Brown can condemn with such authority a film that he has never seen and notes a double-standard at work in his appraisal: the 'shallow images of black men' in films such as *Shaft* (1971) and *Superfly* (1972) were rewarded with 'top-forty songs of worship.'[62] Brown refused to revise his position. Speaking to *Newsweek* magazine later that year, he denounced Spielberg's adaptation as 'the most racist depiction of Black men since *The Birth of a Nation* and the most anti-Black family film of the modern film era,' but he refused to confirm whether or not he had seen it.[63]

Spielberg's film has also been derided as an 'infantile abomination,'[64] 'the first Disney film about incest,'[65] a 'superbly realized feminist cartoon,' and a 'hate letter to black men.'[66,67] Upon its release the film was boycotted by the NAACP, although the organization eventually altered its position, giving Spielberg the Image Award in 1986. Many critics complained that the film's departures from Walker's text had distorted its identity politics. They took exception to the evasion of the sexual intimacy between Celie and Shug – this crucial development in Celie's life takes the form of a single, chaste kiss – and deplored an added scene that sees Shug, a character who requires no redemption in the novel, appeal to her preacher father for forgiveness.

Jacqueline Bobo's research, presented in 'Black Women as Cultural Readers' (1988) and 'Sifting Through the Controversy' (1989), sheds an interesting light on the film's reception. Bobo views the controversy surrounding the film and the novel as a construction that conditioned subsequent responses to both works and gave licence to those unfamiliar with either to dismiss or attack them. She writes that both Walker's novel and Spielberg's cinematic adaptation 'became inflammatory subject matter because there were those who did not like them rather than because the content of the works was offensive to everyone in the audience.' She adds:

■ The distinction is a subtle and fine one, yet is important. If a cultural product is presented as controversial, this view affects the way in which it is perceived and its worth evaluated, initially, by an audience. The predominant reading, or meaning construction, of *The Color Purple* is that the works negatively depict black people, especially black men. Although the works are open to a variety of readings, this particular reading became 'relatively fixed' at the moment they were constructed as controversial. This interpretation is especially true for those who have not seen the film and/or have not read the book.[68] □

Tracing the reception of the film, Bobo observes that the negative responses of some black people were initially of little concern to reviewers. However, as protests against the film increased, 'the tone of the critiques changed.'[69] The most vocal protestors were black men. In '*The Color Purple*: Black Women as Cultural Readers' (1988), Bobo records the responses of the black women viewers she interviewed, emphasising the 'different perspective' that they brought to the film.[70] Their responses confirmed that Walker had achieved one of her primary aims in supporting the adaptation: aware that 'their specific experience, as Black people, as women, in a rigid class/caste state, has never been adequately dealt with in mainstream media,' these viewers 'were able to form a positive engagement with *The Color Purple*.'[71]

In 'Sifting Through the Controversy' (1989), Bobo reports one woman's statement that the reason why so many people took exception to the film was that they 'felt it was an airing of black people's dirty laundry.' This prompted another woman to respond: 'We don't always have to pretend that everything is hunky-dory. It could be that if I tell somebody and they tell somebody else then maybe I can get some answers to some problems I have.' Another response was to ask why outrage at sexist portrayals had been saved for this film: 'Where was all this hue and cry when the Blaxploitation films came out?' one woman viewer asked.[72]

This subchapter closes with a consideration of a review-essay by Wayne J. McMullen and Martha Solomon, 'The Politics of Adaptation: Steven Spielberg's Appropriation of *The Color Purple*' (1994). The essay suggests reasons for the disparity between the public's response to the film and its critical reception, arguing that Spielberg 'reframes' Celie's story 'through the lens of comforting American mythologies.' Drawing from the terminology of critic Kenneth Burke (1897–1993), McMullen and Solomon identify the film as a ' "terministic screen" for Walker's novel,' stating that 'it selects and reflects certain elements in that work, but it also deflects our attention from other themes and aspects.'[73]

McMullen and Solomon identify two main reasons why the film appealed to American audiences: the film 'stimulates a sense of satisfying repetition of a work, a pleasure inherent in adaptations,' and 'adaptive changes' made by Spielberg 'simplify psychological and social issues in Walker's novel,' thus 'promot[ing] a sense of psychological reassurance about persistent tensions in American life.'[74]

This reading explores two 'significant' departures from the novel: 'a shift to a different type of narrative from epistolary to melodrama and a shift in emotional focus through the eclipsing of Celie's voice.' While Celie's story is 'one of growing self-empowerment against the forces of sexism and racism,' the film offers a '*melodramatic* narrative of an individual who successfully triumphs over interpersonal and economic adversity. Like other melodramas, the heroine's success results not only in personal glory, but also in the restoration and reaffirmation of the social order' (McMullen and Solomon's italics).[75] This 'melodramatic cinematic strategy' manifests itself in the opening credits: 'Whereas the reader of the novel is immediately introduced to Celie's bleak, desperate plight, the viewer of the film sees a rural idyll, full of flowers, tall grasses, and children at play': this 'contrast [...] illustrates Burke's terministic screens; Spielberg selects out certain elements in the work but deflects our attention from other themes.'[76]

According to McMullen and Solomon, concerns about Spielberg's handling of the novel's gender politics are justified: the ending of the film sees the 'restoration' of patriarchy: Shug goes to her father's church to seek forgiveness, singing 'a Christian hymn,' thus giving 'the patriarchal voice' back to 'the white father'; and it is Albert who single-handedly organizes Nettie's return. This sense of 'restoration' is compounded by the overlapping of both scenes:

■ Spielberg cross-cuts Shug's procession into the church and subsequent reconciliation with her father with a sequence of shots depicting Albert's actions to bring about Nettie's return from Africa. He sustains the thematic connection between these shots aurally: the singing voices of Shug and the congregation are the soundtrack for Shug's reconciliation as well as Albert's efficacious actions. □

However, the film ignores Celie's new friendship with Albert and his assimilation within her womanist community: '[s]eparate from the reunion he helped instigate, Albert's exclusion from Celie's extended family seems to be atonement for his "crimes."'[77]

Other crucial elements of the novel are displaced through the 'obscuring of [Celie's] voice,' which 'occurs in three ways: removing Celie's distinctive and crucial angle of vision, obliterating her sexuality, and oversimplifying her emotional life.' In key scenes that do not directly involve Celie, such as the castigation of Albert by his father, she is 'marginalize[d] to the position of an onlooker.' Moreover, the viewer is 'deprived of Celie's evolving sense of herself,' in particular her sexuality:[78] 'Shug's arrival in the film is delayed, and her relationship to Celie is largely devoid of erotic tension.' By the time Shug kisses Celie, the film 'has left the viewer unprepared for the display of physical affection. The eros of this scene comes as a surprise to some viewers, who have had no clue to Celie's latent lesbianism, nor to Shug's bisexuality.'[79]

McMullen and Solomon do not lay the blame entirely at Spielberg's feet but recognize that his tactics were informed by '[v]arious social and cultural factors': 'his adaptations are largely typical of Hollywood practices that are guided by an acute sensitivity to the marketability of a film.'[80] By stifling Celie's 'dialogue with God and herself,' the film 'obscures' her story of 'self-empowerment through relationship and community'; instead, Spielberg presents Celie as 'an example of the American dream. Persistence, hard work, and capitalistic acumen secure her eventual triumph. In short, for Celie the patriarchally controlled system works.' Ultimately, Spielberg's film 'recasts Celie's story to fit cultural myths rather than highlighting her alternate path to power in its racial and sexual specificity.'[81]

Walker herself has been asked many times to justify her involvement with the film and to explain why she approved the addition or editing of particular scenes. *The Same River Twice: Honoring the Difficult* features a journal entry dated December 6, 1985, that documents Walker's concerns about the film's handling of the novel's identity politics: having watched the film once, she describes it as 'slick, sanitized and apoliticial' and picks up on some of its 'anachronisms' such as the buggy driven by Shug's father.[82] She regrets the lack of recognition of 'Celie's industry' and all that it entails, and she 'resent[s] the imposition of Shug's father between her and "God,"' but at the same time she finds the music to be 'wonderful.'[83] Although the final scenes were 'moving,' she was disappointed that Albert was not 'up on the porch.'[84] Regarding the film's handling of Celie and Shug's sexuality, Walker has stated that she would not have tackled it in the same way as Spielberg but that she was not particularly perturbed by his approach which did not prevent viewers from using their 'imagination.'[85]

The Color Purple: **The Broadway Musical**

Some of the concerns raised by critics of the film version of *The Color Purple* resurfaced nineteen years later with the presentation of the Broadway musical. The idea for this latest incarnation of the novel came from television and theatre producer Scott Sanders. When he read *The Color Purple*, he sensed immediately that it 'had music in its soul.' On watching the film, he felt that 'Steven Spielberg and Quincy Jones could feel the music trying to break out.' Sanders presented Walker with the idea of a musical adaptation but she 'politely declined,' expressing her desire to 'move forward rather than go back to something she had spent considerable time with.'[86] However, she finally gave her endorsement, as did Spielberg. The musical's official website recognizes the influence of the film as well as the novel; this theatrical adaptation comes 'from the classic Pulitzer Prize-winning novel by Alice Walker, and the moving film by Steven Spielberg.'[87]

The musical opened in September 2004 at Atlanta's Alliance Theatre and moved to Broadway in December 2005. It closed in February 2008. It was nominated for eleven Tony Awards (winning one) and was recognized by the NAACP Theatre Awards. Oprah Winfrey (b. 1954), who played Sofia in the film, Quincy Jones and Harvey Weinstein (b. 1952) joined Sanders as producers. The music, which consisted of a range of genres including jazz, blues, gospel and African music, was written by Brenda Russell (b. 1949), Allee Willis and Stephen Bray (b. 1956). Marsha Norman wrote the script.

Promotion for the musical again played on the universal appeal of Celie's story. The website tells us that *The Color Purple* is 'The Musical About Love' and describes it as 'an inspiring family saga that tells the unforgettable story of a woman who – through love – finds the strength to triumph over adversity and discover her unique voice in the world.' Through its 'joyous score,' it tells 'a story about hope, a testament to the healing power of love and a celebration of life.'

Audiences flocked to the musical adaptation of Celie's story, emerging from theatres with warm reviews. Critics were less enthusiastic and queried the omission of particular dimensions of the novel and even the film. In his review, Wendell Brook notes that the Broadway version of the musical writes out the pivotal scene in which Millie, the mayor's wife, clashes with Sofia: a scene that made its way into the film and the production at the Alliance Theatre. LaTonya Holmes, the understudy for the parts of Celie and Nettie, has asserted that the musical deals more directly with Shug and Celie's sexual relationship, but many reviewers agreed that it did not go far enough. Speaking to Holmes, Brook concurs that the musical 'show[s] more of the relationship,' but adds that 'Shug's breakout song, 'Push Da Button,' is more about catching a man than satisfying a woman.'[88] Writing for *New York* magazine, Jeremy McCarter found that 'the lesbian element in Celie's story gets swept aside. The love she shares with Shug in Walker's book is dispatched here with a couple of timid kisses and some platitudinous lyrics.' He also felt that the musical gave too much emphasis to Celie's status as entrepreneur: 'The show leaves the impression that Celie's redemption comes mainly from entrepreneurial zeal.'[89] Ben Brantley (b. 1954) of the *New York Times* agreed: 'Devotees of Ms. Walker's novel would be better off thinking of this show less as *The Color Purple* than as, say, "Celie: A Woman of Independent Means."' Brantley found much in the musical to remind him of the film but could detect few traces of the novel: 'there's a sumptuousness throughout that, while hardly true to the harrowing bleakness of the early chapters of Ms. Walker's novel, does bring to mind the enjoyably hokey cinematic ravishments of Steven Spielberg's 1995 version.'[90]

It is clear from this chapter that the novel and its adaptations continue to provoke strong reactions and to polarize opinions. The rest of this Guide focuses primarily on critical readings of the novel. It begins with one of the most contentious issues that emerged from early reviews: the question of the novel's generic identity.

CHAPTER TWO

Defining *The Color Purple*: The Question of Genre

This chapter presents a wide range of readings exploring Walker's engagement with various generic traditions. One would be hard pressed to find a critical reading of *The Color Purple* that does not address the question of its generic identity to some degree. Critics continue to draw on Walker's use and subversion of generic premises and conventions to sustain readings of the novel's identity politics.

Writing about 'transformations of genre,' Alastair Fowler observes that the 'most important factor separating modern from earlier genre theory' is 'the perception that literary genres are dynamic rather than static entities – that they change or "evolve" over time.'[1] Early reviews of *The Color Purple* revealed the highly significant role that preconceptions of genre play in shaping responses to literary texts. Some reviewers had no reservations about locating the novel firmly in one specific generic category and then proceeding to point out ways in which it failed to adhere to that category's particular conventions. These hasty categorizations prompted more helpful readings that demonstrated how Walker's engagement with various oral and literary traditions served to counter 'static' notions of genre.

In her essay 'Writing the Subject: Reading *The Color Purple*' (1988), bell hooks takes issue with readings that identify the novel with a single generic tradition: she sees the limitations imposed on the novel by criticism that categorizes it as 'a modern day "slave narrative" ' or aligns it with 'the literary tradition of epistolary sentimental novels.'[2] In *Alice Walker* (2000), Maria Lauret states that the novel's 'metafictional layers' work to form an 'embedded critical dimension [...] which comments on the (white) Western literary tradition.'[3]

The readings chosen for this chapter examine some of the ways in which *The Color Purple* has contributed to the development of particular traditions and illuminated the dynamism of genre.

As was noted earlier, several reviewers have based their evaluations of *The Color Purple* on the assumption that it was written as a piece of traditional realism and, within this context, found it wanting. Walker's revelation that she conceived *The Color Purple* as a 'historical novel' further prompted critics to contest its realist credentials. They were quick to note the absence of historical references in the novel, to question its handling of chronology and to highlight the difficulty of contextualizing its narrative.

Other critics have taken their cues from Walker's womanist aesthetic and have viewed the novel as a revision of patriarchal notions of history. Maroula Joannou concludes her study *Contemporary Women's Writing: from The Golden Notebook to The Color Purple* (2000) with an analysis of Walker's most famous novel. In 'To *The Color Purple,*' Joannou acknowledges that 'the novel contains no dates, and only a handful of verifiable historical facts' and that '[t]his makes it impossible for it to be repositioned accurately in history.' However, she reminds us of the limitations of historical narrative for those writers wishing to give expression to experiences that official, but partial, versions of history have distorted or written out:

■ historically precise narratives are not the only narratives that women who wish to counter oppression have at their disposal. If, as is so often the case, history is the history of the defeated, it is necessary to resort [...] to allegorical form, myth, fantasy and fairy tale in order to redress injustice, and to envision the triumph of democratic and egalitarian principles. □

Thus, 'Walker takes liberties with the notion of historical truth, and subordinates this to myth, because, at its best, history is inspirational myth and, at its worst, it is either irrelevant or damaging to black people.'[4] The following readings consider Walker's engagement with several related traditions, assessing the credentials of *The Color Purple* as a piece of utopian fiction, a fairy tale, a folk tale, a blues narrative, a parable and a romance.

A UTOPIAN NOVEL?

Keith Byerman is one of Walker's most prolific critics and has produced several illuminating readings of *The Color Purple*, placing particular focus on the relationship between Walker's womanist politics and her engagement with generic traditions. In his essay ' "Dear Everything": Alice Walker's *The Color Purple* as Womanist Utopia' (1988), Byerman considers the interaction of various generic conventions in *The Color Purple*. While critics judging the novel through the lens of traditional realism have chafed at its utopian qualities, Byerman argues that the realistic and the fantastic inform each other in *The Color Purple*: realistic aspects 'establish the conditions of the present world and [...] lend credibility to an alternative one'; 'fantastic elements provide the mechanism by which the reader is moved from one world to the other.'[5]

Drawing from a number of definitions of utopian fiction, Byerman finds that *The Color Purple* fits only some of the criteria:

- 'redefinitions' of 'male–female relationships [...] race, work, religion, art, and family' in *The Color Purple* 'often occur in discussions rather than in dramatic action'
- the narrative 'moves from a strong sense of history to timelessness and from profane to sacred space'
- 'the change in the story is gradual rather than sudden' and 'is presented as [...] irreversible.'[6]

Byerman finds that strong parallels emerge with Jean Pfaelzer's definition of utopian fiction as a 'category of prose fiction in which the author's political statement controls the narrative structures.'[7] Using Pfaelzer's terminology, Byerman identifies Walker's novel as a 'retrogressive utopia' – one that places emphasis on 'the land, the family, religion, and domestic creativity' – underpinned by a 'womanist ideology.'[8]

The Color Purple also emulates the conventions of utopian literature in its identification of 'greed as a fundamental evil of the writer's contemporaries.'[9] However, while many utopian novels offer socialism as an alternative model for its characters and readers, Walker offers 'arts and crafts capitalism'[10]: she demonstrates 'the evils of both traditional and modern systems of exploitation' and 'would have us believe that it is possible to create a self-sufficient, non-exploitative, woman-based local capitalism' and that '[t]he creation of a feminized economy, one which privileges women's work, would transform the world into a womanist utopia.'[11]

Underpinning this womanist utopia is 'the discovery of female bonding, the joining together of women for mutual nurture.' This utopia also has space for men who can look beyond social inscriptions of masculinity but has no room for institutionalized religion. It is this rejection of mainstream ideology that qualifies the novel as a 'retrogressive utopia':

■ Its characters are artisans with close connections to the land and family. The world that has been made has no connection with the world of racism and exploitation. Most of the whites have disappeared, the only capitalism practiced is Celie's cottage form, and there are no men except those who have accepted womanist principles. The religion practiced is that of natural piety, not church dogma. It is a completely self-contained world separated from the history that generated it. All of its members have come to full self-awareness and, we are convinced, have perfected themselves.[12] □

The novel's ending furnishes the strongest parallels with the utopian novel as the final scenes place Celie's community safely out of reach of history: 'Despite Walker's hints to the contrary, we sense that no further development is possible. The dialectical struggle necessary to achieve the good place ends with its realization.' Byerman suggest that 'it is in this very condition that this novel becomes most fully utopian' as 'its very ability to resolve historical conflicts places it outside of history. Celie's world is no longer one of change and growth, but one of timelessness.'[13]

FOLK TALE OR FAIRY TALE, BLUES NARRATIVE OR PARABLE?

Reading Celie's story, some readers and critics have been reminded of the characters and narrative structures of the folk tale and its European counterpart, the fairy tale. In her essay 'The Enchanted World of *The Color Purple*' (1987), Margaret Walsh draws on Bruno Bettelheim's study, *The Uses of Enchantment* (1976), and Iona and Peter Opie's comments in their collection, *The Classic Fairy Tales* (1981), to read Walker's novel as a postmodern revision of the fairy tale.

By viewing *The Color Purple* within this framework, Walsh aims to counter some of the criticisms that surfaced continually in early reviews. While some critics accused Walker of relying on stereotypes in her characterization, Walsh sees her characters as 'inventive incarnations' of the '[s]implified situations and figures' common to the fairy tale. She argues that Walker's engagement with fairy tale conventions is both sustained and modified by her use of the epistolary form: the fairy tale offers 'no character development or deep analysis,' yet we 'view [Celie's] experiences from inside her psyche as she grows intellectually and matures emotionally.' However, 'Walker's choice of epistolary form does allow her to take certain liberties: our knowledge is limited by the interpretive and communicative abilities of the letter writer, thereby permitting Walker to tell her story with almost folk tale plainness and lack of complexity.'[14]

According to Walsh, the novel engages 'two delightful aspects of fairy tales': 'fantastic happenings and improbable endings: separated siblings reunited, a heroine restored to former glory, the renewal or rebirth of formerly debased or degraded characters.'[15] The metamorphoses of characters such as Harpo, Squeak and Albert testify that 'love transforms and can make all things new and beautiful' – which is the 'message' that, according to Bettelheim, 'is at the heart of all fairy tales.'[16] Parities with the structure and tropes of the Cinderella story are clearly evident: Walker presents an oppressed heroine who must overcome her oppressors before receiving her just reward; Shug and

Nettie fulfil the functions of the fairy godmother. However, Walker subverts the ideology and structure of the Cinderella story by presenting her heroine in the opening scene as a victim of *sexual* oppression.

Walsh draws on a further parallel with the fairy tale to defend one of the most maligned elements of the novel. Recognizing that Nettie's letters are often the target of critical derision, she asserts that they are crucial to the elaboration of an 'enchanted world': they deliver an embedded fairy tale that introduces stock elements of the genre otherwise missing in the novel: 'Not only do they tell of Celie's "Cinderella" past, but also they contain a mini–fairy tale of their own and two of this tale's hard-to-find good black men.' Nettie plays 'fairy godmother [. . .] to Celie's two children.' Walsh identifies the 'princely men' as Samuel and Celie's son, 'bearing the appropriate name of Adam, foreshadowing his role as an idealized new man at the story's end.'[17]

Walsh examines the handling of Celie's return to her childhood home – a further staple of the fairy tale – to show how Walker breaks from the conventions of the genre to dramatize one of life's hardest lessons. Although Pa appears to have changed – he is 'a picture of courtly love, with servants, manners and a new child bride' – Walsh reminds us that he 'had always been "a fine looking man"' [*CP* 15].[18] Pa is therefore comparable to the 'kindly old woman or a deceptively appealing gingerbread house' in that he 'is not what he seems' yet he goes unpunished in a touch of realism: 'Here Walker again deviates from a fairy tale convention, namely, that in which evil is not rewarded: we know from life experience that virtue often goes unrewarded while wickedness flourishes.'[19] Walsh concludes that 'reading *The Color Purple* in the context of a fairy tale is not the same as presuming that it was written as such and it is not to suggest that what happens to Celie is trivial or impossible.' However, like the fairy tale, Walker's novel has a message for all readers:

■ If *Purple's* violence is unrelenting and prominent and if the few good black men seem too little [. . .] or too late [. . .] such under- or overstatement (as the case may be) can be justified or seen as necessary for pointing the tale's moral, which is that personal redemption and rebirth are possible in spite of all that has gone before. That message, Bettelheim reminds us, is the reason why, even though we know that fairy tales are not stories of actual or real events, we intuitively recognize that they speak to us of things true and universally experienced within the human family (73).[20] □

In ' "Preachin' the Blues": Bessie Smith's Secular Religion and Alice Walker's *The Color Purple*' (1994), Thomas F. Marvin finds readings of the novel as fairy tale 'more convincing than those' that 'try to force the novel into a "realistic" mode,' but adds that interpretations such as

Walsh's emphasize Walker's engagement with a European tradition and thus 'divert attention from [the novel's] African-American content.'[21]

In a further essay on *The Color Purple*, 'Walker's Blues,' first published in his book *Fingering the Jagged Grain: Tradition and Form in Recent Black Fiction* (1985), Keith Byerman examines the novel's engagement with the structures and tropes of both the folk tale and the fairy tale. References to Byerman's reading come from the critical collection *Alice Walker* edited by Harold Bloom (b. 1930) in 1988. Byerman argues that, for the most part, the related traditions of the folk tale and fairy tale complement each other in Walker's novel:

> ■ Since the fairy tale is a folk form, albeit a European one, there is no obvious contradiction between it and the Afro-American and African materials that enrich the narrative. In fact, such materials enhance the sense of a faerie world where curses, coincidences, and transformations are possible. The power for healing and change latent in folk arts and practices important to black women – quilting, mothering, blues singing, 'craziness,' and conjure – fit the pattern of the female character in the fairy tale who is victimized but then saved through love and magic.[22] □

Where Byerman's reading is particularly illuminating is in its discussion of the relationship between Walker's genre and gender politics. Unlike her earlier works of fiction, *The Color Purple* is, specifically, a ' "womanist" fairy tale.'[23] It is the first of Walker's novels to 'set [] up [...] an opposition between male and female folk wisdom; the former wisdom, passed from father to son, claims, in Walker's view, the natural inferiority of women and the need to keep them under control, through violence if necessary.'[24] The novel's African-American women challenge this view, drawing inspiration from the folk tradition; they 'develop with models for resistance as well as healing.'

Sofia enacts one such model, taking the role of what Byerman calls the 'crazy' woman who rejects 'the rules of an oppressive order.'[25] Further forms of resistance lead to her release from the local prison: a 'Brer Rabbit scheme' that results in her working as a maid for the mayor's wife. The Br'er Rabbit story originated from the African oral tradition and tells how Br'er Fox uses a tar baby to trap the hero. Then Br'er Rabbit tells his captor that his worst fear is to be thrown into the briar patch; Br'er Fox falls for the trick and Br'er Rabbit sets himself free.

When Sofia is imprisoned for punching the mayor, Harpo's new girlfriend Squeak visits the prison warden, a man she knows as her 'cousin' and who has refused to recognize his parentage of three of her siblings. She tells the warden that Sofia is hardly suffering in prison and that a greater punishment would be to have to work for the mayor's wife. The warden arranges Sofia's release in exchange for sexual favours.

Byerman argues that Sofia's appropriation of the 'crazy' woman role helps her because the mayor's wife 'has already seen what she considers the black woman's crazy behavior' and is therefore 'intimidated and Sofia suffers much less than she would have otherwise. "Craziness," then, is a form of resistance that allows for the expression of the frustrated humanity and creativity of black women.'

It is blues singer Shug Avery who emerges as 'the most important of the folk figures' in *The Color Purple*.[26] While Walsh sees Shug as fairy godmother to the heroine, Byerman sees her as a realistic, fully-fledged character who plays a crucial role in Celie's development. She cannot be regarded as 'pure fantasy' as she is 'connected with [Celie's] reality through Mr.—' and 'opens for Celie the realms of the unconscious.'[27]

Unlike the traditional fairy godmother, Shug embodies the tensions of the blues, awakening Celie to the joys of love and the realities of pain that she has not experienced before. Shug is haunted by the death of Albert's first wife, who had a fatal affair with an abusive lover in response to Albert's betrayal with Shug. Byerman characterizes Shug's 'inability to stay with one man' as 'a tale of loneliness.' Her love of freedom surpasses her love for Albert. Byerman reads in her story 'the classic blues dilemma she describes in her songs' and argues that Shug 'creates the same tension for Celie, whose very love for Shug makes her vulnerable to despair when her beloved finds another man.' Shug's role as 'folk figure' is to present 'possibilities' rather than to 'construct [...] completed orders of reality.'

Complicating this understanding of Shug is her contribution to the novel's denouement: it is here that the conventions of fairy tale and folk tale diverge. Walker opts for the happy ending, which distinguishes the European fairy tale from the African-American folk tale. This ending, primarily orchestrated by Shug, removes the narrative from its historical context completely, undermining its folk credentials. Celie's pantsmaking enterprise, inspired by Shug, 'works' initially 'in a folk manner': 'she puts her energy into sewing instead' of 'kill[ing] Albert'. However, when her anger subsides, this activity 'becomes a business and Celie a petty capitalist,' and once we learn of Albert's fondness for sewing, 'any lingering hostility vanishes.'[28]

For Byerman, 'this very liberation contradicts the nature of the folk sensibility on which it is based. History [...] cannot, in the folk worldview, be transcended; it must be lived through.' In *The Color Purple*, 'Walker seeks to resolve the dialectic by making all males female (or at least androgynous), all destroyers creators, and all difference sameness.' In order to engineer this kind of resolution, Walker 'must move outside the very conflicts that generated the sewing, the blues singing, and the voice of Celie herself.' By 'mov[ing] to allegorical form,' Walker has 'neutralized the historical conditions of the very folk life she values.'[29]

Thomas F. Marvin acknowledges the innovation of Byerman's reading and draws attention to the ways that Shug's blues philosophy is informed by the narratives and tropes of African religion. He argues that Shug embodies the philosophy outlined by fellow blues singer Bessie Smith in her song *Preachin' the Blues*, bringing Celie to a fuller realization of her potential.[30] Marvin identifies Shug and Smith with Legba, 'a West African spirit closely associated with musicians, who opens the door to the spiritual world and provides opportunities for the social and psychological growth of the individual.'[31] Through her contact with Shug, Celie undergoes a 'blues conversion.'[32]

In her reading of the novel, Diane Gabrielsen Scholl identifies formal affinities with another theological model: the Christian parable. She explores these connections in her essay 'With Ears to Hear and Eyes to See: Alice Walker's Parable *The Color Purple*,' first published in 1991 in the journal *Christianity and Literature*. References to this reading come from the collection *Alice Walker's The Color Purple* (2000) edited by Harold Bloom. Acknowledging that many readers might contest this kind of interpretation by referring to the 'vague spiritualist cast' of the philosophy espoused by Shug, Scholl highlights the novel's 'qualities of extended parable, its movement through a realistically improbable sequence of narrative reversals toward a conclusion that defies realistic expectations.'[33] Through these reversals, Walker transports 'us beyond the comfortable assumptions of our culture-bound lives.' Scholl compares the reversals that see Sofia offering guidance to the mayor's family and Albert transforming into a trusted friend to moments of subversion in Christian parable, reminding us that 'it is not the priest or the Levite who offer aid to the traveler set upon by robbers but the unlikely Samaritan' and that 'the prodigal son gets a warm welcome when he returns, overshadowing his dutiful brother.'[34]

Scholl responds to Byerman's observation that Walker 'neutralize[s] the historical conditions of the very folk life she values' by suggesting that he has 'overlook[ed] the obvious figurative implication of the ending.' The 'ahistorical' dimension of the ending is, she argues, in keeping with the novel as a whole and 'consistent with the requirements of its nature as parable': 'biblical parable [...] transcend[s] the precise historical moment without avoiding the historical implications of the story and its multiple ways of being heard and understood.'[35]

A ROMANCE?

In her comparative reading of *The Color Purple* and Zora Neale Hurston's *Their Eyes Were Watching God*, Molly Hite delivers a highly innovative analysis of both writers' engagement with the conventions of romance.

'Romance, Marginality, and Matrilineage: *The Color Purple* and *Their Eyes Were Watching God*' was first published in 1989 in Hite's book *The Other Side of the Story: Structures and Strategies of Contemporary Feminist Narrative*. Hite's analysis of thematic resonances between the two novels is explored further in Chapter 7 of this Guide where we take a closer look at Walker's intertextual relationship with Hurston. The discussions presented in this subchapter focus primarily on the question of Walker's use and subversion of the romance genre in *The Color Purple*.

Hite proposes that we approach the 'ostensible violations' of realism in both novels as 'calculated subversions of conventions that the authors regarded as permeated with white, masculinist values.' She suggests that Hurston and Walker were 'writing not realism but romance,' purposefully engaging with an established, 'highly conventional' genre in which 'ideological implications are easier both to underscore and to undermine.'[36] The romance genre 'formally encodes a system of hierarchical relations that have ideological repercussions': this system 'is also the ideology of racism and patriarchy that the two novels expose and, ultimately, invert.'[37]

The romance genre has its roots in European courtly narratives of the twelfth century, but the term has come to represent narratives that transport the reader beyond 'everyday reality' by incorporating dimensions of fantasy. It is Shakespeare's adaptation of the romance genre that provides the model for Hite in her analysis of novels by Hurston and Walker. Shakespeare's late plays, often classified as romances, are characterized by improbable turns of event that are engineered through fantastical transformations and interventions and abrupt leaps in time and space.

Hite refers us to the term Frank Kermode (b. 1919) uses for the late plays – *pastoral tragicomedy* – in his introduction to the New Arden edition of *The Tempest*.[38] The utility of Kermode's term for Hite lies in the way that it 'invokes the tradition of the pastoral and thus a set of conventions celebrating a rural, "natural" community' that is 'often explicitly identified with the nonwhite inhabitants of Africa or the New World and constituted in implicit opposition to a dominant urban community.' In *The Color Purple*, 'Walker makes a group of black farmers the central social unit, and uses this community as a vantage point from which to deliver a blistering critique of the surrounding white culture.'[39]

Consideration of the novel's trajectory opens up further connections with the Shakespearean romance. Firstly, Celie is 'an exemplary pastoral protagonist,' because her 'defining quality [...] is innocence.' Her movement toward 'experience' is mirrored by her surrounding environment: this development 'implicitly restores a submerged Edenic ideal of harmony between individual human beings and between humanity and the natural order.'[40] As Hite notes, Kermode stresses how the writer of romance presents 'the action of magical and moral laws in a version of human life so selective as to obscure [...] the fact that in reality their force is intermittent and only fitfully glimpsed.'[41] He does this 'for the special purpose of concentrating attention on those laws.' Hite sees a parallel with Walker's novel, where 'the moral laws [...] subtitled in the original hardcover edition *A Moral Tale*, have magical power, producing consequences that are not in naturalistic terms remotely credible.'[42] By viewing the novel in terms of its engagement with the conventions of romance, then, one can account for the implausible elements and inconsistencies that so troubled early reviewers of the novel.

The observations of Northrop Frye (1912–91) on the denouements of Shakespearean romantic plots shed further light on Celie's narrative. In *A Natural Perspective: The Development of Shakespearean Comedy and Romance* (1965), Frye states that the endings of Shakespeare's romances are not 'a logical consequence of the preceding action, as in tragedy, but something more like a metamorphosis.'[43] Hite observes that '[t]he metamorphoses of romance are not limited to the social order' and finds that 'they have an analogous metaphysical dimension in *The Color Purple*, where Celie's progress also serves to redefine the proper relation between human beings and the natural world they inhabit.' Moreover, Shug's pantheistic reflections 'are consonant with the pastoral's characteristic fusion of reverence and hedonism, and with a long tradition that uses pastoral convention to attack the excesses and misconceptions of established religious practice.'[44]

Hite then turns to the evocation of Africa, which both critics and readers have found structurally incongruous. She identifies the purpose of the ' "Africa" Section' as being 'to provide analogies and contrasts to the dominant action.' She sees 'parallels' between Walker's representation of Africa and 'scenes in the romances taking place in what Frye has called the "green world," a pastoral landscape that serves as a "symbol of natural society, the word natural referring to the original human society which is the proper home of man," and that is "associated with things which in the context of the ordinary world seem unnatural, but which are in fact attributes of nature as a miraculous and irresistible reviving power." '[45,46] In romance this world is, according to Frye, the site of the heroine's death and reinvention. In *The Color Purple*, however, it is the site of 'Nettie's reincarnation as correspondent and co-narrator.'

Hite explores further parallels between the Olinka village and Bohemia, the pastoral realm to which King Leontes' daughter Perdita is banished in Shakespeare's *The Winter's Tale*. She alerts us to 'one signal difference': while Perdita gains inspiration from her time in Bohemia, Nettie, who initially sees the Olinka 'as a natural and self-determining black community,' is stripped of her illusions, finally viewing it as 'sexist and vulnerable to incursions by the encompassing white empire.'

Meanwhile, Celie's world becomes more idyllic, 'finally containing and assimilating even elements of the white community in the person of Sofia's former charge, Miss Eleanor Jane.'[47] Walker overturns expectations regarding the 'ordinary' and 'green' worlds and therefore 'inverts the emphasis of the romance, suggesting the extent to which [she] unsettles this structural paradigm in the process of applying it.' *The Color Purple*, then

■ not only reveals the central preoccupations of the tradition within which it locates itself but succeeds in turning a number of these preoccupations inside out, at once exposing the ideology that informs them and insinuating the alternative meanings that, by insisting on its own centrality, the paradigm has suppressed. □

TWO FURTHER TRADITIONS: THE SLAVE NARRATIVE AND THE EPISTOLARY NOVEL

In 'Who's Afraid of Alice Walker?' (1987), Calvin C. Hernton (1932–2001) attributes much of the criticism that has been levelled at *The Color Purple* to misreadings of its generic identity: '[n]obody,' he declares, 'recognized that *The Color Purple* was, and is, a slave narrative.'[48] Slave narratives formed the foundation of African-American letters. They were written with a specific purpose in mind: to record the devastating impact of slavery and to persuade white readers of its many injustices. Slave narratives were often framed by letters or prefaces of recommendation written by white men to assure white readers of the authenticity of their contents. Many incarnations of the form emphasize the centrality of education and literacy to the fight for freedom. Henry Louis Gates, Jr., who argues that the search for a voice is central to African-American literature, perceives the legacy of the slave narrative in *The Color Purple*. He also draws connections with the autobiographical writing of Rebecca Jackson (1795–1871), a free black woman whose work, reviewed by Walker, was also influenced by the slave narrative. Gates observes that the 'spirit' to whom Walker 'dedicate[s]' her novel is the same one that 'taught Rebecca Jackson to read.'[49]

Hernton identifies several structural and thematic parallels between black fiction and the slave narrative genre: both 'focus on key individuals' and explore 'the collective situation of the group with whom the key individuals share a common oppression'; they 'portray the process of overcoming that oppression, both in concrete terms and in terms of the self-negating emotions of the protagonists.' Regarding Walker's novel, there is, however, 'one all-important difference': where the slave narrative foregrounds 'white-on-black oppression,' Walker's novel portrays 'black-on-black oppression.'[50] Like many critics, Hernton finds that Walker's manipulation of generic conventions in *The Color Purple* is informed by her gender politics:

■ Specifically, *The Color Purple* portrays black men as oppressors and brutalizers of black women. This means, in this instance, that a black woman took possession of a black-invented literary form that black men have always dominated and have always assumed as being exclusively their own property. If black women were to use this powerful literary vehicle, they were supposed to use it in defense of the 'whole' race – i.e., in defense of black men – to expose and decry white racism, white capitalism, and so on. Instead, Alice Walker utilizes the slave narrative to reveal the enslavement that black men level against black women.[51] □

Structurally, Hernton argues, *The Color Purple* emulates the slave narrative: it is 'in a sequential progression of episodes, incidents and scenes that depict physical brutality, torture, trials and tribulations, economic and sexual exploitation, and the inequality and injustice of it all,' that 'Walker shows the extreme barbarity of Celie's oppression and evokes heartrending moments of pathos.' Further parallels emerge when we consider the relationship between the novel's engagement of public and private issues: 'Celie's situation is not merely an individual "isolated incident." This is in keeping with the generic imperatives of the slave narrative tradition' the primary 'purpose' of which 'is to make *public* the injustices suffered by the protagonist' and 'to show the connection of the protagonist's suffering with the suffering of the entire group of which the protagonist is a member' (Hernton's italics).[52]

For Hernton, Walker's use of the slave narrative constitutes a 'radical leap forward': 'Walker repossessed the genre, for it belongs as much to women as to men, and she *womanized* it' (Hernton's italics).[53] While women such as Harriet Jacobs (1831–1897) have made important contributions to the genre, Walker is the first to write a 'womanist' slave narrative. However, the epistolary form of the novel causes problems for Hernton who sees a conflict between the subject matter of Celie's story and the form that it takes: 'the *writing* of the letters is incongruous with the texture and substance of Celie's narrative' (Hernton's italics).[54] Furthermore, Nettie's letters disconcert the reading of *The Color Purple* as slave narrative. While they 'provide needed information,' they are 'simply too much of a departure from the slave-narrative genre in which the rest of *The Color Purple* is decidedly written.'[55] Furthermore, doubts concerning the authenticity of Nettie's voice complicate the categorization of *The Color Purple* as the first 'womanist' slave narrative: Nettie's writing 'sounds too much like the stylized rendering of a middle-class romantic-heroine do-gooder.'[56]

The poet and critic bell hooks has expressed reservations about the categorization of *The Color Purple* as a post-modern slave narrative, highlighting the incompatibility of its utopian dimension with the genre. In 'Writing the Subject: Reading *The Color Purple*' (1993), she writes that Walker's 'fictive autobiography [...] parodies' the slave narrative. Problems with the novel's approach to history resurface in hooks' reading. In the slave narrative 'oppressed African-American slaves moved from object to subject, from silence into creating a revolutionary literature'; they 'worked to convey as accurately as possible the true story of slavery' and to 'creat[e] [...] a radical discourse on slavery that served as a correlative and a challenge to the dominant culture's hegemonic perspective.' In contrast, Walker's novel focuses 'less on historical accuracy and more on an insistence that history has more to do with the interpersonal details of everyday life at a given historical moment.'[57] Nettie's letters from Africa offer the most compelling evidence of Walker's true agenda:

■ Historical documents, letters, journals, articles, provide autobiographical testimony of the experience and attitudes of nineteenth-century black missionaries in Africa, yet Walker is not concerned with a correspondence between the basic historical fact that black missionaries did travel to Africa and providing the reader with a fictive account of those travels that is plausible. □

Walker, hooks argues, sacrifices '[h]istorical accuracy [...] to teach the reader history not as it was but as it should have been.'[58]

In her essay, hooks takes the opposing view to Hernton in her evaluation of the wider significance of the novel's central narrative, arguing that it does *not* reflect the concerns of the wider community as a slave narrative would: like Hernton, she notes that one of the 'revolutionary' elements of the slave narrative was 'the insistence that the plight of the individual narrator be linked to the oppressed plight of all black people so as to arouse support for organized political effort for social changes.' However, hooks finds that Walker 'appropriates' the genre only to 'legitimize and render authentic Celie's quest without reflecting this radical agenda.' Celie's story is, she insists, 'not representative.' For a start, there are significant differences between the experiences of the novel's women: Shug is not, like Celie, 'a victim of male domination'; in contrast to Celie, Sofia has not 'allowed patriarchal ideology to inform her sense of self.' Therefore:

■ [b]y de-emphasizing the collective plight of black people, or even black women, and focusing on the individual's quest for freedom as separate and distinct, Walker makes a crucial break with that revolutionary

African-American literary tradition which informs her earlier work, placing this novel outside that framework. □

Readings of *The Color Purple* as a neo-slave narrative are also problematic for hooks because of the novel's structural affinities with a Western literary tradition – the sentimental novel. Placing the emphasis on personal feelings arising from domestic experience and intimate relationships, sentimental novels often take an epistolary form. *Pamela; or, Virtue Rewarded* (1740) and *Clarissa; or, The History of a Young Lady* (1747), both by Samuel Richardson (1689–1761), are often identified as paradigms of the genre. hooks expresses unease with the association between the slave narrative and the novel of sentiment. She argues that 'by linking this form to the sentimental novel as though they served similar functions, Walker strips the slave narrative of its revolutionary ideological intent and content connecting it to Eurocentric bourgeois literary traditions in such a way as to suggest it was merely derivative.' In the slave narrative, '[l]iteracy is upheld [...] as essential to the practice of freedom.' According to hooks, however, Celie's writing is 'a gesture of shame.' It is the 'spoken word' that 'empower[s]' Walker's heroine: it is not her letters to God that foster 'self-legitimation' but her oral narration of her experience to Shug. Only when Celie 'has made the shift from object to subject' and begun to write to Nettie does writing become truly empowering.[59]

Several reviewers and critics, while reading *The Color Purple,* have been reminded of the strategies of nineteenth-century novelists. Diane Gabrielsen Scholl observes that, as a 'story of [...] changing fortunes,' the novel 'displays a kinship to Victorian novels,' which made liberal use of coincidental events and encounters in their engineering of plot; indeed, Scholl argues that *The Color Purple* surpasses the Victorian novel in terms of its 'dizzying series of ironic reversals.' Is Celie, Scholl wonders, 'a black Jane Eyre [1847, by Charlotte Brontë, 1816–55]?'[60] In '"Show Me How to Do Like You": Didacticism and Epistolary Form in *The Color Purple,*' Tamar Katz explores the novel in relation to its sequence of 'failed, misguided, or insidious models of instruction' and yet concludes that it is 'above all, a type of *Bildungsroman.*' This 'instructional model,' Katz notes, has its 'roots' in the 'didactic form' of the 'epistolary novel.'[61] While critics such as Marjorie Pryse argue that Walker merely 'pays lip service to the eighteenth-century roots' of the epistolary novel, others, such as Linda S. Kauffman, read her engagement with this tradition as part of her womanist project.[62]

Kauffman's essay 'Constructing Otherness: Struggles of Representation in *The Color Purple*' comes from her book *Special Delivery: Epistolary Modes in Modern Fiction* (1992). The book places *The Color Purple* in the company of other twentieth-century variations on the genre such as

The Golden Notebook (1962) by Doris Lessing (b. 1919) and *The Hand-maid's Tale* (1986) by Margaret Atwood (b. 1939). Kauffman's reading of *The Color Purple* illuminates how Walker both emulates and revises a genre initially dominated by white, male writers. She identifies *The Color Purple* as 'an intricate patchwork of different novelistic codes and genres' but, like hooks and Hernton, foregrounds the influence of two genres in particular, viewing the novel as a 'hybrid blending of epistolary and slave narrative.'[63,64] Kauffman raises no objection to this hybridity, but recognizes that racial politics separate Walker's novel from the epistolary tradition:

■ Race is nevertheless an irreducible difference between Walker's novel and epistolary predecessors, for initially Celie can only envision her Maker as a white patriarch, punishing her for crimes she did not commit but for which she nonetheless feels guilty. She is a cursed 'daughter of Ham,' victim of a racist biblical rhetoric as well as of an implacable social order.[65] □

Kauffman perceives the influence of the epistolary tradition in the following elements of Walker's novel: the 'injunction' which instigates Celie's letter-writing, Pa's warning that she can tell only God about their sexual contact;[66] the predominant 'discourse of pathos' that 'links Celie to Ovid's heroines, Héloise, and Clarissa';[67] the 'omnipresent threats' of 'silence, absence, and loss' that are 'paradoxically endemic in epistolary transmission.'[68] Kauffman notes that, like the letters of Richardsons's *Clarissa*, 'Celie's letters recount an unfolding moral development and spiritual epiphany utterly at odds with religious doctrine; both heroines forcibly confront the differences between letter and spirit, church dogma and faith.'[69]

Like Hernton, Kauffman examines the relationship between Walker's manipulation of genre and her gender politics. She builds on earlier explorations of Walker's engagement with the slave narrative by analy-zing her appropriation of particular *types* of this genre: the 'criminal confessional' in which 'the slave confesses to forbidden desires' such as 'the yearning for freedom' and in which 'slavery is presented as a system of benevolent controls' and the conversion narrative which 'similarly tend[s] to rob the slave of free will, by emphasizing that all suffering leads to a heavenly reward.' Kauffman identifies both varia-tions of the genre in *The Color Purple*: 'at various points Celie confesses her crimes, some real (like urging Harpo to beat Sophia[*sic*.]) and some imagined.' Kauffman notes that Celie seeks comfort by reminding her-self that 'Heaven last all ways' (*CP* 39). However, Celie writes herself out of these confessional and conversion narratives by developing her own 'conception of divinity': here the 'hybrid blending' of the two genres emerges most clearly, as the epistolary form plays an essential part in this transformation, providing the reader with insight into 'how Celie wrests language from those who would persecute and silence her.'[70]

Kauffman responds to the objection of Hernton concerning the epistolary form of the novel, arguing that 'writing is an act of specifying, a defiant testimony to Celie's growing ability to comprehend the injustice of her fate and to rebel against it.' Like hooks, she points out that 'literacy' in the slave narrative 'has been a vital source of liberation and salvation.' Unlike hooks, she argues that it performs the same function in *The Color Purple*: 'It is the only thing that keeps Celie from being "buried" alive' [*CP* 18]. Moreover, 'Walker reproduces the epistolary convention of writing-to-the-moment, complete with errors and crossings-out, in order to represent Celie's rebellion in process. The slow evolution of Celie's historical consciousness is accompanied by changes in her style as she masters reading and writing.'[71]

Furthermore, Kauffman argues that the much-maligned ending of the novel, in which Celie is reunited with her sister and achieves financial prosperity, is in keeping with its womanist agenda and its engagement with both genres: '[w]here tragic epistolary novels like *Clarissa* end with the heroine's death, comic ones end with reunions among the correspondents whose separation made writing necessary in the first place. Generic precedents can also be found in slave narratives.' She notes that from the work of Gustavus Vassa (1745–97), *The Life of Olaudah Equina, or Gustavus Vassa, the African: Written by Himself* (1789), 'onward, the economics of slavery is one of the major motifs in the plot.' She adds:

■ Vassa's economic shrewdness enables him to secure his freedom and to survive thereafter. Slaves had to master the mercantile system in order to set themselves free and to free their families. They had to shift paradigms, to learn how to exploit the exchange value of money rather than being exchanged themselves. Since such shrewdness is traditionally attributed solely to males, slave narratives reinforced the dominant culture's patriarchal bias; by showing Celie's transformation into a savvy businesswoman, Walker subverts that bias by shifting the gender paradigm as well as the economic paradigm.[72] □

In her essay '*The Color Purple*: Revisions and Redefinitions,' first published in *Sage: A Scholarly Journal on Black Women* (1985), Mae G. Henderson considers the juncture between Walker's use of particular generic conventions and her gender politics. Henderson's reading explores Walker's revisionist aesthetic with particular reference to her engagement with the epistolary novel and the fairy tale. She examines Walker's use of the epistolary form as a means of dramatizing a womanist approach to authorship: she argues that the novel 'subverts the traditional Eurocentric male code which dominates the literary conventions of the epistolary novel' and that Walker, '[by] appropriating a form invented and traditionally controlled by men, but thematicizing the lives and experiences of women [...] asserts her authority, or right to authorship.'[73]

The Color Purple offers a full expression of the possibilities for female intimacy that eighteenth-century male practitioners of the form only hint at: 'In the sentimental novel, the women frequently expire or ultimately succumb in form – if not always in spirit – to the patriarchal condition. The women in Walker's novel, however, reform the essential bases of the relationships, codes, and values of their world.'[74]

Henderson also points out that the epistolary form provides Walker with a means of engaging with the African oral tradition:

■ Celie's letters transpose a black and oral mode into a Western epistolary tradition (a form also adapted effectively by modern African writers such as Camara Laye [1928–80] and Ferdinand Oyono [b. 1929], whom Walker acknowledges as influences). Walker's use of the vernacular (sometimes called Black English) has invested an old and somewhat rigid form with new life.[75] □

Thus, 'Walker creates a new literary space for the black and female idiom within a traditionally Western and Eurocentric form. In the process of merging two forms and two traditions, *The Color Purple* extends both.'[76]

In her reading of *The Color Purple,* Maria Lauret illuminates how Walker not only revitalizes Western forms such as the epistolary novel and the *Bildungsroman* but also 'signifies on' them. Drawing from Henry Louis Gates, Jr.'s, definition, Lauret explains that signifying 'can be a way of covert, indirect communication between members of a group who understand its particular code, and it can be a form of playing tricks on someone outside the group by a devious use of words.'[77] She adds: 'To "signify on" a text (or a person) is to talk negatively about it, often in hyperbole and with either a light touch (in jest) or a heavier, more serious didactic intention.'[78]

By presenting Celie's experience in the form of letters, Walker ' "signifies on" the earliest novels in English, where white women's suffering in trying to protect their most precious commodity – their chastity – motivates plot and form.' As Lauret notes, 'such suffering pales somewhat in significance when compared with Celie's and that of numerous black women over the last three centuries.' Walker's 'signifying' is 'both heavy and light': it is 'heavy, in that it teaches us as readers about dominant assumptions regarding what is great literature and what is not.' Lauret points out that: '*Clarissa* and *Jane Eyre*'s legitimacy as canonical novels about (and by) "our" literary foremothers is taken for granted, whereas Celie's has to be established' both 'through a catalogue of suffering and Walker's heavily accented alternating use of standard and non-standard (African, American) English in the epistolary exchange.'

Walker's 'signifying' is 'light, because some of the familiar motifs of the eighteenth-century epistolary and nineteenth-century realist novel (absent mothers, lost and found relatives on different continents, surprise inheritances and initially recalcitrant lovers) are rewritten in *The Color Purple* to tragi-comic effect.' Lauret adds, however, that this kind of 'signifying' 'is done so obliquely that we cannot even say that this or that feature is clearly comic, whereas another is tragic: both elements criss-cross each other with the tragic dominating at the beginning and the comic at the end.'

The Color Purple also revises the gender and sexual politics of the epistolary tradition which initially limited its scope to 'fixed gender roles' and 'compulsory heterosexuality.' Unlike earlier epistolary novels or incarnations of the female-centred *Bildungsroman* such as *Jane Eyre*, Walker's novel features 'no female rivals' who must 'be killed off in order to establish [the heroine's] moral superiority.' Moreover, 'the love triangle,' a stock element of these traditions, 'is resolved in, first, a lesbian relationship between the women which bypasses the man and only later, once the villain has redeemed himself, in tripartite respect and harmony.'[79]

The Color Purple features in Claudine Raynaud's essay 'Coming of Age in the African-American Novel' (2004), where she notes that Celie's relationships with other women are in fact central to her growth: '[h]er coming of age [...] is the gradual understanding through the help of other protagonists, Sofia, Shug Avery, and her sister, Nettie, that she can claim her own beauty, her own self.' She observes also that readers might find that the mature Celie 'is much older than might be expected' and continues that the 'trait is common to a lot of heroes and heroines of the black novel. The deferral into adulthood of achievement and accomplishment is in direct relation to the weight of the burdens.'[80]

This chapter closes with extracts from Carolyn Williams's essay ' "Trying to Do Without God": The Revision of Epistolary Address in *The Color Purple*' (1988), which comes from *Writing the Female Voice: Essays on Epistolary Literature*, a collection edited by Elizabeth C. Goldsmith. For Williams the novel's epistolary form is central to its womanist agenda: indeed, it constitutes the novel's 'most fundamental representation of a concern with women isolated from one another within the patriarchal network, a concern that is also elaborately thematized within the novel.'[81] However, one of the most interesting lines of enquiry pursued by Williams involves the novel's departure from traditional incarnations of the epistolary novel – deviations that illuminate the novel's proximity to other, closely related autobiographical forms.

Williams draws from the research of Janet Gurkin Altman (b. 1945) on 'epistolarity' to explore the significance of Celie's choice of addressees. In *Epistolarity: Approaches to a Form* (1982), Altman explores what Williams terms the 'play of absence and presence' in 'epistolarity.'[82] Williams notes that by presenting a heroine who writes to God and receives no direct reply, Walker 'implicitly draws attention to a similarity between epistolary desire and prayer; both represent attempts, through language, to conjure presence from absence.'[83] Williams explores the implications of this parallel for the generic categorization of the novel:

■ In addressing God, Celie prays to read a sign of his presence in order to feel her own more clearly; if he were to answer her prayers, she would know herself, would know 'what is happening to [her]' [*CP* 3]. Of course, God never answers, and the epistolary relation remains incomplete. For Celie, the practice of addressing God simply reaffirms her solitude; she is essentially writing to herself. *The Color Purple* is thus an example of an epistolary novel with close affinities to the journal, diary, or autobiographical confession. As in those genres, here the practice of introspective letter writing records the disciplined process of increasing self-knowledge. In this case, however, self-revelation is at first referred to a principle of absolute exteriority – God – which is always paradoxically close to sheer interiority, and prayer always an exercise in attempted self-possession.[84] □

This reading of Celie's letter-writing opens up parallels with further genres. Williams likens the 'effect' of her address 'to that of the poetic strategy of apostrophe or prosopopoeia [...] in which the lyric address of something absent, inanimate, or dead conjures the illusion of presence and voice but at the same time has the uncanny effect of reflecting absence back upon the lyric "I." ' Williams adds: 'this feature of epistolary address [...] cuts across and complicates the fiction of increasing self-knowledge and self-presence, which is the generic mark of autobiography.'[85]

Celie and Nettie must 'accomplish the transformation, internalization, possession, and negation of God' and 'achieve a similar sort of faith in relation to the other; the sister, too, must be internalized.' This process ultimately hinges on 'absence.' The novel therefore can only gesture toward a fully-fledged epistolary dynamic, and thus its 'epistolary form' is 'ironic.' Williams argues that 'the most profound motives' of the novel 'depend upon [the] fact' that '[a] full epistolary exchange is never established, either with God or with Nettie,' but notes that 'the hope and faith that epistolary desire *might* be internally fulfilled sustain the epistolarity of the second half of the novel' (Williams' italics).[86] According to Williams, we must bear 'this lesson of epistolarity, its fictive trick of conjuring presence' in mind as we approach the novel's ending: 'Celie's internalized recreations of "Everything" and everyone eventually issue in their external appearances in the plot [...]. Celie is complete [...] [t]he parallel and divided plots of the two sisters are reunited. Time is figuratively reversed, and everyone feels young again.' At this point, 'epistolary address ceases altogether, for Celie's correspondent has returned.'

Finally, Walker's representation of her own position and status in the margins of the text serves as a meta-commentary on the play of absence and presence that grounds the novel: the epigraphs 'break the fiction of presence and refer us to [the novel's] author': by signing off with thanks to the characters and as 'author and medium,' Walker 'closes the book as if it had been one long letter to the reader and this were her signature.' Thus, '[t]he usual effects of epistolarity are set in motion again at the edges of the text in order to assert authorial presence and at the same time to deny it.' Walker's representation of herself as author and medium suggests that while she views the novel 'as artifice, an aesthetic form created by her own letter-writing hand,' she also 'refers authority to a power external to herself, who speaks through her.'[87]

Considering Walker's politics it is perhaps strange that this 'conception of the artist as mediating the voice of a higher power is but one step removed from the conception of the artist as analogous to or a surrogate for God' and that 'both conceptions are traditional in romantic literature where, as feminist critics have pointed out, they operate to reserve authorial power in the male line.'[88] However, Williams reminds us that in the novel 'the notion of God has been detached from the patriarchal chain of authorization' so that Walker's 'claim' to the status of 'medium' is 'at once more humble and at the same time more vast than the traditional male claim.' Walker's 'closing signature returns us to the opening epigraph of the novel': a dedication to '*the Spirit:*/Without whose assistance/Neither this book/Nor I/Would have been/Written.' Here, Walker 'introduces this epistolary fiction of presence with a gesture of deferring her own. Her dedication strikingly conflates life outside and inside the text; and it invites the reader to consider epistolarity as a paradigm for all creation.'[89]

The issue of *The Color Purple*'s generic identity is clearly a highly contentious one and remains very much open for debate. As the readings covered in this chapter demonstrate, several literary traditions resurface continually in explorations of Walker's use of genre. Many illuminating readings have emerged from these explorations. While critics have recognized Walker's engagement with particular genres, they have differed widely on the extent to which the novel emulates or subverts the codes and conventions of these genres as well as on the political implications of this engagement. For many critics, it is Walker's engagement with generic traditions that provides the key to the most contested and maligned elements of the novel.

The next chapter takes a closer look at Celie and Nettie's letters and shifts the focus to Walker's linguistic and narrative strategies.

CHAPTER THREE

Language and Narrative Poetics in *The Color Purple*

In her interview with Gloria Steinem, Walker identified the language of *The Color Purple* as her 'first language' and revealed the 'real rage' that she experienced at the thought that 'black people or other people of color who have different patterns of speech can't just routinely write in this natural, flowing way.'[1] Many critics who differed widely in their responses to Walker's novel found common ground in their engagement with what Trudier Harris terms the 'pattern and nuances of Celie's voice.' In an otherwise negative review of *The Color Purple*, Harris concedes that '[t]he form of the book, as it relates to the folk speech [...] is absolutely wonderful,' before taking issue with the plausibility of Celie's prowess as a writer. For Harris, Celie's language is the only realistic dimension of the novel: it evokes memories of her childhood in Alabama where 'black women [...] made art out of conversation' and 'created poetry out of cotton fields and rivaled the blues in the domestic images that came so readily to their tongues.'[2] For many reviewers, the language of *The Color Purple* elevated Walker to the status of 'poet.'[3] Robert Towers praises Walker for 'know[ing] how to avoid the excesses of literal transcription while remaining faithful to the spirit and rhythms of Black English,' and he singles her out as the novelist who has most effectively 'tapped the poetic resources of the idiom.'[4]

Walker's use of black folk speech has not been without its detractors.[5] In the essay 'Coming in from the Cold: Welcoming the Old, Funny-Talking Ancient Ones into the Warm Room of Present Consciousness, or Natty Dread Rides Again!' (1984), Walker describes events of the previous summer when a mother tried to ban *The Color Purple* from Oakland public schools. After reading only the first five pages of the novel, a Mrs. Green found much to condemn, not least its use of black vernacular: Walker's novel, she argued, 'degraded black people by its "exposure" of their folk language.'[6]

Other readers and critics have questioned the authenticity of the novel's language. In the same essay, Walker reveals that she initially sent *The Color Purple* to a black women's magazine in the faith that its editors 'would recognize its value better than anyone.' They rejected the proposal of publishing an extract from the novel on the grounds that 'Black people don't talk like that.'[7] In response to this declaration, Walker asserts that Celie shares the voice and language of her step-grandmother, Rachel. To deprive Celie of her own language would constitute an act of disempowerment; her language is the most compelling manifestation of Celie's burgeoning autonomy:

■ Celie is created out of language. In *The Color Purple* you see Celie because you 'see' her voice. To suppress her voice is to complete the murder of her. And this, to my mind, is an attack upon the ancestors, which is, in fact, war against ourselves. For Celie's speech pattern and Celie's words reveal not only an intelligence that transforms illiterate speech into something that is, at times, very beautiful, as well as effective in conveying her sense of her world, but also what has been done to her by a racist and sexist system, and her intelligent blossoming as a human being despite her oppression demonstrates why her oppressors persist even today in trying to keep her down. [...] She has not accepted an alien description of who she is; neither has she accepted completely an alien tongue to tell us about it. Her being is affirmed by the language in which she is revealed, and like everything about her it is characteristic, hard-won, and authentic.[8] □

This chapter focuses on readings that give thought to the political implications of Walker's treatment of both the spoken and written word in *The Color Purple*. In *The Signifying Monkey: A Theory of Afro-American Literary Criticism* (1988), Henry Louis Gates, Jr., observes that 'black letters' since the earliest slave narrative have 'represented and thematized' the 'curious tension between the black vernacular and the literate white text, between the spoken and the written word, between the oral and the printed form of discourse.'[9] Is there a 'tension' between orality and literacy in *The Color Purple*, a novel that delivers the heroine's folk speech to the reader in the form of letters? What are the functions and effects of Celie's folk speech? What is the impact of the shift to standard English with the arrival of Nettie's letters? This chapter closes with a discussion of Gates's reading of the novel, which illuminates Walker's contribution to the African-American literary tradition by analyzing its 'bivocality.'[10]

ORALITY AND LITERACY: READING CELIE'S LETTERS

In her comparative reading of 'imposed silences' in *The Color Purple* and Maxine Hong Kingston's short story cycle, *The Woman Warrior: Memories of a Girlhood Among Ghosts* (1976), King-Kok Cheung notes that both writers must make the choice of whether to write in the language of the mainstream or 'in a mode that reflects their multicultural legacies.' Both 'seek ways to transplant their native dialects to their texts, even if they risk being occasionally unintelligible to the reading majority.' Cheung adds that the 'stakes are high' for these women writers because 'reclaiming the mother tongue is much more than reproducing a dialect or marshaling a new vocabulary; it is also bringing to life a rich oral tradition in which women have actively participated.'[11]

For Maroula Joannou, Celie's folk speech plays a crucial role in shaping responses to a novel so frequently celebrated for its cross-cultural appeal: it is one of several factors that prevent readers from adopting Celie's narrative as one of female oppression. Walker's use of letters places the novel in the epistolary tradition but '[t]he reader is made critically aware of the dangers of universalizing white women's experience and of the distance which separates Celie's use of the vernacular from the elegant sentiments which characterised the earlier letter writers.'[12]

In 'The Dialect and Letters of *The Color Purple*' (1985), Elizabeth Fifer analyzes the functions of folk speech in relation to Walker's positioning of herself as 'medium' rather than controlling creator of the novel's world. Fifer observes that 'for Walker, dialect provides its own world view, its own answers, its own determination: it does not reduce, it compresses; it does not simplify, it focuses.'[13] Celie's letters secure her the position of 'main author'; they are 'an elaborate literary mask, subjective, emotional, affording Celie all the advantageous intimacy of first-person narration and Walker all the distance and control of omniscient narration.'[14] By following the evolution of her language – a development that fills Celie herself with wonder – Celie's letters maintain the 'remarkable illusion [...] that they are shaped by outside events, that they are created without authorial manipulation of reality by a powerless person buffeted by forces she can hardly control.'[15]

Not all readers are convinced by this illusion. In 'Writing the Subject: Reading *The Color Purple*,' bell hooks argues that the letters are little more than a disguise for Walker's didacticism. Like Harris, she casts doubt on the viability of Celie's writing regime, noting that Walker offers no context for it. This is read by hooks as a deliberate omission by Walker to conceal an inherent conflict within Celie's self-conception: '[Celie] must remain invisible so as not to expose this essential contradiction – that as dehumanized object she projects a self in the act of writing even as she records her inability to be self-defining.' This 'fiction' of 'Celie as writer,' however, enables Walker to 'oversee [...] her creation, constructing a narrative that purports to be a space where the voice of an oppressed black female can be heard even though the valorization of writing and the use of the epistolary form suppress and silence that voice.'

On the surface, Celie's language elides the gap between speech and writing. She is allowed to express herself through letters in 'the voice of a black folk idiom,' suggesting that she has 'enter[ed] a discourse from which she has been excluded – the act of writing.' In reality, hooks argues, 'her voice remains that of appropriated other – interpreted – translated – represented as authentic unspoiled innocent.' Indeed Celie as writer is the 'perfect foil' for Walker the 'creator.' Walker undeniably 'pays tribute to the impact of black folk experience as a force that channels and shapes her imaginative work,' but 'her insistent authorial presence detracts from this representation.'[16]

For Maria Lauret, writing functions as a last resort for Celie. Lauret agrees with bell hooks whose thoughts on this issue were outlined in the last chapter of this Guide. Lauret points to an 'often overlooked' moment in the novel when Shug reveals that she has fallen in love with Germaine, a nineteen-year-old man, and that she plans to leave Celie for six months. Celie does not offer a verbal response but uses the written word to express her grief, writing the words: 'Shut up' and 'He's a man' [CP 211]. This incident, Lauret argues, 'makes it clear that Celie's writing is not in itself an act of liberation or even self-expression, but rather an escape valve when all else fails. Celie writes [...] when telling is impossible.'[17] She obeys the opening edict not to tell until halfway through the novel 'when she tells Shug that Mr.— beats her. "Telling" is thus confined to spoken, human communication, whereas writing to God does not count as an act of self-empowerment.' Lauret marks this as a highly significant 'distinction,' because of its wider political implications: the distinction between the functions of writing and speech in Celie's personal experience 'defines the difference between the dominant (white) culture's valorisation of writing as against speech.'[18] The novel's 'privileging of speech and other cultural practices [...] over writing' extends to Walker's gender politics: this distinction is a way of 'engaging with white women's literature, which tends to take *writing* as the mark of liberation from patriarchal oppression' (Lauret's italics).[19]

In the previous chapter of this Guide, we saw how Linda Kauffman in her reading of *The Color Purple*'s engagement with the slave narrative and epistolary tradition views Celie's writing as essential to her understanding of her situation and the world around her. Celie's writing is 'a defiant testimony to [her] growing ability to comprehend the injustice of her fate and to rebel against it.' By tracing the shifts in Celie's writing style, Kauffman argues, the reader can follow the development of her 'historical consciousness.' Learning to read and write is a 'necessary struggle' for Celie who 'must first wrest the alphabet if she is to wrest mastery from the forces that oppress her.'[20] Kauffman emphasizes how speaking and writing inform each other: 'The vibrancy of Celie's written expression comes from its proximity to speech';[21] its 'orality [...]

remains in her phonetic spelling, her syntax, grammar, speech patterns, and her use of proverbs, repetition, and antithesis.'[22]

In her essay, '*The Color Purple*: Writing to Undo What Writing Has Done' (1986), Valerie Babb delivers a detailed analysis of the characteristics of Celie's vernacular narration and argues that it destabilizes the boundary between orality and literacy, fulfilling the functions of both: Walker not only uses literacy as a tool for challenging oppression, but, by fusing literacy and orality, also dismantles the polarisation of speech and writing which accords power to the literate, white male. Drawing on the research of Walter Ong, 'while ignoring the ethnocentricity shadowing his literacy/orality contrasts,' Babb analyzes features of Celie's language to show how orality informs her writing. She notes 'characteristics of oral expression' such as 'rhythmic balanced patterns, repetition-antithesis, assonances, use of proverbs known to a large body, [and] conservative use of language due to the need for repetition of tried and true expressions,' finding examples of all of them in Celie's letters.[23] For Babb, Celie's use of writing to express her pain concerning Shug's new lover is an act of release rather than suppression. Writing has become a crucial outlet for Celie through which she broadens her means of expression:

> ■ In Celie's hands, an antagonistic device once used to conquer and repress her now becomes an instrument assisting in her deepest self-examination. As she creates her own writing form, she also becomes more artistically expressive. She no longer merely states situational facts, she invents metaphors for her feelings. □

The natural world provides much of the inspiration for Celie's metaphors. Nature, 'like Celie [...] has been exploited by man.' As Babb notes, Celie draws comparisons with nature, telling herself that she is a tree when Albert beats her.[24] Babb attributes what Walker terms Celie's 'intelligent blossoming' to the fusion of orality and literacy in her letters: 'By imbuing written words with her own oral forms, Celie creates a new literacy which enables her to explore her own consciousness, create a new world vision.'[25]

NETTIE'S LETTERS: THE SHIFT TO STANDARD ENGLISH

Several reviews of *The Color Purple* bemoan the loss of Celie's folk voice to Nettie's studied standard English. Some critical readings have tried to account for this shift and explore its ramifications for the novel's politics. Elizabeth Fifer argues that Nettie's letters perform an important role, transporting the reader 'beyond Celie's microscopic world.' They bring balance to the novel by 'put[ting] Celie's letters into perspective':[26] 'their emotional coolness helps us bear Celie's trials, intersecting, juxtaposing, providing counterpoint and parallel lines of development.'[27] By elaborating two 'distinctly different narrative voices,' Walker enables the reader to reach an appreciation of 'Celie's plight within a larger cultural context.'[28]

Both sets of letters 'possess personal interior voices, but Celie's dialect adds an insider's language that immediately establishes a sense of community, an efficient capacity to express forbidden subjects, and a disarming exterior effect.' According to Fifer, the shift to standard English has important political implications: 'Since Nettie has been educated and has changed her diction, leaving behind the world of private language Celie inhabits, when Nettie's letters are finally opened and read, many years after their separation, it is the educated language of the outside world that must be translated, not the other way around.'[29]

By reading Nettie's letters, however, Celie develops a more expansive vision of her identity, her relationships and her future; while she learns about Nettie's life experiences in a different culture, she also 'learns about herself and understands how she appears to others, even what she can become.' Moreover, 'the language of [Nettie's] letters' transports Celie 'beyond the arbitrarily set limits of her culture, strengthening a self barraged by the claims and traditions of patriarchy.' Indeed, Fifer attributes Celie's breakthrough – her confrontation with Albert and her moment of self-assertion – to 'her power in union with Nettie.'[30]

In '"A View from Elsewhere": Subversive Sexuality and the Rewriting of the Heroine's Story in *The Color Purple*' (1991), Linda Abbandonato writes that Celie faces the 'burden' that all women share:[31] trying to construct an identity beyond the confines of patriarchal ideology. In the words of feminist critic Teresa de Lauretis (b. 1938), Celie must find another perspective: 'a view from "elsewhere."'[32] One of the means through which *The Color Purple* provides this alternative view is through its 'displacement of standard English.' Abbandonato notes that praise for the novel's linguistic properties centres primarily on the accuracy of Walker's ear, but that critics who 'insist on confining the novel to the genre of realism and thus evaluate the Southern black vernacular solely for its authenticity' miss the true 'significance' of Walker's 'achievement.' The true power of Celie's language is manifested in the responses of millions of readers who claim identification with her. Celie's voice is 'so compelling' that 'we participat[e] in her linguistic processes' and we 'begin to *think* as Miss Celie' (Abbandonato's italics). Therefore we are 'distracted from the extreme skill with which Walker exploits her formal and linguistic resources, and thus we underestimate the degree to which the text is language as performance.'

Like Gates and Lauret, Abbandonato reads *The Color Purple* as 'an elaborate act of signifying.' It is a signifying text because '[t]he apparently impoverished and inarticulate language of the illiterati turns out to be deceptively resonant and dazzlingly rich.' The text's signifying credentials inhere in the contrast between Celie's folk language and Nettie's standard English:

> ■ By incorporating Nettie's letters into Celie's text, Walker illuminates the contrast between Celie's spare suggestiveness and Nettie's stilted verbosity. Thus the expressive flexibility of the black vernacular, a supposedly inferior speech, is measured against the repressed and rigid linguistic codes to which Nettie has conformed; the position of standard (white) English has been challenged, and Celie's vitality is privileged over Nettie's dreary correctness.[33] □

Babb's reading of Nettie's letters sheds further light on their purpose. She agrees with Fifer that they play a crucial role in Celie's development which 'grows out of a coupling of her own written expression and the reading of Nettie's letters.' Once she has found the letters and Shug has 'place[d] [them] in temporal order [...] the cohesion and order Celie seeks in her life begin to take form.'[34] Where Abbandonato shows how Nettie's letters illuminate the richness of black folk speech through contrast, Babb sees subversive potential in the letters in their own right. In her reading, *both* sisters create new forms of literacy, Celie by undermining distinctions between the written and the oral word and creating a new linguistic system for herself, Nettie by subverting the traditional functions of standard English.

Babb draws from Walker's comments on the use and abuse of writing: in a 1984 interview Walker suggested that 'white male writers are more conscious of their own evil' precisely because it has been 'documented for several centuries – in words.' In the essay 'In Search of Our Mothers' Gardens' (1984), she expresses wonder at how the 'creativity of the black woman' has survived without the outlet of writing.[35,36] Walker is, Babb observes, 'very aware of the power of writing, and by extension, literacy, to preserve and value one culture while destroying and devaluing another.' She therefore directs her 'concern' toward 'the particular experience of black women under a system in which writing is used for cultural devaluation.' This concern emerges clearly in *The Color Purple* where both sisters 'change [writing] into an implement that is no longer solely the property of men and whites, but one used by black women to gain a greater awareness of themselves and to preserve their oral history.'[37] Both sisters consciously choose writing as their medium of self-expression because they initially associate the written word with power. Babb notes that 'overtones of literacy as an element of power are present' in the 'dominance' of Pa who claims that he won't give Nettie to Albert as he plans for Nettie to 'git more schooling':[38]

■ Here her stepfather shows that he not only has the power to barter them into marriage, but should he choose, also the power to decide on the availability of literacy to them. The power of literacy to provide an escape from sexual subjugation is also evident as illustrated by the events following Celie's rape. When Nettie seems to be next in line for the same violation, Celie vows to protect her sister, and realizes the best way to do so is to insure that Nettie has power, the power of literacy: 'I see him looking at my little sister. She scared.... But I say I'll take care of you.... I tell Nettie to keep at her books' [*CP* 6].[39] □

For Babb, Nettie's letters constitute a successful move to 'formulate[] a new text' for both sisters.[40] Like Celie, Nettie 'alters literacy and takes it out of its imperialistic function of dominating oral cultures.'[41] By committing her observations of the Olinka tribe to paper she 'allows' literacy 'to record an oral history that would otherwise be lost.' The standard language that distinguishes her letters from those of her sister is, Babb argues, deceptive. While the 'traditional[]' function of 'standard form[s]' is to create a sense of 'unity' this aim can be overturned so that they are used to categorize and alienate social groups.[42] In her letters to Celie, however, Nettie uses standard English to expand, liberate and preserve rather than to divide and contain: her 'use of the standard [...] give[s] cohesion not only to her and her sister's experience, but also to African and Afro-American experience.' Through her letters 'Nettie has changed the use of the written word from traditionally obliterating oral cultures to preserving histories which if not written down would ultimately be forgotten in a literacy-oriented society.' Babb adds: 'Ironically it is Nettie's writing, the tool used to debase them, which ultimately frees the sisters from the confines of a world which tells them they have no history, and their culture is of little value.' It is through writing that Nettie 'is able to record the many cultural wrongs committed by European cultures against African, so that these wrongs will be recognized, evaluated, and remembered.'[43] Through the written word Nettie is also able to challenge the biblical discourse which is often invoked by the white oppressors in Africa. In her letters she alerts Celie to the fact that the Ethiopians in the Bible were black. Babb also notes that Nettie's letters register connections between African and African-American culture, such as the oral narratives that originated in Africa and reached America.

Babb concludes her reading by considering how the absence of an addressee affects the functions of literacy in the novel: 'The capacity of writing as a communicative link is [...] overshadowed by its capacity to lend stasis to human experience so that it can be assessed and its capacity for recording and creating permanent history.'[44]

It is when the letters have been read in succession that this latter capacity emerges. '[A]s a unified body' they

■ echo the larger themes that are part of Afro-American history. The cycle of rape or attempted rape, oppression, escape, and awareness that each sister becomes a part of is a smaller representation of these elements within the course of black history.[45] □

While some early reviews of *The Color Purple* regarded Nettie's letters as little more than an unwelcome intrusion or a tool for Walker's didacticism, close scrutiny of Nettie's language opened up fruitful interpretations of its impact on Celie's development and on the novel's wider engagement with the politics of speech and writing. This engagement is one of the main concerns of the final reading in this chapter.

NARRATIVE STRATEGIES: *THE COLOR PURPLE* AND FREE INDIRECT DISCOURSE

The closing section of this chapter looks at Henry Louis Gates, Jr.'s, seminal readings of narrative poetics in Zora Neale Hurston's *Their Eyes Were Watching God* and Walker's *The Color Purple*. Walker's intertextual relationship with Hurston is explored in more detail in Chapter 7, which considers Walker's place in the African-American women's canon. Gates's reading features here as it pertains to the politics of both writers' formal and narrative strategies.

In the essay 'Color Me Zora: Alice Walker's (Re)Writing of the Speakerly Text,' first published in 1988, Gates demonstrates how Walker takes her cue from Hurston in a number of ways. Excerpts from Gates's reading come from 'Color Me Zora,' published in 1993 in Gates and Appiah's *Alice Walker: Critical Perspectives Past and Present*. This subchapter focuses on Gates's enquiry into both writers' exploitation of the possibilities of free indirect discourse.

The functions and effects of free indirect discourse have caused much debate amongst narratological theorists. In his study of narrative poetics, *Transparent Minds: Narrative Modes for Presenting Consciousness in Fiction* (1983), Dorrit Cohn writes that free indirect discourse 'may be most succinctly defined as the technique for rendering a character's thought in their own idiom while sustaining the third-person reference and the basic tense of narration.'[46] In *Narrative Fiction: Contemporary Poetics* (1983), Shlomith Rimmon-Kenan observes that free indirect discourse 'enhances the bivocality or polyvocality of the text by bringing into play a plurality of speakers and attitudes.'[47]

We have already seen that Gates points us to a dominant concern in African-American literature, to engage the 'curious tension between the black vernacular and the literate white text, between the spoken and the written word.' In 'Color Me Zora' Gates states that, given this concern, the 'central trope' of black writing becomes 'the quest of the black speaking subject to find his or her voice.' In his reading of *Their Eyes Were Watching God,* Gates credits Hurston with instigating a shift in the way that this quest is represented in black fiction. She used the 'bivocality' of free indirect discourse to dramatize her heroine's 'divided consciousness.'[48] Gates designates Hurston's novel a 'speakerly text': one that 'would seem primarily to be oriented toward imitating one of the numerous forms of oral narration to be found in classical Afro-American vernacular literature.'[49]

Hurston's *Their Eyes Were Watching God* takes the form of a frame narrative. When heroine Janie Crawford returns to her home town the local people speculate on the story of her life. A third-person voice sets the scene in standard English, but the black folk speech of the characters is preserved in written form. Janie decides to tell her life story to her friend Pheoby Watson, but the story itself is delivered to the reader in the standard English of the third-person voice. On the surface, it is only the dialogue between the characters within Janie's story and those speculating on it which renders this novel a 'speakerly text.' However, Gates draws our attention to a blending of voices within the third-person narrative discourse itself.

We have looked at various interpretations of Walker's manipulation of narrative levels in *The Color Purple.* Gates observes that in Hurston's novel the language of the characters 'comes to inform the diction of the voice of narrative commentary' as the heroine grows more self-aware. The novel, then, ultimately 'resolves that implicit tension between standard English and black dialect.'[50] Noting how novelists Ishmael Reed (b. 1938) and Ralph Ellison (1914–94) later elaborated on Hurston's exploitation of bivocality, Gates observes that their own groundbreaking strategies seem to leave little room for further 'narrative innovation.'[51] However, he sees in *The Color Purple* a revision of Hurston's narrative tactics and identifies this revision as 'an act of ancestral bonding that is especially rare in black letters.'[52]

For Gates, the innovation of Walker's strategy lies in the absence of division in Celie's narration. This absence eradicates readerly concerns that have often arisen from the use of free indirect discourse: questions about the location of narrative authority or the 'ironies of self-presentation.' Gates finds that Walker's manipulation of form – her use of letters – and style – the innocence of Celie's voice – forestall any readerly scepticism:

■ We read Celie reading her world and writing it into being, in one subtle discursive act. There is no battle of voices here, as we saw in *Their Eyes*, between a disembodied narrator and a protagonist; Celie speaks – or writes – for Celie and, of course, to survive for Nettie, then for Shug, and finally for Celie. □

Walker shapes our response to Celie by presenting us with a 'writing style of such innocence' that 'only the most hardened would not initially sympathize, then eventually *empathize* with her.' She 'manipulates our responses to Celie without even once revealing a voice in the text that Celie or Nettie does not narrate or repeat or edit' (Gates's italics).[53]

According to Gates, Walker's formal and narrative poetics furnish the reader with a particular kind of agency. Celie's growth, in contrast to that of Janie who reflects back on her experience, is in thrall to 'the tyranny of the narrative present'; only the reader can 'overthrow[]' this tyranny and 'reread Celie's text of development, the text of her becoming.' It is the reader who then 'suppl[ies] the coherence necessary to speak of a precisely chartable growth, one measured by comparing or compiling all of the fragments of experience and feeling that Celie has selected to write.'

Although Celie presents herself in 'a continuous written present,' the events of the novel are in the past.[54] It is through this movement between past and present that the opportunity arises for free indirect discourse. Celie is the author of her letters and the narrator and protagonist of the novel. As protagonist she is both 'Celie, the character whose past actions we see represented in letters' and 'that other Celie, who – despite her use of written dialect – we soon understand is a remarkably reflective and sensitive teller, or writer, of a tale, or her own tale.' It is owing to this 'interplay of the narrative past [...] and a narrative present' that she 'emerges as both the subject and the object of narration.' Thus, '[t]he subject–object split, or reconciliation,' represented through 'Hurston's use of free indirect discourse, in *The Color Purple* appears as the central rhetorical device by which Celie's self-consciousness is represented, in her own capacity to write a progressively better-structured story of herself.' This leads to a further difference in the nature of the bivocality of both novels:

■ Whereas Hurston represents Janie's emergent self in the shifting level of diction in the narrator's commentary and in the black-speech-informed indirect discourse, Walker represents Celie's dynamism in her ability to control her own narrative voice (that is, her own style of writing) but also in her remarkable ability to control all other voices spoken to Celie, which we encounter only in Celie's representation of them.[55] ☐

As readers we take it for granted that we are being presented with language in its original form when in reality we have only Celie's report of this language. Her use of black folk speech plays a crucial role in this assumption: as readers 'we believe that we are overhearing people speak, just as Celie did when the words were in fact uttered.' Gates reminds us however that 'we can never be certain whether or not Celie is showing us a telling or telling us a showing' as, '[i]n the speeches of her characters, Celie's voice and a character's merge into one, almost exactly as we saw happen in *Their Eyes* when Janie and her narrator speak in the merged voice of free indirect discourse.' Gates identifies this 'innovation' as Walker's 'most telling Signifyin(g) move on Hurston's text.'[56]

Gates examines a number of examples of this discursive conflation, such as the merging of Celie's voice with those of Albert's sisters, Kate and Carrie, in her twelfth letter to God and a remarkable blending of several discourses in an account of one of Nettie's letters: when Nettie writes that it is '[h]otter than July' and compares the effect of the heat to 'cooking dinner on a big stove in a little kitchen in August and July' Gates asks:[57]

■ Who said, or wrote, these words, words which echo both the Southern expression 'a cold day in August' and Stevie Wonder's album *Hotter Than July*? Stevie Wonder? Nettie? Celie? All three, and no one. These are Celie's words, merged with Nettie's, in a written imitation of the merged voices of free indirect discourse, an exceptionally rare form in that here even the illusion of mimesis is dispelled. ☐

Gates credits Hurston with demonstrating the possibility of merging dialect with standard English 'to create a new voice, a voice exactly as black as it is white.' She showed her contemporaries in 'the New Negro Renaissance that dialect not only was not limited to two stops – humor and pathos – but was fully capable of being used as a literary language even to write a novel.' Walker goes one step further. She exploits the possibilities of free indirect discourse introduced to her by Hurston but 'avoid[s] standard English almost totally' and demonstrates 'how one can write an entire novel in dialect.'[58] Gates urges us to recognize the significance of this development: it is 'as important a troping of *Their Eyes* as is the page-by-page representation of Celie's writing of her own tale. If Hurston's writing aspired to the speakerly, then Walker's apparently speaking characters turn out to have been written.' Gates goes on to explore the 'Signifyin(g) relationship' between Hurston and Walker in great detail.[59] His reading has become an essential reference point not only for critics interested in Walker's engagement with Hurston's novels but also for those interested in the responses of African-American writers to white society's hierarchical polarization of speech and writing.

Most critics are captivated by the authenticity and lyricism of Celie's voice on their first reading of *The Color Purple*. While many agree on the effect of Celie's words on the reader, they often disagree on the function of her black folk speech and her literacy in relation to the politics of the novel. Some of the readings in this chapter stress the crucial role that language and literacy play in Celie's self-realization. The following chapter takes a closer look at what Celie's language can tell readers about her conception of her identity, her relationships, her body and her history.

CHAPTER FOUR

Language and Subjectivity in *The Color Purple*

In her review of *The Color Purple*, Maryemma Graham defines the novel as 'a "coming out" story' in which 'the heroine achieves total self-realization.'[1] Readers from a range of cultural matrices continue to claim identification with Celie and her journey toward independence and fulfilment. For some critics this has proved problematic; they have argued that Walker prioritizes the personal over the political and claim that the novel does not take sufficient account of the impact of racial, sexual and social ideology on the development of the self. This chapter presents readings that explore Walker's handling of this development. Readings in the first section address the function of language in shaping Celie's understanding of her social relationships, her body and her sexuality. The second section examines two psychoanalytical readings: a Lacanian interpretation of Celie's progress by Daniel W. Ross (b. 1952) and Charles L. Proudfit's developmental analysis of Celie's anterior identity.

FRAGMENTATION AND UNITY: MODELS OF SELFHOOD IN *THE COLOR PURPLE*

In an early reading of the novel, 'Alice Walker's Celebration of Self in Southern Generations' (1983), Thadious M. Davis places Walker's treatment of Celie's development within the context of her other novels and finds that *The Color Purple* offers her richest representation of self-realization and fullest exploration of the relationship between self and society. The novel is Walker's 'strongest effort so far to confront the patterns in a specified world and to order and articulate the codes creating those patterns.' After she has established these 'patterns' Walker uses them 'to connect, assimilate, and structure the content of one human being's world and relationship to that world.'[2] Davis notes that the 'social interactions and institutions' that 'typically define human reality [...] do not ultimately define Celie's.' Her 'reality is [...] based upon her singular position and the abstractions she herself conceives in the course of her everyday life. Her inner life is unperverted by the abuse and violence she suffers.' Moreover, her relationships with others only inform her 'sense of social codes in the public world' once she 'has formulated the outlines of her private identity in writing.'[3]

In Celie's much-celebrated assertion to Albert that she is 'pore [...] black' and 'may be ugly and can't cook' but is 'here,' Davis hears an echo of 'folk philosopher' Jesse B. Semple, from the poetry of Langston Hughes (1902–67):[4] 'I'm still here.... I've been underfed, underpaid.... I've been abused, confused, misused.... I done had everything from flat feet to a flat head.... but I am still here.... I'm still here.'[5] Davis reads this 'verbal connection' as an 'actualization' of self 'rather than the potentiality that most often appears in Walker's work.' Celie's 'actualization' constitutes the 'first "happy ending"' in Walker's fictional world and is therefore 'an achievement deserving of celebration.'[6]

Later interpretations cast doubt over such positive readings of Celie's development by scrutinizing the tensions inherent in her self-conception. The following readings look at the tension between unity and fragmentation in Celie's conception of her identity and her body. Wendy Wall's 'Lettered Bodies and Corporeal Texts' was first published in *Studies in American Fiction* in 1988. References to the essay in this Guide come from the collection *Alice Walker: Critical Perspectives Past and Present* (1993). Wall's essay examines the strategies deployed by Celie to come to terms with the corporeal identity imposed on her by Pa and Albert. Wall takes as her starting point the theory of radical feminist philosopher Mary Daly (b. 1928), who 'describes how one ideological group establishes power by imprinting its traces on the bodies of other people'; such imprinting 'often involves invading, cutting, impressing, and fragmenting.'[7] Walker's novel 'abounds with instances in which authority is inscribed on the human body.' By writing letters, Celie 'acquires a means of re-inscribing the imprints and the contours of her body in such a way as to allow self-expression.' However, Wall sees Celie's writing as being fraught with ambiguity. The fragility of Celie's corporeal identity has its correlative in the novel's composite, epistolary form: *The Color Purple* 'presents a strange conflation of text and body; both the novel's form and the main character's corporeal existence are disjunct entities with malleable, tenuous boundaries.'[8]

Wall reads Celie's letters as 'the culmination of a series of anti-selves that [she] creates to mediate between herself and her oppressive environment' and as a mechanism for the displacement or containment of those feelings that she senses she must conceal. The letters constitute a 'surrogate body for Celie,' which both 'fends off pain by siphoning off her feelings of degradation' and enables her 'to express and thus feel the intensity of her emotions.' Wall points out that although Celie is not responsible for her bifurcation, she sustains it 'by displacing a part of herself onto this second body.'[9] By confining her secret thoughts to letters, she 'perpetuates' the 'initial fragmentation' caused by others. However, writing also enables Celie 'to remember her violated body through language.' Her letters are 'poised against self-destruction; they are an attempt to preserve a "real" self by burying it within a diary.' Therefore, they account for Celie's apparent passivity in the face of abuse and oppression: she 'can survive these abuses only by recording them in a diary which acts as her second memory. She displaces her voice onto this silent, uncommunicated text.'[10] Walker, then, presents Celie as 'a serial being, struggling to unite herself in a form that necessarily fractures (and makes tenuous) an identity.'

The form of the novel 'produces an analogue to the female body within the text, as both are continually fragmented and remembered.' The interplay of corporeal and discursive identities is also figured by Albert's trunk, which contains Nettie's letters, underwear belonging to Shug and some pornography. The trunk 'frames together the stolen letters and the fetishized female body, connecting the disrupted linguistic text and the dismembered body.'[11] Nettie's account of genital mutilation in Africa features further images of division of the female body: genital mutilation is 'an attempt to recodify gender distinctions, to write sexual differentiation on the body through ritual.'

Walker challenges these essentialist codifications of gender and sexuality through her portrayals of Shug and Sofia. Only when Celie witnesses their 'usurp[ation] of masculine power,' is she able to pursue her lesbian relationship with Shug, assume the traditionally masculine role of entrepreneur and revise her conception of her body. At this stage, 'language' becomes her most potent tool: 'Celie learns that the socially circumscribed body can be dissembled and reconstructed by re-imagining the self and projecting that image onto the world through language.' Wall finds that this 'shift in focus away from the physical body onto a dispersed self follows a pattern in the text of denying the "imagized" body.'[12]

As Celie's apprehension of her body changes, so does the function of her writing: it no longer serves as a means of displacing pieces of a fractured self, but as an expression of a coherent, authorized self. Wall summarizes:

■ Because Celie no longer writes what she cannot say but *records* her active self-authorization, her letters cease to act as an 'other' confined self. The differences between inside and outside lessen as she no longer has to compartmentalize in letters a radically different internal self; instead she can release this self to interact with the external world. She can refuse to act as slave to her family, she can demand personal satisfaction in her relationships, she can realize her significance. The body is released into the form of her 'lettered' text: an identity that is porous and disjunct (Wall's italics).[13] □

Wall suggests that Walker's novel 'addresses the current rift between Anglo-American feminism and French feminist theories concerning the notion of bodily fragmentation and gender construction.' Whereas '[m]ainstream American feminists' such as Daly 'concentrate on the powerlessness of the fragmented woman,' French feminists 'see disjunction and disunity as a desired state.' Walker 'walks a thin line between these two notions'; she demonstrates the 'horrors of Celie's violent division by rape, yet she indicates that Celie's control of this division serves as a tool for reworking her position.'[14]

Nevertheless, much remains unresolved in the novel. Divisions continue to threaten Celie's environment and she will continue to block or displace them with silence. For Wall, the novel's conclusion offers an optimistic outlook on gender divisions in 'black culture', but little hope of resolving racial conflict in America. Like many critics, Wall finds that the impact of Celie's celebrated development is limited to the personal narrative: it does not empower her to tackle the ideological tensions in the world around her. Drawing on the terminology of philosopher W. E. B. Du Bois (1868–1963), who stated that the African-American is 'gifted with second-sight in this American world, – a world which yields him no true self-consciousness, but only lets him see himself through the revelation of the other world,' Wall argues that Celie is able to 'resolve her double-consciousness' but she will 'still have to suppress her desires within the culture at large.'[15,16]

Wall points to the final exchange between Sofia and the mayor's daughter, Eleanor Jane, whom Sofia cared for. By the end of the novel Eleanor Jane has a baby boy, Reynolds Stanley Earl. When she makes the assumption that Sofia loves him, Sofia responds that she does not. Shocked by Sofia's negation, Eleanor Jane declares that there must be 'something unnatural' about Sofia, telling her: 'All the other colored women I know love children.'[17] Sofia tells Eleanor Jane that she loves children but that any black woman who claims to love a white woman's children does so only out of fear. Sofia has her 'own troubles' and, when he becomes an adult, Reynolds Stanley will 'be one of them.' Eleanor Jane protests: 'I won't let him be mean to colored,' and Sofia responds: 'You and whose army?'[18] Celie reports this exchange but offers no comment on it. According to Wall, this tells us that 'Celie, like the others, will once again silently acquiesce externally while revolting internally.'[19]

Judy Elsley pursues some of the issues raised by Wall concerning Celie's fragmentation in her essay ' "Nothing can be sole or whole that has not been rent": Fragmentation in the Quilt and *The Color*

Purple' (1999). Elsley considers Celie's development from a feminist perspective. *The Color Purple* has generated an abundance of feminist readings, some of which are featured in Chapter 7 of this Guide. Elsley's reading appears here because it pertains specifically to the issue of self-construction. Her reading posits that Walker, through her elaboration of Celie's narrative, rejects the traditionally masculine emphasis on self-containment and strong ego boundaries and presents fragmentation as a form of empowerment. As Wendy Wall notes, French feminist theory views 'disunity as a desired state.' Elsley reads Celie's oppression as confirmation of the proposal of second-wave feminist Luce Irigaray (b. 1932), delineated in *This Sex Which Is Not One* (1977), 'that patriarchal society puts value on women only to the degree that they serve the purpose of commodities of exchange between men.'[20] Celie's narrative shows that a woman can achieve autonomy only by 'taking apart the patriarchal ways of being to create a space for herself' which enables her 'to accept her own fragmentation [...] and thus validate herself.'[21]

This possibility surfaces in the opening words of the novel. While many readers and critics have found the apparent denial of self, the 'I am' that opens the novel unsettling, Elsley perceives 'deep wisdom' in Celie's 'early refusal of a sense of self as single and whole':[22,23] it constitutes a refusal to enter into a system that 'already categorizes her as "other." ' Elsley argues:

> ■ The single 'I' forces a woman to make choices, not only between self and other, but also between the different pieces of herself. A woman in Celie's position is damaged not strengthened by embracing one part of herself at the expense of denying other parts. □

In her formative years, Celie retreats into 'autism' when she is abused, telling herself that she is a 'tree.' She continues to 'dissociate[] herself from her body' and does not experience sexual fulfilment until she meets Shug. Celie must neither resign herself to this disembodiment nor seek to formulate 'a single "I" '; instead, she must take a 'route that lies between those alternatives.' It is through her relationships with women that Celie 'begins to connect the fragments of herself.'[24]

Walker uses various symbols in the novel to figure the kinds of identity available to her heroine. Celie and Sofia's quiltmaking enterprise sets the standard for Celie's movement from passive object to active subject. Elsley observes: 'Quiltmaking turns being torn into tearing, turns object into subject. Active creation replaces passive victimization as the two women, their sisterhood reaffirmed, set about constructing a pattern of their choice out of the fragments of their lives.'

Two further symbols figure the crucial shift in Celie's perception of herself: the scissors held by Pa when he approaches Celie, claiming that he wants her to cut his hair, and the curtains that provide the material for Celie and Sofia's quilt. Elsley explains that the scissors represent the unhealthy division that alienates facets of the self: 'Like the material cut by a pair of scissors, [Celie's] sex has been sharply separated, cut into by Pa's rape and then forced open by the birth of her two babies.' The curtains, like the scissors, 'open and close,' but they represent the possibility of constructing a self that is relational and autonomous, fragmented and coherent: they 'fulfill [...] their function, paradoxically, through their ability to find wholeness while also being fragments. They are complete in themselves as they draw together or softly separate, unlike the scissors which need an object to cut to do their work.'

Elsley views Celie's 'association with the curtains' as 'the beginning of her sexual identity.' Here, Irigaray's theory comes into play: in *This Sex Which Is Not One*, 'Irigaray describes a woman's sex as two lips in continuous contact with each other.'[25] Thus, '[m]ale oneness or wholeness is alien to woman. If she tries to attain that oneness, she is, like Celie, "put in the position of experiencing herself only fragmentarily, in the little-structured margins of a dominant ideology, a waste or excess." '[26,27] Only by rejecting the model of the contained, totalizing 'I' can Celie attain emotional and sexual fulfilment.

PSYCHOANALYTICAL READINGS OF CELIE'S DEVELOPMENT

The following section focuses on interpretations of Celie's development that draw on various dimensions of psychoanalytical theory. Psychoanalysis is concerned with the influence of early experiences and relationships on the construction and development of sexual identity. It is not surprising that *The Color Purple*, a novel that opens with an uncompromising account of the rape of a girl by the man she knows as her father, has attracted the attention of psychoanalytical critics.

This section begins by looking at Daniel W. Ross's essay, 'Celie in the Looking Glass: The Desire for Selfhood in *The Color Purple*' (1988). Ross illuminates the ways in which Walker's fictional account of female development counters and revises psychoanalytical theories about the formation of identity. He argues that the theories of French psychoanalyst Jacques Lacan (1901–81) are particularly relevant to readings of the development of Celie, a subject who is initially denied a social role, confined to a very limited environment and defined by her body.

Lacan emphasizes the role of language in the construction of sexual identity. He argues that the human subject moves through three 'orders': the imaginary, the symbolic and the real. As the subject passes through the imaginary order he goes through a stage of *méconnaissance*, or misrecognition: he mistakenly sees himself as a coherent and fully formed self, but does not recognize his place in the symbolic order that encompasses those meanings and codifications that predate the subject. When the subject enters the symbolic order, he tries to express himself but must first recognize that language is a shared entity. The real order constitutes what lies within and beyond the self but which defies signification through language.[28]

In this reading of Celie's development, Ross directs us to her first mirror scene with Shug Avery as a pivotal moment. When Celie tells Shug that she has never experienced sexual fulfilment, Shug tells her to look at herself 'down there' in the mirror. Reassured by Shug's presence, Celie places the mirror between her legs and is reminded of a 'wet rose' and immediately claims this part of her body as her own. She experiences 'a shiver' when she touches her clitoris.[29] For Ross, this moment marks the 'discovery of desire – for selfhood, for other, for community, and for a meaningful place in the Creation.'[30] Ross reads Celie's mirror scene as a revision of the Lacanian concept of the misrecognition stage. In describing the misrecognition stage Lacan uses the image of the infant seeing itself as a unified entity in the mirror for the first time. However, in *The Color Purple* the mirror scene enables Celie to claim facets of her identity that she has hitherto been denied.

Like Elsley, Ross illuminates the advantages of bifurcation for Celie: Lacan argues that 'the mirror stage offers the child only an illusion of whole selfhood, when in fact the subject is always split.' In *The Color Purple*, Walker offers an 'optimistic revision' of this model: the novel 'endorses another view prevalent in modern thought – that such illusions are not destructive but are positive accommodations that allow one to find meaning in life.'[31] Celie experiences Lacan's *méconnaissance*, the misrecognition that is an essential step toward selfhood, but 'for [her] the mirror opens the door of her imagination, helping her envision a world of new possibilities for herself.'

In her opening letters to God, Celie is 'arrested in the pre-mirror stage of development': she has no recognition of herself as subject. Had she 'elid[ed]' the mirror stage, she would have been 'trapped in a very early stage of development,' left 'without an awareness of externality or otherness' and, according to Lacan, unable to socialize and enter the symbolic order.

In the previous two chapters of this Guide we have seen that critics such as bell hooks and Maria Lauret have identified the spoken word as Celie's most powerful tool. It is through her conversations with Shug – not her letters – that she uncovers the possibility of self-realization. Ross identifies speech as one 'area of development' that is 'retarded if the mirror stage is elided.' Celie's 'inability to find a listening audience for herself is another sign of her autism, another result of her arrested development.' Only when she can find a listening audience will she develop a healthy, full sense of self.

Shug is the one person who is 'able to draw Celie out of her autism.'[32] She fulfils the role of 'sympathetic mentor and friend' and the possibility of 'a relationship that psychotherapist Sharon Hymer calls a "narcissistic friendship."' Quoting Hymer, Ross explains: 'In the earliest stage of such a friendship, the narcissistic friend serves as "the initiator of activities as well as the provider of a value system and lifestyle which the patient embraces as a germinating ego ideal."' It is Shug who 'initiate[s] such activities for Celie, helping her through the mirror stage to a discovery of her own body, her capacity for speech, and her ability to love an other.'[33]

Shug rescues Celie's corporeal identity from its 'arrested development.' As a result of sexual abuse, Celie apprehends her body in fragments; from a psychoanalytical perspective, such fragmentation is anything but empowering. According to Ross, Celie must find a new way of experiencing this fragmentation in order to achieve even 'a desire for selfhood':[34] 'Rather than defining herself in terms of fragmentation or of lack, she must learn to define herself synecdochally, seeing *part* of her body, specifically her genitalia, as a sufficient symbol of herself as a whole' (Ross's italics).[35]

Shug inspires this new mode of seeing in a number of ways: she allows Celie to nurse her through an illness, enabling Celie to 'come to grips with the complicated feelings of separation and ambivalence that characterize her thoughts of both Olivia [her daughter] and her mother';[36] by naming a song for Celie, Shug 'assures the integrity of Celie herself' and enlightens her to the idea that 'language need not come under the jurisdiction of male authority.' This brings Ross to the mirror scene which prompts a shift in Celie's perception of her corporeality and, in particular, her genitalia. Shug shows Celie how to masturbate, giving her a new conception of her 'entire body' and enabling her to 'view her genitalia synecdochally.'[37]

Shug also fulfils the role of surrogate mother, or '(m)Other,' in Lacanian terms: the figure with whom the 'I' first 'identif[ies]' itself.[38] At this point in his reading, Ross turns to the theories of Sigmund Freud (1856–1939) about female identity and sexuality. Explaining his theory of the Oedipus complex, Freud writes: 'It is the fate of all of us, perhaps, to direct our first sexual impulse towards our mother and our first hatred and our first murderous wish against our father.'[39] He posits that the male infant focuses his sexual attention on the mother, but the threat of castration leads him to sublimate this desire, which he focuses on a different adult female. This brings about identification with the father. Freud is less confident in diagnosing the formation of female sexual identity. He finds that the female infant also begins by projecting sexual desire onto the mother. However, when she realizes that she has already been castrated, she directs this attention to the father.

Ross draws on the novel's back story to show how Walker recasts Freud's theories about female identity and sexuality. In her letters Nettie tells Celie that their real father was lynched by racist white men when Celie was two years old. Their mother married their stepfather, Alphonso, known to them as 'Pa,' when Celie was, Ross estimates, 'three to four years old': it is at this age that the 'Oedipal drama' recurs. In her first letter Celie tells us that her mother curses her before she dies. For Ross, 'Celie's early life proves to be a perverse rewriting of the Oedipal script, with Celie aware of her mother's ambivalence about yielding her wifely role to her daughter. [...] Celie's guilt is augmented by her mother's questioning her pregnancy and her cursing Celie on her deathbed.' Ross concludes: 'Given the profound guilt and confusion that Celie must have felt about replacing her mother, in addition to the disruption of her own psychic growth and the continued brutalization to follow, it is little wonder that Celie would seek to annihilate self.' However, Nettie's discovery and 'the intervention of Shug as (m)Other' enable Walker's heroine 'to reimagine the possibilities of selfhood.'[40]

Other Freudian theories of female subjectivity are undermined by Celie's development. In particular, Shug's multifaceted role in Celie's development debunks Freud's categorization of male and female love:

■ As (m)Other, Shug gives Celie an unusual form of identification, at least for a woman. One of Freud's most controversial ideas is his suggestion that women tend to develop inferior object-choices to men's: where men transfer their narcissism to an other, women tend to rechannel love back into the self. Such women love themselves more than anyone else, and they seek not to love but to be loved ('On Narcissism' 89). Man's 'superior' object-choice is 'anaclytic,' in other words, based on the mother-imago; but, as we have seen, Celie also grounds her attachment in an other – Shug – who represents for her a mother-imago.[41] □

Celie's apparently 'masculine' choice of Shug as lover is the first of 'several such choices' that galvanizes her development. Ross returns to the theories of Lacan, who identifies two signs which mark the end of the mirror stage: the 'coherent use of language' and 'the development of aggressivity.' We have seen how Shug facilitates Celie's use of language, but 'aggressivity,' according to Ross, 'poses more sinister possibilities' for Celie. When she has developed her sense of self and has discovered Nettie's letters, she feels compelled to avenge herself and vows to destroy Albert. Shug prevents Celie from acting on this urge. As she moves toward autonomy, Celie learns to sublimate her aggression in two ways: through 'assertive speech' and sewing.[42]

Sewing enables Walker to explore the possibility of collapsing gender boundaries, thus debunking Freud's view of sewing outlined in his essay 'Femininity' as 'evidence of woman's shame, caused by her castrated genitals.'[43] Ross argues that '[f]or Celie the sewing of unisex trousers represents not a means of covering up her castrated genitals but of binding together the sexes.' Celie's sewing places her in the company of women characters in American literature such as Nathaniel Hawthorne's Hester Prynne who 'use their art not to reveal their shame, as Freud suggests, but to transplant it, placing it where it really belongs – on their male oppressors.'[44]

The final mirror scene in the novel occurs after Shug has left Celie for Germaine. Ross reads this scene as the litmus test of Celie's development: 'Standing naked before the glass, Celie asks herself, "What would she love?.... Nothing special here for nobody to love" [*CP* 220]. That Celie comes through this depression signifies that she has broken free of Shug, further establishing her independence and identity.'[45]

In his essay 'Celie's Search for Identity: A Psychoanalytic Developmental Reading of Alice Walker's *The Color Purple*' (1991), Charles L. Proudfit stakes out new territory in his investigation of Celie's progress by placing it within the context of psychoanalytic developmental psychology. He makes the back story of the novel the focus of his exploration, engaging with Freudian theories about the significance of the human subject's early orientation toward the mother. In his reading of Walker's novel Proudfit hopes to draw attention to 'the importance of the mother for the female infant, child and adult as she struggles to separate, to individuate, to develop her own identity, and to make a final choice of love object.'[46] The points presented in this chapter represent one aspect of a detailed reading; they have been chosen because they shed an interesting light on some of the criticisms levelled at *The Color Purple*, in particular those delivered by Trudier Harris.

Drawing from the theories of analyst and paediatrician D. W. Winnicott (1896–1971), Proudfit defines 'the study of the infant's and the child's development,' or object relations theory, thus: 'the study of the infant or child's development that focuses upon the unconscious, conscious, and maturational processes that *occur within the mother–infant/child matrix*' (Proudfit's italics).[47] Proudfit applies the basic principles and features of Winnicott's theories to Walker's representation of female relationships in *The Color Purple*. One key feature of these theories is the ' "good-enough mother" [...] who is empathetically

attuned to her infant's needs' and who 'provides a "holding environment" ' for the child.[48] It is in this environment that the child makes the
transition from attachment to the mother to independent subject. The
'good-enough mother' functions as the 'auxiliary ego' and the 'mirror'
in which the child 'sees itself reflected' until, if the reflection remains
positive, it eventually begins to see what Winnicott terms a 'True Self.'
If the mother does not reflect a positive image 'we have the beginning
of a compliant "False Self." '[49] According to Proudfit, Celie and Nettie
exemplify these opposing models of selfhood, with only Celie achieving an authentic identity. He speculates that both Celie and Nettie were
deprived of "good-enough mothering" after the arrival of Pa and that
Celie 'became mother surrogate to' her brothers and sisters as well as a
'sexual replacement' for her mother.

Drawing on the back story of the novel and the theories of psychoanalyst Leonard Shengold, Proudfit responds to one of Harris's doubts
concerning Celie's development: that she does not react against abuse
and oppression. He argues that the 'portrait of Celie as a traumatized
and depressed survivor-victim of parent loss, physical and emotional
neglect, rape, incest, and spousal abuse [...] is in fact a clinically accu-
rate description of what Leonard Shengold calls "soul murder." '[50] In
Soul Murder: The Effects of Child Abuse and Deprivation (1989), Shengold
defines 'soul murder' as the 'trauma imposed from the world outside
the mind that is so overwhelming that the mental apparatus is flooded
with feeling.' His theory posits that '[o]ur identity depends initially on
good parental care and good parental caring – on the transmitted feeling
that it is good that we are there.' He adds: 'What happens to the child
subjected to soul murder is so terrible, so overwhelming, and usually so
recurrent that the child must not feel it and cannot register it, and resorts
to a massive isolation of feeling, which is maintained by brainwashing
(a mixture of confusion, denial, and identifying with the aggressor).'[51]
Proudfit finds that Celie's behaviour manifests several signs of 'soul murder': her reliance on strategies to deal with isolation such as making
herself into a 'tree'; her tendency to 'identif[y] with her male aggres-
sors'; her 'harbor[ing]' of 'murderous rage' which threatens to emerge
when Albert's father criticizes Shug and when Celie discovers Nettie's letters.[52] Proudfit moves on to discuss how Celie overcomes these
feelings. Like Ross, he highlights the importance of those 'surrogate
mother' figures in the novel who enable Celie to work through 'several
developmental processes that were traumatically halted at age two and
that need to be readdressed in her skewed and delayed adolescence.'[53]

Proudfit finds that Celie's experiences in her early, pre-trauma years
account for her gravitation toward women: first of all, 'Celie's father's
adoration of his pregnant wife and mother of his daughter [...] strongly
suggests that femaleness and femininity were highly valued by both

mother and father, and that Celie's core gender identity is femaleness.' Furthermore, Celie does not complete a crucial 'developmental phase that occurs roughly between six and twenty-four months':[54] a phase during which the infant experiences an urgent need for the mother. Thus, Celie gravitates toward 'the ministrations of women' in order to 'resume the developmental tasks of separation, autonomy, and identity formation': tasks that the loss of her mother curtailed.

Proudfit recognizes a number of ways in which Shug helps Celie to complete this process. By initiating a dialogue about Celie's experience of rape and incest, she offers what Winnicott terms a 'holding environment':[55] this 'enables Celie to verbalize and to get in touch with long-repressed memories and feelings and work them through.'[56] Shug also saves Celie from herself when she is assailed by anger upon the discovery of Nettie's letters. Finally, her desertion of Celie for a nineteen-year-old man forces Celie to reach coherent selfhood on her own and leads her to 'unconsciously experience Shug's separateness, uniqueness, and autonomy, as well as her own.'[57]

Proudfit also uses his psychoanalytical approach to address criticism of Nettie's characterization. He draws here on Winnicott's theory that the 'False Self' dominates when the ' "not good-enough mother" mirrors her own self to the infant rather than mirroring the infant back to itself, thereby making the infant perceive rather than apperceive' so that it 'complies with mother and her needs.'[58] In contrast to Celie, who is part of 'an intact, loving, traditional family with "good-enough mothering," ' during her early years, 'Nettie spends the first several months of her life experiencing severe physical and emotional deprivation and the first several years complying with the emotional needs of a depressed and mentally unstable mother.' Proudfit concludes that 'it is reasonable to speculate that Nettie, in order to survive, quickly learned to comply with her environment; out of necessity she developed a "False Self" at the expense of her "True Self." '[59]

According to Proudfit, the novel sustains this reading of Nettie. He draws our attention to the contrasting status of the sisters at the end of the novel to support his psychoanalytical diagnosis. When they are finally reunited we see the difference between the models of identity embodied by the two sisters. Nettie arrives with her new husband Samuel, confirming his first wife Corrine's intuition that Nettie still needs to express 'love for the oedipal father.' Proudfit reminds us that 'Nettie, unlike Celie, was not traumatized at the height of the rapprochement period, when a child *needs* its mother' (Proudfit's italics). Nettie therefore 'passes through' the Oedipal complex 'as a "False Self." '

In the reunion scene we know that Celie has an 'authentic' existence because '[e]verything that she brings to the reunion is truly hers.' Proudfit notes that Celie 'is supported by her symbolic preoedipal family of origin as well as her lover Shug and now friend Albert.' Nettie, however, is surrounded by 'a dead woman's husband and a living woman's grown children.' Proudfit asserts: 'Celie's "True Self," forged out of years of abuse and suffering and "female bonding," is face-to-face with Nettie's "False Self," created through compliance with the outside world in order to survive a chaotic infancy and childhood.'[60] Thus 'the reunification scene offers a psychological validity that transcends the contrivance of plot' and that 'consists in offering closure to the developmental processes that began with the sisters' births.'[61]

Toward the end of his essay, Proudfit recognizes that his reading is 'limited in scope.'[62] However, it is clear that psychoanalytical readings of Celie's story can open up new ways of accounting for those actions and reactions which have tested the credulity of some readers and critics such as her silence and apparent passivity. They also shed new light on the roles played by the women surrounding Celie in her development.

Many critics have argued that Walker's representation of Celie's personal story is flawed because it does not engage sufficiently with the social ideologies that must surely have had a profound effect on her development. The remaining chapters in this Guide address Walker's handling of these wider issues in *The Color Purple*, beginning with the novel's engagement with racial politics.

CHAPTER FIVE

Reading Race in *The Color Purple*

In 'The Black Writer and the Southern Experience' (1984), Alice Walker urges the black Southern writer to use 'double vision' to engage simultaneously with the private and the political: he is 'in a position to see his own world, and its close community' and to 'know[], with remarkably silent accuracy, the people who make up the larger world that surrounds and suppresses his own.'[1] Some critics have struggled to find evidence of this double vision in Walker's work, especially *The Color Purple*. As we have seen, bell hooks finds that Walker 'de-emphasiz[es] the collective plight of black people' by 'focusing on the individual's quest for freedom as separate and distinct.'[2] Elliott Butler-Evans argues that Celie's letters function as a 'textual strategy by which the larger Afro-American history, focused on racial conflict and struggle, can be marginalized by its absence from the narrative';[3] speaking more generally of Walker's fictional oeuvre, Keith Byerman contends that '[t]he question of race is less important in Walker's work than it is in that of many other black writers.'[4]

Academics who have shared their experience of teaching *The Color Purple* have emphasized the importance of engaging with its racial politics. In 'Keeping the Color in *The Color Purple*' (1986), Cora Kaplan (b. 1940) notes the challenges of teaching texts by African-American writers to white, middle-class, British students who, '[m]ore often than not' approach them with 'minimal attention to their cultural specificity.'[5] Kaplan stresses the need to read and teach Walker's novel in ways 'so that its cultural and political conditions of production are not deracinated' and so that it 'retains its rich, polychromatic texture, its provocative politics.' Kaplan notes that readers of the novel must ensure that it is not 'bleached into a pallid, progressive homily, an uncontentious, sentimental, harmless piece of international libertarianism.' She recognizes that some readers have referred to the novel's handling of history and chronology to sustain this kind of reading: 'The fact that "history" as a series of dated events is not employed in the novel, but appears obliquely collapsed in its narrative chronology, makes it hard to use internal evidence to give the book back its wider history.'[6] It is essential that one reads *The Color Purple* 'in a three-dimensional, diachronic and dialectical manner': such an approach will safeguard the text from 'ideological bleaching [...] into an all-purpose human garment.'[7]

One of the ways in which Kaplan reinforces the 'cultural specificity' of *The Color Purple* is to direct us to its intertextual dialogue with novels by other black writers. Critics have been quick to place Walker's novel within the context of 'dominant Amercian ideologies of family, community and self.' Comparisons have been made with Harriet Beecher Stowe's best-selling sentimental novel *Uncle Tom's Cabin* and the popular television series *The Waltons*. Kaplan urges us to examine Walker's 'intertextual relationships' with writers such as Zora Neale Hurston, Richard Wright (1908–60), Ralph Ellison and James Baldwin (1924–97).[8]

In particular, it is fruitful to consider Walker's representation of black women within the context of the gender politics in texts written by the aforementioned black male writers: 'Celie, Shug, Sophia [*sic*.] [...] need to be read in relation to these prior constructions of southern Black social relations that represent women as either powerless or repressive, and which focus (with Baldwin as an honorable exception) on the imperilled masculinity of Black men.' Kaplan argues that the novel's 'seemingly apolitical model of change as a familial dialectic looks rather less simple when read as a polemic against the deeply negative imaginative interpretations of southen Black life in much male Black fiction and autobiography.'[9]

Alison Light pursues some of Kaplan's concerns in her essay 'Fear of the Happy Ending: *The Color Purple*, Reading and Racism' (1990). Light's exploration focuses on the engagement of white, British, women readers with *The Color Purple*. Her findings offer valuable insight into the novel's susceptibility to readings that 'reduce' the novel. Speaking to these white women readers, Light noted a dramatic shift when the conversation moved from identification with Celie to the novel's wider political significance. Light detected the influence of 'liberal humanist values' in discussion of a novel that 'is not primarily concerned [...] with black struggle against white racism but with experience within the black community, within familial and sexual relationships.' Light observes:

■ This foregrounding of 'the private sphere' has made it possible for the question of difference, racial, sexual, social, to be ignored and effaced as a conflictual and political force and to be reformulated in the rhetoric of a liberal humanism (of which English is one discourse) as a repository of essential and eternal truths about a universal human condition.[10] □

Both Kaplan and Light find that the marketing of Celie's story has played a significant part in fostering this '[u]niversalizing' impulse. Light

comments on the absence of the words *black* and *lesbian* on the cover of
The Women's Press edition of the novel and notes that: 'reproducing an
invisibility to which those who are defined as "other" are consigned
by the dominant culture, such homogenizing makes the text more
manageable, more marketable.' Thus, '[d]ifference which is potentially
alienating, frightening and challenging, is written out in favour of a
transhistorical truism.' This homogenizing is clearly at work in the marketing of Spielberg's cinematic adaptation: '[a]s the advertising trailer
for the film puts it, "It's about life. It's about love. It's about us." '[11]

Light draws our attention to the limitations of the 'naturalizing
aesthetic' of literary criticism, which 'collapses [the novel's] cultural
specificity into moral value, emptied of any social or political refer-
ent.' This approach, she notes, informed several reviews of the novel: 'a
"consummately well-written novel" enthused the *New York Times Book
Review*, whilst the US *Tribune* praised its "sweetness of tone [...] the
sweep and daring of its literary ambition." ' Such reactions 'efface the
material and political conditions within which black language emerged
as a *weapon* against, as well as a consequence of, slavery, and as a means
of creating and maintaining a separate and inviolable community for
black people in the face of white oppression' (Light's italics).[12]

In order to give *The Color Purple* a fair reading, one must 'fragment[]
that impulse to homogenize and thereby control the diverse subjects
and subjectivities which come within the boundaries' of the English
language. Light urges white readers to 'press hard upon [their] first
"naïve" readings' and 'return to [their] "selves" not in order to wallow
in guilt but because such selves are historically and socially produced.'
Like many academics, Light hopes that readings of *The Color Purple*
will 'lead into a discussion of racism.' She scrutinizes this desire and
concludes that this kind of reading 'is easier than seeing [her]self as
marginal to [the novel's] concerns.' Like Kaplan, she urges the importance of a 'dialectical' approach to the novel: this entails relinquishing
'the power of naming and of assuming knowledge of someone else's
struggle, accepting that there are things which we cannot share, and ini-
tiatives which we cannot create.'[13] Light argues that the challenge of *The
Color Purple* for the white literary critic is that 'it is not about "us" at all.'[14]

THE COLOR PURPLE **AND RACIAL POLITICS IN AMERICA**

This subchapter looks at readings that explore Walker's representation of
race relations in rural Georgia and consider the nature and extent of her
engagement with racial politics in America. It begins with the provocative and influential essay 'Race, Gender, and Nation in *The Color Purple*'
by Lauren Berlant (b. 1957), which first appeared in the journal *Critical*

Inquiry in 1988. It has since appeared in various collections of essays on Alice Walker's work. References in this Guide come from Henry Louis Gates, Jr., and Kwame Anthony Appiah's collection, *Alice Walker: Critical Perspectives Past and Present* (1993). Berlant gives a trenchant analysis of the interaction of class, race and gender politics in *The Color Purple*. Her comments on the novel's socioeconomic politics are considered in Chapter 6 of this Guide.

One of the many innovations of Berlant's reading is its detailed examination of the novel's 'discourse on the problematics of Afro-American national-historical identity.' Berlant traces the development of national and personal discourses in the novel and finds that it 'problematizes nationalism itself, in both its Anglo- and Afro-American incarnations.'[15] Nationalism is a broad term that has taken on many different meanings and connotations. One of its functions is to oppose colonial ideology through the assertion of national culture and identity. In her reading of nationalism in Walker's novel, Berlant directs us to the scene where Nettie tells Celie that the only way that she can recall the name of the man who discovered America is to think of the word 'cucumbers.'[16] Their conversation debunks America's 'self-mythification [...] by revealing the manifest irrelevancy of the classic American myth to Celie.'[17]

Berlant goes on to explore Walker's representation of the interaction of racism and sexism in the 'negating context' of white America.[18] She examines Celie's response to the back story concerning her father, noting that she does not engage with its wider implications. Indeed, the back story functions to 'repress the scene of history insofar as the extrafamilial elements of social relations are concerned.'[19] Moreover, Nettie's choice of language solicits this kind of response: her 'fairy-tale rhetoric' – she opens her account with the phrase '[o]nce upon a time' – places the focus firmly on 'the personal [...] components of social relations.'[20,21] This is paradigmatic of the novel itself, in which 'the burden of operating within a racist social context [...] is generally deflected from Celie's tale onto events in the economic and cultural marketplace.'

It is the other female characters in the novel who must fight for 'legitimacy' in the wider world.[22] Sofia responds to the mayor's wife's proposal that she work for her as her maid with 'Hell no,' and follows the mayor's slap with a punch.[23] However, 'her effort to stay honest in the face of the white demand for black hypocrisy' results in imprisonment in jails 'that work by a logic similar to that of lynching: to racialize the scene of class struggle in the public sphere and to deploy prejudice against "woman" once behind the walls of the prison and the household.'[24]

In order to liberate Sofia, Harpo's new girlfriend, known initially to the reader as Squeak before she claims her original name of Mary Agnes, must participate in the racist discourse of the 'negating context.' Squeak engages in a 'comedy of double-and quadruple-talk that includes [her] asking for (and getting) the *opposite* of what the warden incorrectly *thinks* she wants' (Berlant's italics).[25] Only after she has been subjected to abuse 'in the name of communal solidarity' can Squeak reclaim her name, assert her sense of identity through song: she must 'learn[] to ironize the already-doubled double-talk that marks the discursive situation of the female Afro-American subject in the white patriarchal public sphere.'

Berlant relates the various strategies deployed by these characters fighting for legitimacy to black political theory, drawing first on philosopher W. E. B. Du Bois's assertions from his 1903 speech 'The Souls of Black Folk' regarding the 'double consciousness' imposed on African Americans. In Walker's novel '[t]he degree of discursive self-alienation' experienced by the characters is 'expressed in the multiple inversions of language that become the violated ground of both rape and humor.'[26]

In *The Color Purple*, female conversation provides refuge from these contexts. However, the conflict between personal and national discourses reasserts itself in the final scene, which re-appropriates the discourses its characters have struggled against. In the end, Walker 'reinstates nationalist discourse as the proper context for Celie's autobiography.'[27] On the Fourth of July, Henrietta, the youngest child of Sofia, asks why family reunions take place at a time when it is 'so hot.' Harpo explains that white people take this day to 'celebrate they independence from England'; therefore black people do not have to work and 'can spend the day celebrating each other.'[28]

Berlant offers several readings of Harpo's response: perhaps his notion of history conveys a sense that 'Afro-American culture exists confidently in the interstices of Anglo-American historical time.' Another possibility is that the re-emergence of 'American consciousness' at the end of the novel 'represents a historical change [...] in the modes of cultural reproduction.' After all, Celie has moved from a life that 'mainly involved the black community' to one that 'overlaps the circulation of blues culture throughout both black and white urban communities.' Berlant speculates that a 'traditionally national language' is 'the only discourse available to describe this variegated cultural landscape.' This reading suggests that the novel ultimately 'abandon[s] the project of specifically representing an Afro-American national culture for a less racially delimited, more pluralistic model.'

Another way of viewing the return of national discourse is as a means for the community to register 'its own separate, specifically Afro-American recolonization of American time, American property, and mythic American self-help ideology by casually ironizing it.' In this reading, Harpo's explanation of the rationale behind the celebration of July Fourth 'reduc[es] the holiday to a racial and not a national celebration.'[29] Perhaps Walker ended the novel in this way in order 'to illuminate the real poverty of a politically established Anglo-American national identity when set next to that of the Afro-American community that has fought on all grounds for the right to have everything.'[30] Berlant insists, however, that the 'alliance' of the two perspectives 'implicitly represents American racism as a condition of Afro-American celebration.'[31] She concludes: 'if *The Color Purple* clearly represents anything, it is the unreliability of "text" under the historical pressure to interpret, to predict, and to determine the cultural politics of the colonized signifier.'[32]

In her book *Down from the Mountaintop: Black Women's Novels in the Wake of the Civil Rights Movement 1966–1989* (1991), Melissa Walker pays particular attention to the novel's handling of racist encounters in America. As we saw in Chapter 1, Dinitia Smith stated in her review of *The Color Purple* that, '[n]o writer has made the intimate hurt of racism more palpable than Walker.'

In his review of the novel and the film for the *Revolutionary Worker,* Carl Dix dismisses as absurd those readings that criticize Walker for 'focusing on women's oppression and not dealing with national oppression.' As counter-evidence he cites the examples of Sofia's suffering at the hands of white society, the lynching of Nettie and Celie's father and the absence of a resting place for Shug as she tours the South. Dix writes that those complaining about the lack of condemnation of racial oppression in the novel are in reality 'arguing that *The Color Purple* should not have taken as its *focus* the oppression of women as it occurs *among the oppressed*' (Dix's italics).[33]

Melissa Walker takes a different view. She objects that Celie merely reports incidents of racism and sexism without pondering them at any length or offering any commentary on their implications. Celie's story unfolds during the Depression 'in a rural society where for most African Americans daily survival was a struggle.' According to Melissa Walker, Celie 'never reports suffering' the 'consequences' of the Depression.[34] Moreover, other characters do not speak out against racial oppression and abuse. Even Sofia, who tells Celie that she must learn to fight back, moves to the back seat of the car without complaint after giving the mayor's wife a driving lesson and hearing her assertion that she will not tolerate 'a white person and a colored sitting side by side in a car.'[35] There is no trace of 'rancour' in Shug's comment that she and her new husband, Grady, had to drive all night because no resting place would receive them or that there was no place to wash during her tour of the South. Celie tells Nettie that she and Shug have to use the bushes on their way to Memphis but offers no further comment. Melissa Walker points out that similar incidents and experiences cause 'profound humiliation' or provoke 'acts of rebellion' in Toni Morrison's novel *Sula* (1973) and Alice Childress's *A Short Walk* (1979). Celie and Shug register only frustration at the 'inconvenience' caused.

It is left to Nettie to express anger at the oppression and marginal-ization of black people in America. As Melissa Walker notes, Nettie is clearly troubled by the 'Jim Crow train' to New York.[36] Moreover, she tells Celie that the aim of her missionary work is 'the uplift of black people everywhere' and that she shares 'concern about racism [...] and sexism' with Celie's children.[37,38] Nettie is concerned that when the chil-dren come to America they will be unable to cope with the country's pervasive racism and Adam's wife Tashi, who has very dark skin and scars on her cheeks, looks at the images in American magazines and worries that her husband will leave her when he sees 'light-skinned women.' Melissa Walker also points out that Nettie's letters feature evocations of Harlem, reports on the cultural traditions of the Olinka people, stories involving figures such as King Leopold of the Congo and W. E. B. Du Bois and revelations concerning 'the British role in the slave trade';[39] however, Celie's letters offer no sign of engagement with 'Nettie's lessons in public history.' It is only when she learns from Nettie about the past experiences of their family that she 'realizes the persistence, range, and historical context of racism.'[40]

Taking an opposing view, Lean'tin Bracks delivers a historical reading of the novel. Her essay 'Alice Walker's *The Color Purple*: Racism, Sexism, and Kinship in the Process of Self-Actualization' was first published in her book *Writings on Black Women of the Diaspora* in 1998. Bracks opens her essay with the assertion that

■ *The Color Purple* has a special place within the process of historical reclamation for it discusses continuing attitudes of resistance to the dom-inant culture's political and social agendas while revealing silences within the community that have been unavailable to historical renderings of any kind.[41] □

Through close textual analysis, Bracks demonstrates how the stories of Celie and the men and women in her community engage issues of race and are in fact a powerful reflection of the realities of life for black people living in the American South in the early decades of the twenti-eth century: 'It is to emphasize Celie's disenfranchisement that Walker locates *The Color Purple* in the early twentieth century, a time of legal seg-regation as well as economic and political limitations for blacks' when 'interaction' between black and white communities 'occurred only from specific intentions or intrusions of whites into black affairs.'[42]

Bracks gives a detailed analysis of the various forms of intrusion dra-matized by Walker in her novel. She identifies lynching as the 'most severe' form of intrusion, noting that 'the lynching of Celie's father' was based on a 'real incident in Memphis in 1892.' The novel's back story, therefore, 'roots the characters within the social and political conditions of the time.'[43] The novel also registers the 'divisive legacy' of slavery through its exposure of the absorption of 'racist beauty standards in America.'[44] As Bracks notes, it is the women in *The Color Purple* 'who are the major recipients of the idea that skin tone is a visual barometer of worth.'[45]

Bracks's reading of the many forms of intrusion in *The Color Purple* provides a fertile line of enquiry into its engagement with racial politics. She offers a new reading of the silences within Celie's community that have disconcerted many critics and readers. Silence about the abuse suffered within the community is, according to Bracks, 'a double-edged sword.' While it may be viewed as a strategy commonly adopted to 'forestall further interference' from white people it also 'allowed destructive behaviors within family units to go unchecked and unchallenged.'[46] Bracks identifies Pa's 'moral laxity and [...] disrespect for women' as 'examples of what Walker will interrogate in the novel as internalized racism in the community being directed at women whose abuse is met with the same silence adopted for protection against white abuse.'[47] She continues:

■ This attitude toward women, and Celie in particular, allowed her step-father to intrude upon every aspect of her life just as white society had intruded, unchecked, into the lives of the black community. Furthermore, the failure of the community to confront such behaviors within the family undercuts its potential to band together to confront the abuse everyone suffered from whites. The destructive attitude of the black community toward silence regarding assaultive family behaviors on the one hand and its collective efforts to protect its members from whites on the other reflect the contradictory forces within the community in the wake of slavery.[48] □

AFRICAN CULTURE AND WESTERN COLONIALISM IN *THE COLOR PURPLE*

Speaking to Gloria Steinem in 1983, Walker asserted: 'We're going to have to debunk the myth that Africa is a heaven for black people – especially black women. We've been the mule of the world there and the mule of the world here.'[49] The readings in this subchapter address Walker's depiction of African culture and European imperialism in Nettie's letters to Celie. Many critics of the novel have taken exception to the shifts in narrative voice, language and geographical location that these letters bring to the novel. Some have objected to

Nettie's letters on structural grounds, while others have chafed at their apparent didacticism or have contested the accuracy of their representations. For Maryemma Graham, however, 'Walker portrays colonial Africa more vividly than the terrifying conditions of sharecroppers' in America.[50]

This section examines balanced readings of Walker's representations of African culture and the impact of imperial discourses. It considers further interpretations by Lean'tin Bracks and Lauren Berlant along with Linda Selzer's highly innovative and detailed essay 'Race and Domesticity in *The Color Purple*' (1995).

In 'Alice Walker's *The Color Purple*: Racism, Sexism, and Kinship in the Process of Self-Actualization,' Bracks presents a persuasive case for the thematic relevance of Nettie's letters, arguing that their revelations perform a crucial function in relation to Celie's personal development by awakening her political and historical consciousness. While the protracted account of missionary work in Africa seems to 'be a break from the novel's initial themes of identity and empowerment,' Bracks finds that this account 'extends these issues to the diaspora, encompassing all black communities.' Thus, 'Nettie's experiences in Africa' are presented 'as part of the expanded sense of one's place in the world.' Her 'letters, in turn, equip Celie to embrace and strengthen her own identity, protected from an intrusive force that isolates and restricts her potential for being black and a woman.' In Bracks's reading, Nettie's letters achieve something that many critics have felt was lacking in Celie's progress toward empowerment: they galvanize her political awareness:

■ It is this knowledge about the world outside of Georgia that opens possibilities to a future for Celie. Her realization of an African family beyond the boundaries of America's colonial plan expands Celie's notion of personal struggle to one of common battle with a superior force wielded by the white world over black people as a group. Recognizing her kinship with Africans is the first step in Celie's journey toward a collective, empowering identity that transcends personal isolation.[51] □

Moreover, the experiences of the characters who travel to Africa enable Walker to make '[o]ne of [her] most incisive points': they illuminate 'how intrusions endured by the black community in America are similar to those the African community of the Olinkas were forced to suffer from the European colonizers.' In each case, the 'community has no choice but to submit to the whims and mandates of the dominant group.'[52]

Bracks turns to the 'duality of Corinne and Samuel's missionary work' to show how Walker engages with '[t]he complexities of [...] relations between colonizer and oppressed.' Here Bracks concurs with most critics who perceive some ambiguity in Walker's portrayal of the missionary project. Bracks recognizes the project as 'another form of Western intrusion' because 'it tries to affect lives and communities that are different in many ways from the lives of the missionaries.'[53] She adds: 'Even African American missionaries are imbued with a kind of paternalism to the Africans they attempt to convert.' Yet there is one important distinction:

> ■ [m]issionary work for the African-Americans, unlike the straightforward colonizing efforts of white Europeans, grew out of kinship ties and a sense of community with Africans and sought to mitigate the destructiveness of white intrusion into the lives of black people on both sides of the Atlantic. For the African-American missionary, the sharing of pasts and destinies often moved the colonizer–exploited relationship to one of greater knowledge and reclaimed kinship that had previously been hidden, devalued, or ignored.[54] □

For Berlant, the misguided work of the missionaries in Africa betrays some the problems of Pan-Africanism identified by W. E. B. Du Bois. The Pan-African movement identifies and celebrates African culture as a common foundation that unifies black people across the world, transcending national boundaries. In her reading of *The Color Purple* Berlant identifies Nettie's clear expression of 'pleasure [...] from reading Blackness from a proper and sanctified point of view' as 'the affective origin of the specifically nationalist politics previously repressed in *The Color Purple*.'[55] The missionaries' reaction to this issue is less clear. Berlant finds that Samuel in his efforts 'unintentionally aims to reproduce the normative social relations of Western culture.'[56] She points to the construction of the big road through the Olinka village as symptomatic of the 'failure' of the missionaries' vision. Both the missionaries and the Olinka believe that the road is being built to serve the tribe, but in reality it serves only the interests of the colonizers. Berlant observes that Samuel might have predicted this outcome if he had heeded the warning of W. E. B. Du Bois, whose works he has read, that 'Pan-Africanism requires material transformation of the techniques of power before a new spirit would have any place to grasp.' When the missionaries finally foresee the impact of the road on the tribe and their mission, they are powerless to react.[57]

Berlant then turns to Nettie's 'tributes to the fabulous richness of African culture, read as a pan-national phenomenon' and notes again how discourses in the novel's final pages undermine its revolutionary potential. These tributes to African culture are undercut when the missionaries return to America. Nettie 'unconsciously quotes "America, the Beautiful"' and we hear in the missionaries' thoughts on America echoes of 'seventeenth-century Puritan religious and civil' ideas that posit 'America as the only site where a sanctified and defetishized church might have a chance for survival.'[58]

In the final scenes, then, the 'hybrid, fractured status of Afro-American signification re-emerges in its earliest form.' In the end, the novel does not 'infus[e] the African side of the compound term with the positive historical identification usually denied in the American context.' Instead, it 'returns "Africa" to the space of disappointment and insufficiency, finally overwhelmed by the power of "America" to give form to the utopian impulse.'[59]

This chapter concludes by considering Linda Selzer's essay, 'Race and Domesticity in *The Color Purple*,' first published in 1995 by the *African American Review*. Selzer delivers one of the most detailed analyses of the novel's handling of race and its depiction of interracial relationships in America and Africa. She takes an opposing view to hooks and Berlant, arguing that the novel's elaboration of personal relationships facilitates the exploration of its wider politics.

Like Bracks, Selzer focuses on the ways in which the novel's personal and political narratives inform each other. She identifies two 'strategies' through which 'Walker's domestic novel engages issues of race and class': 'the development of an embedded narrative line that offers a post-colonial perspective on the main action, and the use of "family relations" – or kinship – as a carefully elaborated textual trope for race relations.'[60] Selzer argues that '[a]ny attempt to oppose political and personal discourses in the novel collapses' when the reader considers Walker's use of the 'discourse of family relations': Walker uses this discourse in two ways: 'to establish a "domestic ideal" for racial integration and to problematize that ideal through the analysis of specific integrated family groupings in Africa and America.'[61]

Much of the innovation of Selzer's essay arises from her scrutiny of particular moments in *The Color Purple*, most of which have attracted little critical attention. She identifies Celie's response to the envelope containing Nettie's first letter as an important moment not only in the heroine's personal narrative but for the reader's engagement with the novel's wider politics. Celie looks at the stamps on the envelope and sees that one of them bears the image of a '[l]ittle fat queen of England' while others feature 'peanuts, coconuts, rubber trees.'[62] Selzer argues that Celie's uncertainty regarding the meaning of the image on the English stamp *suggests* that 'her domestic perspective "erases" race and class concerns from the narrative' but that while this cultural encounter is filtered through Celie's perspective, its 'textual features [...] invite readers to resituate her narration within a larger discourse of race and class.' Those readers who identify the woman on the stamp as Queen Victoria 'immediately historicize' this scene. While the images on these stamps, placed side by side, 'suggest[] to Celie nothing but her own ignorance' to readers of her narrative they 'serve as a clear reminder of imperialism. Thus Africa [...] enters the novel already situated within the context of colonialism.'[63] While some critics cite the responses of characters in the novel as evidence of Walker's limited engagement with race, Selzer shows us how moments such as these function as openings onto the wider politics of the domestic narrative.

Selzer also draws our attention to the significance of the Olinka version of the biblical creation story, in which 'Adam was not the first man but the first white man born to an Olinka woman to be cast out for his nakedness – or for being "colorless"' (*CP* 231) and the concept of Original Sin is recast as one of 'breaking kinship bonds.' In her narration of this story, Celie herself articulates 'some rather sophisticated ideas concerning the social construction of racial inferiority, since the myth defines that inferiority as a construct of power relations that will change over time.'[64] As Selzer notes, Celie tells us that the Olinka foresee a time when white people will destroy 'the earth and the colored that everybody gon hate them just like they hate us today.' White people will therefore 'become the new serpent.'[65]

It is through the Olinka version of the creation story that the novel poses one of its most weighty questions: 'Is progress in race relations possible?' Celie tells us that while some of the Olinka tribe foresee a continual 'cycle of discrimination' with each race alternately 'in the position of oppressor,' others can envisage a time of 'racial harmony' and share a sense that 'Original Sin may be ameliorated – through a new valorization of kinship bonds.'[66] They 'express a *domestic ideal* for race relations, one that counters the sin of discrimination – based on an ideology of essential difference – with an ethic of acceptance that is grounded upon a recognition of relation, or kinship' (Selzer's italics).[67]

Walker explores the possibility of this 'domestic ideal' through two interracial relationships in the novel: first, the relationship between Doris Baines, a white, English missionary and her adopted African grandson and second, the relationship between Sofia and Eleanor Jane, the mayor's daughter. Both relationships 'serve to expose and to critique the larger pattern of racial integration found in their respective countries.' The relationship between Doris Baines and her adopted grandson has been largely ignored by critics. Doris Baines distances herself from the agenda of the other missionaries by asserting that she has no interest in trying to 'convert' the African people. However, Nettie's account of this relationship raises questions about 'the possibility of kinship across racial lines.' From her letters we learn that the boy does not engage with his adopted grandmother and is more comfortable with Adam and Olivia.

Through her manipulation of Nettie's voice, Walker places the terms of Doris's missionary work under scrutiny. We discover that her decision to be a missionary was a strategy formed 'to escape the rarefied atmosphere of upper-class England.' As Selzer notes, Nettie's use of 'fairy-tale' language tells us that she 'does not take Doris's hardships very seriously.'[68] Doris's 'self-interest' further manifests itself in the terms of her relationship with the Akwee: while 'ostensibly reciprocal' in reality it 'reflects her imperial power to buy whatever she wants.'[69] Doris speaks of the harmony that existed between herself and the Akwee, asserting that their relationship 'ran like clockwork.'[70] However Doris 'never overcomes a belief in the essential "difference" of the Africans attributed to her by the Missionary Society in England.' Thus, Nettie's account of Doris's 'honorary "kinship" with the Akwee villagers' opens up questions about the terms of interracial relationships in Africa:

■ Stripped of both the religious motivations of the other missionaries and the overt racism of the other whites, Doris Baines through her relationship with the Akwee lays bare the hierarchy of self-interest and paternalism that sets the pattern for race relations in larger Africa.[71] □

The work of the black missionaries is less easily read. Selzer notes that 'missionary work is tied to national interest from the time Nettie arrives in England.'[72] Selzer draws attention to one of Nettie's early letters where she describes her personal impression of England. She tells her sister that England's missionary work in Africa and parts of Asia stretches back over a hundred years. She describes a visit to an English museum where she sees items from these continents on display. Nettie marvels at the artistry of the items and wonder at the idea that their makers are no longer 'exist,' as the English insist.[73] Again, political questions arise from a description of an ostensibly private experience. For Selzer, Nettie's letters offer a powerful demonstration of 'Walker's ability to maintain the integrity of the narrative's personal perspective [...] even as she simultaneously invites the reader to resituate that perspective in a wider context of race and class.'

Nettie's account of her experiences in Africa 'enables readers to sympathize with the hopes and disappointments of the black missionaries' but also 'exposes the limitations of their point of view.'[74] The representation of Samuel and Corrine's aunts, Theodosia and Althea, is a case in point. The aunts are portrayed as 'representatives of a group of black women missionaries who achieved much against great odds' and yet Aunt Theodosia is the target of the novel's 'harshest criticism of missionary work.' When a young man named DuBoyce arrives at one of Theodosia's social gatherings he tells her that she should view the King Leopold medal of which she is so proud 'as a symbol of [her] unwitting complicity with' the 'despot' responsible for the abuse, oppression and murder of 'thousands and thousands of African peoples.'[75] Again, a personal setting becomes a scene for the engagement of political issues:

'[t]he appearance of Du Bois in Aunt Theodosia's domestic sphere recontextualizes Nettie's narrative.' Moreover, his response to the medal 'serve[s] as an authoritative final judgement upon the entire missionary effort in Africa.'[76]

Selzer goes on to examine how the relationship between Sofia and Eleanor Jane in America's South works as an 'analogue' to the interracial relationships in Africa. The 'affection' between Sofia and the mayor's daughter 'has been shaped by the perverted "kinship" relation within which it grew.' Through this 'relationship' the novel 'expose[s] plantation definitions of kinship in general and to [...] explode[s] the myth of the black mammy in particular.'[77] Selzer compares the white people in the novel from Georgia's rural South to the 'apologists for slavery' who sustain 'a counterfeit definition of family while denying the real ties that bind them to African Americans.'[78]

Walker gives Sofia the role not only of debunking these myths and definitions but also of 'articulat[ing] a strong position counter to the Olinka kinship ethic of treating everyone like one mother's children.'[79] Having asserted that she does not love Eleanor Jane's son Reynolds Stanley, Sofia adds that 'all the colored folks talking about loving everybody just ain't looked hard at what they thought they said.'[80] Again, Walker engages us in political issues through her elaboration of one character's personal experience:

■ In subverting the plantation model of kinship in general and the role of mammy that it assigns to black women in particular [...] Sofia's position as an unwilling domestic in the mayor's household underscores the importance of the personal point of view to the novel's political critique of race relations.[81] □

When Selzer turns to the novel's concluding vision of kinship she finds 'arresting images of racial segregation in both Africa and America that complicate the idea of progress and ultimately move the narrative toward a final definition of kinship based on race.'[82] The 'small steps towards progress in race relations' do not stem from a sense of 'identity *between* the races but from an evolving separatism and parallel growth *within* the African and African American communities' (Selzer's italics). The final scenes present 'images of an emerging Pan-Africanism in Africa and a nascent black nationalism in the American South.'[83]

Two further stories of attempted integration suggest that race remains a highly significant factor in the development of notions of kinship: Shug's son's failed attempt to enter the American Indian community and Mary Agnes's 'successful integration with the mixed people of Cuba' where if you '[t]ry to pass for white, somebody mention your grandma.'[84] Selzer writes that in each context of the novel, 'feelings of racial identity among marginalized peoples become the basis for definitions of kinship by the novel's end.'[85]

From the readings considered in this chapter, we can see that the issue of racial politics in *The Color Purple* has generated divergent responses. Much depends on where the reader looks for meaning: does the apparent absence of deep reflection on racial politics in rural Georgia or Africa compromise the reader's grasp of the wider implications of the novel's cultural encounters? Some critics attribute the novel's limited political engagement to its domestic emphasis. For others such as Selzer, Walker's vivid dramatization of personal experience is a highly effective means of engaging readers in the novel's historical and political contexts. This issue remains central to readings of the novel's socioeconomic politics which are the focus of the following chapter.

CHAPTER SIX

Class and Consumerism in *The Color Purple*

At the end of the novel *The Color Purple*, Celie, like many oppressed heroines before her, is rewarded with financial independence. After she confronts Albert and declares her intention to 'enter into the Creation' she moves to Memphis with Shug.[1] She lives comfortably in Shug's stylish home, performing domestic duties and designing and making trousers for members of the community. Each pair of trousers is tailored to the individual's needs. Celie begins to look for paid work and Shug encourages her to turn her sewing enterprise into a business. When Celie returns to Georgia she finds that Albert has changed dramatically; he now performs the labour that Celie was forced to undertake, looking after the house and working on the land. Once he recognizes Celie, he welcomes her and they build a new friendship. Alphonso, Celie's stepfather, has also died, leaving her property – her father's original house and store – and some land. Celie settles in her childhood home, running her business, 'Folkspants, Unlimited,' from the store. She employs women from the local community to manufacture her designs of unisex trousers. Her workers include Sofia and a white man initially hired by Alphonso to run the store. The readings in this chapter consider how Celie's economic progression fits into the novel's wider socioeconomic politics.

When asked to explain the rationale behind Celie's economic prosperity, Alice Walker has stated that Celie's long-term happiness was foremost in her mind. In one of her final, joyous, letters, Celie describes her life to Nettie and acknowledges the importance of money and work: 'I'm so happy. I got love, I got money, I got work, friends and time.'[2] However, Celie's happy ending has troubled many readers and critics. Some critics have questioned the viability of her sudden elevation to the position of successful entrepreneur, reading her economic progression as evidence of the novel's utopianism; others have scrutinized its political implications and accused Walker of capitulating to bourgeois codes. Many readings have struggled to reconcile this outcome with the novel's overarching rejection of mainstream values. In her review of the novel, Maryemma Graham expresses concern that 'Walker has imbued her rural Georgia females with the strivings and potential for self-indulgence of the urban middle class' and wonders if this is one of the reasons for the novel's popularity amongst readers with mainstream values.[3]

There are few interpretations of *The Color Purple* that view the novel from a strictly Marxist perspective. In the nineteenth century, German philosopher Karl Marx argued that the marginalization of particular social groups has its basis in economics: the 'base' of social relationships is constituted by the economic system in place. The ideology that emerges from this base – the values, institutions and belief systems – forms the 'superstructure' of society. Marx examined the relationship between the base and the superstructure and found that a system founded on capitalist values led to the alienation of the human subject not only from his community but also from his authentic desires and needs. He proposed that a communist society, in which everybody is rewarded equally for their labour, would enable human subjects to reach their potential. Writers who represent alienated or oppressed groups might use literature deliberately to expose and challenge the dominant ideology that underpins social hierarchies. Marxist literary critics view texts in terms of their engagement with and representation of socioeconomic systems.[4]

Walker's social criticism reveals strong socialist sympathies. She has always claimed that her allegiance lies with working-class subjects. She tells Claudia Tate:

■ I am drawn to working-class characters as I am to working-class people in general. I have a basic antagonism toward the system of capitalism. Since I'm only interested in changing it, I'm not interested in writing about people who already fit into it. And the working-class can never fit comfortably into a capitalist society.[5] □

Walker has recognized the validity of concerns regarding the novel's economic politics and has welcomed readings of *The Color Purple* that pose important questions about the future for the disenfranchised and impoverished. In her essay 'In the Closet of the Soul,' Walker responds to criticism 'by a black man offered *with* love' (Walker's italics):[6] Carl Dix's review of the novel and film of *The Color Purple* for the *Revolutionary Worker*. Dix writes: 'This vision of liberation as a woman having her own property (a democratic right) is not the outlook and aspiration of the revolutionary proletariat.' For women such as Celie to 'break the chains of women's oppression' would require 'the revolutionary overthrow of the imperialists who dominate the globe' and the 'obliterati[on]' of 'every foul social relation of this dog-eat-dog setup and every reactionary idea that it has spawned.' He adds, however, that by 'typify[ing] crucial contradictions of the imperialist system,' Walker's novel and Spielberg's adaptation 'contribute to bringing this about.'[7]

Walker supports Dix in his assertion that 'the inheritance of private property is not a viable solution in terms of the masses of poor people' and praises him for delivering a reading that 'project[s] our thoughts forward into the realm of better solutions for the landless, jobless, and propertyless masses.'[8] She justifies Celie's prosperity by emphasizing its specific context. The novel's main action takes place during the early decades of the twentieth century after the Civil War and the period known as 'Reconstruction,' which failed to improve opportunities for African Americans, and before African Americans had civil rights.

The novel's back story transports the reader to the beginning of the century.[9] Celie's stepfather and husband are sharecroppers: tenant farmers who work and use rented land but who must hand over some of its yield to the land's owner. Celie herself is treated as a commodity of exchange between 'Pa' and Albert. 'Pa' sells her to Albert, who makes her labour on the land for no reward. Only when Celie finds Nettie's letters does she discover that her real father was a prosperous businessman who was lynched by racist white men. Responding to Dix, Walker writes that 'for Celie's time – the post-Reconstruction era in the South, whose hallmark was the dispossession of blacks – this solution was in fact progressive' because 'it spoke eloquently of the foresight of her father in his attempt to provide for her in a society where black people's attempts to provide for their coming generations were brutally repressed.'[10]

Some of the critics who have found themselves confounded by Celie's ultimate prosperity have looked to the novel's contemporary context for answers: they have wondered how far the political climate of the early 1980s informed the shaping of Celie's economic trajectory. In the 1980s an economic boom led to an intensification of capitalist values in mainstream America. Notions of progress, success and empowerment were linked directly to acquisition and accumulation. Individual pleasure and instant gratification were openly promoted and sought. The term 'yuppie' entered public discourse to describe young urban professionals who reached high levels of prosperity in their twenties or early thirties. The word 'buppie' was used to describe young urban black professionals. It was the affluent who benefited most from the economic surge; many Americans, particularly those from marginalized groups, were left behind as the boom broadened the gulf between the rich and the poor.

While many critics expressed reservations about Celie's happy ending, others had little difficulty reconciling her prosperity with the novel's wider message. Critics who champion the novel's revolutionary potential often refer to Celie's success as verification that *The Color Purple* is concerned, first and foremost, with representing new models of growth and fulfilment. They stress how the ethos of Celie's business differs from the capitalist ethos that dominated mainstream 1980s America.

'A NOVEL FOR YUPPIE AND BUPPIE AMERICA'?

One of the most critical and provocative readings of Walker's socioeconomic politics features in Cynthia Hamilton's essay, 'Alice Walker's Politics, or the Politics of *The Color Purple*,' which first appeared in the *Journal of Black Studies* in 1988. Hamilton argues unequivocally that Celie's economic progress quashes any revolutionary potential in the novel by suggesting that the only way to escape oppression in its many different forms 'is to assume bourgeois values and style.'[11] Hamilton finds that the novel is in key with the ethos fostered by the Republican government of the 1980s and goes so far as to assert that Walker's novel sustains Republican attitudes toward those who were left behind by their economic policies. For Hamilton, *The Color Purple* 'has become, intentionally or unintentionally, the best handle the Republicans have for demonstrating that the problem of the black poor is not "their problem." '[12]

Hamilton criticizes Walker for assigning the blame for the continuing oppression of black women solely to black men. She claims that Walker takes no account of reasons for their oppression 'other than race and gender' and presents only one solution for black women: a 'transformation that produces a duplication of relations and manner of the petty bourgeoisie.'[13] *The Color Purple* is therefore a 'classic "victim" melodrama where the oppressed are both targets and perpetuators of oppression.' At the end of the novel, the victims achieve their dream of 'assum[ing] the roles, possessions, and values of the oppressor.'

Hamilton hears echoes of the tenets of early feminist philosophy in Walker's novel. She refers us to the arguments of eighteenth-century philosopher Mary Wollstonecraft (1759–97), who voiced concerns over the impact of capitalist ideology on women's lives. In her feminist tract, *A Vindication of the Rights of Woman* (1792), Wollstonecraft challenges the sentimental rhetoric and imagery that informs abstract notions of womanhood and argues that women should be granted the same educational opportunities as men. As Hamilton notes, Wollstonecraft's main concern is the 'emergent class of women of the new bourgeoisie or middle class.'[14] While this new social stratification offered men the chance to gain prosperity through their 'talent' rather than their family background, the 'new standards of capitalist society strapped [women] as ladies of leisure or household workers.'[15] Socialized expectations forced women to forego their capacity for reason and focus instead on attracting male admiration.

Wollstonecraft posits that the reasoning faculties of women will flourish only in the absence of men: therefore the widow and the abandoned wife have the best chance of learning 'self-sufficiency' and passing it on to their children.[16] In regard to those women who are trapped in working-class environments, Wollstonecraft can only hope that education will reach them and give them the tools for effective self-expression and moral development. Hamilton argues that, like Wollstonecraft, Walker blames men for women's oppression and offers no alternative model for those people without the means to acquire an education: she can only find a place for the disenfranchised working woman in the dominant system. Walker fulfils this vision in her novel by giving her working women a 'transformed bourgeois existence.'

Hamilton also consults the work of Wollstonecraft's daughter Mary Shelley (1797–1851), best known for her novel *Frankenstein*, which first appeared in 1818. The novel tells the story of Dr. Victor Frankenstein who tries to manufacture human life after the deaths of beloved family members. He creates a creature who, owing to physical deformities, is rejected by society. As a result, the creature is denied an education and goes on to murder members of Frankenstein's family in revenge. The novel has been interpreted as a dramatization of tensions between the ruling and working classes, the dispossessed creature embodying the anger of oppressed workers denied the possibility of upward mobility. Hamilton defines the novel as 'an allegory of the French Revolution,' a cautionary tale of what might happen if the working classes were given a voice and society was forced to change. In Shelley's novel, as in Wollstonecraft's tract, hope for the 'mob women' lies not in revolutionizing the system, but in the unlikely possibility of joining it.[17]

According to Hamilton, Walker has capitulated to the myth that all narratives are available to any dispossessed subject who is willing to strive for them. She refers us to W. E. B. Du Bois's 1926 speech, 'Criteria of Negro Art,' in which he speaks of a growing tendency amongst white people to tell black people that they must stop 'fighting and complaining' and need only 'do the great thing' to receive 'the reward.' He notes that 'many colored people are all too eager to follow this advice'; there are 'those who are weary of the eternal struggle along the color line, are afraid to fight and to whom the money of philanthropists and the alluring publicity are subtle and deadly bribes.'[18] Hamilton perceives this kind of mentality in Walker's writing:

■ Beyond the societal constraints that even Alice Walker cannot escape there is the ideology of submission. It is not the ideology of defeat because this social realist, Walker, says to us there is nothing to fight against; what we want, what we need is within our midst. We have kept ourselves from it through our mythologies of difference. It is not a new society that we require, but release from the bounds and constrictions of community that have prevented us, women, from finding our individual identities alone in the world. It is the philosophy of narcissism that she offers us as salvation, the philosophy of self-indulgence, of gratification, of consumption, the philosophy of postindustrial society.[19] □

For Hamilton, those readers who respond favourably to Celie's happy ending betray their investment in a powerful but apocryphal vision of America: they 'are responding with one last gasp, to hold fast to America, a society of mobility and accumulation, the likes of which they see nowhere else.' These readers 'seek to belong, to become one with, to find a place, knowing the "mob," in the Third World and within their midst, waits, growing impatient at the gates.'[20]

In Chapter 5 we looked at Melissa Walker's argument that *The Color Purple* prioritizes the personal over the public and writes out 'historical contingencies.'[21] She draws comparisons with Toni Morrison's first novel, *The Bluest Eye* (1970), to query the viability of Walker's definition of *The Color Purple* as a historical novel. Set in the 1940s, Morrison's novel tells the story of a black girl named Pecola Breedlove who comes from an impoverished background and longs for the blue eyes of the child film star Shirley Temple. Parts of her story are narrated by her friend Claudia, who tells us that she senses in her community a 'hunger for property, for ownership'; however, those who succeed in 'creep[ing] [...] up into the major folds of the garment' do so alone.[22] For Melissa Walker, one of the fundamental differences between the two novels is their stance on issues of racial and social identity. Unlike *The Color Purple*, Morrison's novel acknowledges the relationship between personal and public narratives: 'real events [...] impinge on [the novel's] private, fictional world.' *The Color Purple* presents 'patches of pleasure-giving purple scattered by God from time to time' which 'tell the characters that, even if they are poor and black and female, there is pleasure in the world, there for the taking – sometimes.'[23]

For Melissa Walker, the novel's emphasis on personal pleasure resonates with the dominant ethos of 1980s America. She points out that although Nettie's letters acknowledge the influence of historical factors on personal experience, Celie's reception of the letters – she reads them at one sitting, years after the events recorded within them have taken place – removes them from their immediate context. Eventually Nettie 'abandons her mission in the greater world' and, like Celie, dismisses the issues that are discussed in newspapers. This leads Melissa Walker to conclude that, in the world of the novel, 'history is irrelevant and personal life (and pleasure in things purple) are what it's all about.' This 'pleasure principle' was 'the theme of the 1980s "me-generation,"' and 'paved the way for *The Color Purple* when it came on the scene, preaching in its fashion, and perhaps inadvertently, private or "free enterprise" to Reagan's America.'[24]

This ethos finds its most powerful expression in the words and actions of Shug Avery, the woman who helps Celie to develop a new conception of her identity. Weighing up the novel's 'historical and ahistorical reality,' Melissa Walker concludes that the philosophy of Shug – the embodiment of the pleasure principle in the novel – ultimately wins out: 'Through the authority of Shug's behavior and voice, the novel seems to endorse an essential selfishness, to say, "enjoy yourself however you can, even if you hurt people who love you."' The novel's endorsement of Shug's mentality constitutes, according to Melissa Walker, a nod to 'Reagan's America' and a disregard of the real lives of many black people: 'By celebrating lovemaking and money-making in 1982, *The Color Purple* seems to appeal to those on the make in Reagan's America and to gloss over the economic and social realities of many blacks.' Walker's novel 'imagines a kind of miraculous transformation of personality, nurtured by powerful though incomplete personal love, rather than the slow, tedious change that is the result of hard work and commitment to making the most of life.'[25]

In Melissa Walker's reading, the ending of the novel verifies its commitment to personal fulfilment rather than lasting social change. One can only wonder what the future holds for people such as Celie: her story 'affirms a time of reconciliation and consolidation within the black community without proposing a program, plan, or forward thrust.' Melissa Walker shares Maryemma Graham's suspicions about the link between the novel's socio-economic politics and its appeal to white America:

■ For readers in the early eighties, it affirmed the regrouping of the private world that is personal, intimate, and even sexual, one that is free from political and social concerns. At that time it was a novel for Yuppie and Buppie America, an America that was a bit tired, a bit bewildered, driven to cut losses, consolidate gains, and cultivate its own private, profitable gardens. □

She goes on to remind us that few in Celie's position would have the good fortune to inherit property or receive the support of a rich lover like Shug. For Melissa Walker, '[s]peculation' over Walker's rationale in granting Celie economic prosperity opens up questions regarding the impact of contemporary contexts on the class consciousness of fiction writers. After all, Walker herself has recognized that Celie's ending cannot stand as a 'viable solution' to the problem faced by 'the landless, jobless, and propertyless masses.'[26] Melissa Walker wonders if 'the stories novelists tell are so conditioned by the receptiveness of the culture that even a writer like Walker [...] committed to social action on many fronts [...] inadvertently speaks to the values of the audience dominant at the time she composes a novel.' Does *The Color Purple* speak to 'an audience listening for reassurance that seeking economic prosperity and personal gratification are valid enterprises'?[27]

Both Hamilton and Melissa Walker raise interesting questions about the novel's socio-economic politics. While Melissa Walker offers some detailed analysis of the novel itself, Hamilton's reading relies mainly on abstractions and offers little engagement with Walker's language. Neither reading pays close attention to the kind of business which Celie builds. The following interpretations take a different approach, arguing that the relational ethos of Celie's enterprise makes it a viable alternative to the capitalist system.

FOLKSPANTS, UNLIMITED: 'A LABOUR OF LOVE'?

This subchapter opens with reference to an essay by Susan Willis which examines forms of production and consumption in modern America. 'I Shop Therefore I Am: Is There a Place for Afro-American Culture in Commodity Culture?' appeared in the collection *Changing Our Own Words: Essays on Criticism, Theory, and Writing by Black Women* (1989), edited by Cheryl A. Wall. Willis takes Toni Morrison's *The Bluest Eye* as her cue to ask 'whether it is possible for Afro-American culture to find expression in a mass cultural form.'[28] Focusing on the fashion and music industries, Willis examines the effects of mass commodity culture on the African-American consumer. Drawing on research by bell hooks, who 'develops the important distinction between white supremacy and older forms of racism,' she argues that black people have been denied alternative models of consumption.[29] In 'Overcoming White Supremacy' (1988) hooks describes white supremacy as 'the most useful term to denote exploitation of people of color in this society.'[30] Willis elaborates:

■ In contrast to racism which bars people of color from dominant modes of production and consumption, white supremacy suggests the equalization of the races at the level of consumption. This is possible only because all the models are white. As replicants, black versions of white cultural models are of necessity secondary and devoid of cultural integrity. The black replicant ensures, rather than subverts, domination. The notion of 'otherness,' or unassimilable marginality, is in the replicant attenuated by its mirroring of the white model. Finally the proliferation of black replicants, in toys, fashion, and advertising smothers the possibility for creating black cultural alternatives.[31] □

In her reading of *The Color Purple*, Willis argues that Walker 'refuses commodity fetishism and [...] imagines a form of cottage industry that has Celie organizing the collective production of customized pants for her extended community of family and friends.' Walker 'looks back upon commodity production, sees its earliest manifestation in the "slops" produced for slaves, its continuation in the fashion industry [...] and summarily denies the possibility of the mass-produced commodity as having anything to offer Afro-Americans.'[32] For Willis, Celie's enterprise places her beyond commodity culture.

Maroula Joannou, who refers to Willis's essay, also argues that Celie's entrepreneurial success offers an alternative to the capitalist ethos; her company produces pants as a response only to the community's needs. Hamilton sees the novel as a reflection of the 'alienating' forces at work in 1980s America; indeed, she argues that one of the reasons that so many readers and viewers identify with Celie is that she is 'a lonely, isolated, alienated young woman.' For Hamilton, Celie's prosperity does little to mute this impression. Hamilton insists that her 'environment throughout the novel is desolate and empty.'[33] Joannou, however, argues that Celie's industry offers a 'clear' alternative to a world bereft of meaningful relationships: her product is manufactured 'in a non-alienated way, as a labour of love.' Moreover, that very product destabilizes the identity boundaries which have divided that community and prevented authentic, healthy connections throughout the novel:

■ At a symbolic level the trousers are used to break a number of taboos. [...] The idiom 'to wear the trousers' means to be the dominant partner. Celie's cottage industry affirms both the importance of women's devising ways to avoid being financially dependent on men, and the continuance of the African-American woman's traditional skills of sewing and needlework, albeit in an updated form.[34] □

In his reading of the novel as 'womanist utopia' Keith Byerman explores how Walker's socio-economic politics fit into her utopian vision. He argues that Walker expresses her interest in *changing* America's prevailing economic system and exposes its reliance on racist ideology through her representations of two embedded narratives: the story of Celie and Nettie's father, a successful businessman lynched by white men, and Nettie's account of capitalist tyranny in Africa. After

Nettie reveals the true identity and story of their father, Celie visits Alphonso, the man she knew as 'Pa,' now a successful businessman himself. He articulates the 'situation of the Southern black rural middle class.' He tells Celie that 'the key to all [white people] is money' and that when slavery ended black people could only achieve economic success if they gave something to their oppressors: Alphonso gave white men money 'before [he] planted a seed.' He was able to buy a white boy to run the store because, in the eyes of white people, he had 'bought him with whitefolks' money.'[CP 155] Alphonso's account demonstrates that 'those who are successful in agriculture must not act so as to threaten the economic hegemony of whites. The individualism and entrepreneurship of Northern and European capitalism must be modified to fit the necessities of the Southern racial code.' The narratives of Celie's father and 'Pa', then, tell us that black people can enter 'the system' only if they 'pay[] a literal tribute to racism.'[35]

Nettie's letters also show us that the aim of 'the European and American capitalists' in Africa is nothing less than the 'total economic subjugation of groups of people.' The Olinka are initially receptive to the 'intruders' and welcome their plans for a new road. The idea of 'private property' has no meaning in the Olinka's 'communal society'; the people only recognize the reality of corporate greed when they witness the demolition of their homes and disregard for their communal way of life. Byerman reads Walker's exposure of the damaging effects of capitalism on oppressed groups in America's South and Africa as part of her wider utopian project: one of the characteristics of utopian literature is 'its frequent focus on greed as a fundamental evil of the writer's contemporaries.'

Walker's criticism of capitalist systems shifts 'focus' from 'greed' to 'status' when she addresses the issue of work that women are expected to undertake, which 'is viewed as that which is beneath the dignity of men (and sometimes white women) to perform.' In Africa, the Olinka forbid the education of their women; they do not need it in order to fulfil their designated domestic roles. In Celie's rural Georgia, however, the work which constitutes the main source of income 'is not gender differentiated': both Celie and Albert are farmers. Here the issue is one of 'control' over one's working life. While Albert decides on his working hours, resting whenever he feels the inclination, Celie is expected to work without reward or respite. Walker exposes '[t]he irony of such a labor system' by showing how it stifles both men and women: 'Because certain tasks carry negative status connotations, they cannot be performed by those men who might have a talent for them.'[36] When Sofia challenges hegemonic gender ideology by performing traditionally masculine and feminine tasks, Harpo attempts to 'beat' her. As Byerman notes, gender ideology prevents Harpo from doing the cooking which he prefers to farm work; he 'cannot erase the stigma of woman's work.'

At the end of *The Color Purple* Walker presents an 'alternative' to this system: 'the transvaluation of domestic activity.' She stresses the 'therapeutic and creative potential' of tasks usually assigned to women such as sewing, an activity which 'becomes a source of profit, community and selfesteem.' Here she deviates from the tradition of the utopian novel, where alternative economic systems evolve, more often than not, from the principles of 'socialism.' Her new system is 'a locally-based, arts and crafts capitalism.' Therefore Walker's main concern in *The Color Purple* is not with the 'principal [*sic*.] of profit-making' itself but the 'nature of work.' The idea of making money is not anathema to her, as long as it comes from 'non-alienated labor.' It is work generally assigned to women which 'makes possible a non-oppressive, non-self-interested productivity.' Byerman observes that the men also benefit from this system: Harpo uses his culinary skills in his blues club and no longer feels the need to attempt to force women into submission; Albert no longer oppresses Celie and finds a creative outlet in sewing; Samuel's work involves 'preach[ing] about his non-patriarchal, nondomineering [*sic*.] God.' This work is 'non-alienating' because it is no longer based on hierarchical, polarized thinking: Walker's alternative system makes 'no distinctions between usefulness and art, labor and leisure, worker and owner.' Walker 'reinforce[s] this point' by refusing to reveal how Celie uses her profits: she gains property through inheritance but we have no idea what she does with the money earned from 'Folkspants, Unlimited.' Byerman acknowledges that Walker's new economic order leaves many questions unanswered: indeed, she 'largely ignores the implications of her petit bourgeois ideal.'[37]

For example, we do not discover where the fabric for the trousers comes from or how it is purchased or promoted beyond Celie's immediate circle. Byerman expresses doubt about the plausibility of Walker's vision: 'Walker, after showing us the evils of both traditional and modern systems of exploitation, would have us believe that it is possible to create a self-sufficient, non-exploitative, woman-based local capitalism.'[38] Byerman recognizes that this model bears no relation to present realities but, rather than viewing Celie's prosperity as a nod to 'yuppie and buppie America,' he sees it as being beyond history: as we saw in Chapter 2 of this Guide, he views the 'world' of the novel's final scenes as one 'that has [...] no connection with the world of racism and exploitation.'[39]

CELIE'S PROSPERITY: FURTHER TENSIONS

In 'Race, Gender, and Nation in *The Color Purple*' Lauren Berlant sheds new light on some of the apparent contradictions inherent in the novel's social politics. She traces shifts in Walker's representation of familial and communal structures, showing how her treatment of class systems in the novel is largely informed by her womanist project.

Berlant observes that the story of the lynching of Nettie and Celie's father alerts us to 'the white men's *economic* aim to liquidate' black busi-nesses (Berlant's italics). This issue is, however, elided in the novel as Celie shows 'no curiosity about the larger, situational motives' of the revelations.[40] Like Melissa Walker, Berlant notes the absence of his-torical consciousness in Nettie's letters. In rendering the story of their father, Nettie 'reflects – without really reflecting on – the historical prox-imity of racial and sexual oppression to the class struggle that marks Afro-American experience.' Thus, 'the nonbiologized abstraction of class relations virtually disappears from the text.'[41] Nettie chooses to tell the story using 'abstract kinship terms,' referring to her father and uncles as 'the man and his two brothers' rather than specifying their names.[42] Her method of telling and Celie's response 'bracket[] class issues within the context of family relations, as if the capitalist economy is generated by the operations of family ideology.'[43]

When she turns to Celie's pants-making business, Berlant pays close attention to the political implications of Celie's methodology as designer: the product, folkspants, is designed 'to embody the essential person' rather than that person's 'physical body' and to 'release the wearer into authentic self-expression.' Berlant continues: 'this semiotic democ-racy [...] replaces the sexism and racism of "natural" languages of the body and consciousness.'

Moreover, Celie's success earns her a place in her family's entre-preneurial legacy and returns the sisters to their mother who 'protected her daughters from the deadliest penetration of patriarchy by preserving the property for the girls.' Moreover it 'provides closure to the narra-tive genealogy of racism and class struggle inscribed in Celie's family history.' It is highly significant, Berlant argues, that Celie conducts her business from the store which belonged to her father who was lynched 'for presuming the rights of full American citizens' and stepfather who achieved some limited success only by working 'exclusively for and with whites.'[44] Celie's enterprise, on the other hand, is 'biracial' and 'unisexual': 'capitalism, figured as a small (but infinitely expandable) family-style business, provides for the socially marginalized characters [...] the motivating drive for forging a positive relation to social life.'[45]

Nonetheless, Berlant remains uneasy with the novel's 'insistence on the significance of the product in the consumer's self-knowledge and self-expression.'[46] After all, 'the image of the commodity as the subject's most perfect self-expression is the classic fantasy bribe of capitalism.' For Berlant, the novel offers no engagement with this apparent contra-diction at the heart of its socio-economic message: 'the very force that disenfranchises Afro-Americans provides the material for their national reconstruction' yet this conflict 'is neither "solved" by the novel nor raised as a paradox.'[47]

This subchapter closes with consideration of Peter Kerry Powers's reading, ' "Pa Is Not Our Pa": Sacred History and Political Imagination in *The Color Purple*' (1995). Powers explores the implications of Celie's prosperity for her spiritual growth. He identifies a crucial transition from a communal to a commercial ethos in the novel and argues that it problematizes readings which applaud Celie's independence by threatening to undermine the novel's spiritual dimension. He identifies the early stages of Celie's sewing enterprise – her time spent in Memphis tailoring trousers to individual needs – as a period of spiritual fulfilment and unprecedented creativity for Celie. However when she begins to make money from her designs and becomes an entrepreneur she enters an economic system which cannot accommodate her need for spiritual development. The original premise of her business is lost: her 'new religious vision,' which is informed by Shug's philosophy, is subsumed by the 'social and economic organization of the larger culture.' This dominant culture 'assumes that the proper sphere of religious reality is a private one.' This conflict emerges clearly in 'the last third of the novel,' where 'Walker struggles to imagine the place of religion in the world at large.'

Indeed Celie's 'new spirituality is only sporadically evident' after the move to Memphis.[48] While the reader is offered a glimpse of a 'community in which each member provides for others according to his or her own special talents and interests' Celie becomes estranged from her product and her customers. In Memphis Celie tells Shug that she takes great pleasure in making pants, but that she must find a way of supporting herself financially: 'what Celie loves and what Celie has to do to sustain herself cannot coexist.' She 'accepts the inevitability of this asceticism. She puts aside her love, making pants for her friends, so that she can get down to the real business of life, making a living.' Thus, '[t]he spontaneous creativity of the pleasuring God is transformed into an imperative and threatening commandment: Create ... or else.'[49]

Powers recognizes the temptation to 'sentimentalize Celie's newfound freedom' but reminds us that her industry, 'originally an act of love within a community, becomes an abstract business in providing for her freedom.' Thus the 'contradictions' inherent in Celie's status at the end of the novel 'suggest that [her] personal bourgeois revolution is not a utopian fulfillment, that her coming to voice as the producer of her own story is bought at the price of having no clear audience with whom to share that story.'[50] Powers goes so far as to state that 'while conversion occasions Celie's arrival as a producer in her own right, Celie's arrival very nearly empties the novel of any spiritual focus at all.' Indeed 'God, community, spirit, and celebration are subordinated to Celie's triumphant individuality, first as producer and then as heiress.'

While many critics have suggested that Walker purposefully evades the tensions inherent in the ending of the novel in a bid to make Celie happy, Powers detects some engagement with these tensions: had the novel been 'unreflective' about these contradictions, 'Celie's story would have ended plausibly where many critics apparently think it does: with Celie as the triumphant bourgeois entrepreneur.' However Powers finds that her 'triumph as an individual is as deeply problematic as her earlier domination by Albert': her 'hasty retreat to the bucolic domesticity of the rural South' implies 'that the conflicts are not reconcilable within the context of world systems that privilege the public over the private, the work place over the home, the secular over the sacred, the male over the female.' Powers does not believe that true freedom can 'come by Celie's integration into the dominant economic system. Rather, total liberation awaits a different system, a different time, a different manner of living, for which Celie's story has only just begun to create a space.'[51] Here Powers differs significantly from those critics and readers who argue that the novel offers little scope for Celie's further development.

Powers argues that it is in recognition of this 'possibility' that Walker chooses to stage her heroine's liberation on the Fourth of July rather than a work day. Noting that 'the Fourth of July merely represents another holy day affirming the values of American culture, the mythology of freedom and opportunity that the oppression in the book belies on every hand,' Powers nevertheless sees the novel's closing scene as an affirmation of the 'possibility' of a community such as Celie's: it might exist in 'its own realization beyond the present order, not necessarily in some heavenly realm, but at least at a time when different stories will obtain, providing for different practices from those which are presently available.' Moreover, the choice of a holiday date for the final letter moves the focus away from economic progress: it 'suggests that Celie's accomplishments as a business-woman are not the ultimate accomplishments available to human beings, whatever the ways in which her own bourgeois revolution liberates her from slavery to Albert.'[52]

Powers sees plenty of scope for optimism in the novel's closing scenes. In her final letter Celie includes her original addressee in a list of addressees, indicating a significant shift in her conception of God: 'God identifies with a particular community, thereby pointing beyond the false God of the early portion of the book.' There is also political meaning for Powers in the fact that Celie does not sign her name at the end of this letter: this 'suggests that the ultimate human achievement is not in the individualism that the political economy demands [...] [r]ather, individual human significance manifests itself in the development of human community.'[53]

Does Celie's economic prosperity constitute a capitulation to mainstream values and help to account for the novel's cross-cultural appeal or is the ethos of Celie's enterprise radical enough to challenge mainstream values? The readings in this chapter show the range of stances that critics have taken on Walker's handling of socio-economic politics in *The Color Purple*. For many critics, however, the revolutionary potential of the novel lies with its gender politics. Readings in the following chapter focus on Walker's representation of female experience and address a question which has occupied critics' minds since the novel's publication: does *The Color Purple* belong in the feminist canon?

CHAPTER SEVEN

The Color Purple: Feminist Text?

In his study of contemporary American culture, *Loose Canons: Notes on the Culture Wars* (1992), Henry Louis Gates, Jr., notes that 'works by black women novelists, especially Walker and Morrison, are selling in record-breaking numbers, in part because of an expanded market that includes white and black feminists as well as the general black studies readership.'[1] The cross-cultural appeal of Walker's *The Color Purple* is often attributed to her engagement with women's issues that transcend class and race: Alison Light finds that the novel 'can be popular with a whole range of women readers, cutting across the specificity of its black history, in its concern with family, emotionality, sexual relations, and fantasy life.'[2] Judy Elsley affirms that Celie's journey will strike a chord with all feminists: 'Celie's struggle is more dramatic than many women experience, but her journey is a familiar one. All of us in academia, especially those involved in feminist studies, are quiltmakers [...] [w]e have a lot in common with Celie.'[3]

Feminism argues that women should be granted the same rights as men and that gender identity should not be a determinant in the treatment of any human subject. Many black women have distanced themselves from feminism, noting how issues pertaining to their everyday lives have been ignored in feminist debates and stressing the influence of mainstream models and inscriptions – for example, the codification of femininity as white – on the feminist movement.

As feminism has evolved, its concerns have shifted. The development of the movement has been traced through three waves. In the nineteenth century the issue of suffrage was at the heart of first-wave feminism. The second wave, which emerged in the 1960s and 1970s, informs several of the readings in this chapter. Feminist critic Maggie Humm notes that second-wave feminism built on the work of nineteenth-century feminists by taking particular interest in 'women's "everyday" difference from men in the street and in the home' and aiming to 'make[] visible the powerful realities of gender difference.'[4] In the 1990s, third-wave feminists took exception to some of the essentialist notions of gender identity espoused by the second wave and called attention to the resulting exclusion of women from a range of cultures and possibilities. In the twenty-first century, the term *post-feminism* has gained some currency but has also raised concerns because of its implied assumption that the original goals of feminism have been achieved.

Alice Walker has expressed reservations about her association with feminism, arguing that its tenets are often at odds with black women's experiences. For this reason she prefers the term *womanist*, a word that derives from her culture and that she first heard in conversations between mothers who lived in her childhood community. She tells Krista Brewer that she has 'always felt that "feminist" was sort of elitist and ethereal and it sounded a little weak.' The term feminist, she stresses, comes from a different tradition from her own: 'I have trouble with having to say that I'm a black feminist when white feminists don't ever say they're white feminists. They say that they are feminists because it is assumed that they are white feminists, since the word "feminist" comes from their culture.'[5] Furthermore, Walker finds that the definitions and models of white feminism are informed by patriarchal assumptions: it 'is not a tradition that teaches white women that they are capable.' She notes: 'my tradition *assumes* I'm capable. I have a tradition of people not letting me get the skills, but I have cleared fields, I have lifted whatever, I have *done* it' (Walker's italics).[6]

In her essay 'Some Implications of Womanist Theory' (1986), writer Sherley Anne Williams (1944–99) explains her preference for Walker's term. She expresses concern over the 'separatism' of 'current black feminist criticism,' noting 'its tendency to see not only a *distinct* black female culture but to see that culture as a separate cultural form having more in common with white female experience than with the facticity of Afro-American life' (Williams's italics). She finds this idea troubling because 'until quite recently, black women's literary experiences were excluded from consideration in the literature of white feminists.' Walker's definition of womanism, outlined in *In Search of Our Mothers' Gardens*, is, on the other hand, ' "committed to the survival and wholeness of entire people," female *and* male, as well as to a valorization of women's works in all their varieties and multitudes' (William's italics).[7]

Jita Tuzyline Allan's book, *Womanist and Feminist Aesthetics: A Comparative Review* (1995) includes an essay on Walker's novel, '*The Color Purple*: A Study of Walker's Womanist Gospel.' References to this essay come from the collection *Alice Walker's The Color Purple* (2000), edited by Harold Bloom. Allan finds that the distinction between womanism and feminism 'is a matter of intensity': '[w]hile both modes of thought originate from the same wellspring of resistance to patriarchal domination, womanism intensifies the struggle by fighting from several fronts because it believes that patriarchy, like the Gorgon, is many-headed.'[8] Allan, along with other critics, expresses concern about the 'essentialist implication of womanism's self-definition' and wonders about the 'exclu[sion]' of 'those white feminists whose creative vision approximates the womanist ideal [. . .] or those who might choose to incorporate aspects of womanism in their writing, especially in the wake of the recent push for inclusiveness in feminist theory.' She concludes her essay by noting that womanism 'also assumes that by virtue of being black or nonwhite, a feminist is necessarily womanist.'[9]

Walker's identification of herself as part of the womanist tradition has inspired a welter of readings of her fiction, in particular *The Color Purple*, which was immediately seized upon by many reviewers as a feminist classic. Elliott Butler-Evans finds that Walker's fiction as a whole 'can be said to be structured by a complex ideological position that oscillates between her identity as "Black feminist" or "woman-of-color" and a generalized feminist position in which race is subordinated.'[10] He adds that her 'primary emphasis' is 'consciousness of herself as a Black woman empowered to narrate the stories of Black women who are past or present creators of a Black female culture' and that her chief 'role [. . .] is one of enabling Black women, especially those most marginalized by race, caste, and class, to have their voices heard and their histories read.'[11]

Butler-Evans feels confident in identifying *The Color Purple* as an example of a 'specific feminist discourse,' pointing to 'Celie's self-narration,' Walker's engagement with the tradition of the epistolary novel and the 'displacement of broad issues of Afro-American history by a specific feminist ideology largely characterized by images and representations that force the reader to reconsider the plight of the Black woman as oppressed.'[12]

Other critics, however, view the novel as an elaboration of Walker's specifically womanist ideology and contest its feminist credentials. Maroula Joannou argues that Celie's use of black folk English and the 'context' of her story qualify easy identifications with feminist narratives:

■ Because the context of slavery is invoked through the particulars of Celie's situation, her experiences bring to mind collective rather than individual memories and histories, thus rendering problematic any identification that white feminists might make with Celie as a recipient of sexual abuse, since the context in which the abuse takes place involves race as well as gender.[13] □

In the essay 'African-American Womanism: from Zora Neale Nurston to Alice Walker' (2004), Lovalerie King considers how Walker's womanism has informed her fiction. In *The Color Purple*, King argues, 'Walker achieves a previously unrealized depiction of the womanist approach to life in the character of Shug Avery.'[14] King identifies several dimensions of Walker's womanism in her characterization of Shug: she 'choos[es] an alternative to mothering,' embraces 'a free, open, fluid sexuality that is not bound by prefixes,' and articulates and lives by 'a *philosophy* of connectedness and relatedness [...] consistent with her healthy embrace of all sensual pleasures' (King's italics).[15]

In her book *The Erotics of Talk: Women's Writing and Feminist Paradigms* (1996), an investigation of 'feminist criticism's political investment in recovering women's voices and in the difficult and not always progressive pleasures such recovery may provide,' Carla Kaplan places *The Color Purple* alongside 'feminist classics' from a range of contexts and cultures.[16] Kaplan notes that these 'classics' have been read as 'model[s] of coming to voice.' In her study she draws attention to 'the presence of a competing topos in women's literature [...] the search not for a voice, but for a listener capable of hearing that voice and responding appropriately to it.' She notes that 'this topos takes the form of a repeated and structuring metaphor – a performative trope,' the term for which is '*the erotics of talk*.'[17] In the essay ' "Somebody I Can Talk To": Teaching Feminism Through *The Color Purple*,' Kaplan compares Walker's novel to Hurston's *Their Eyes Were Watching God*. She finds that it 'signifies' upon the earlier novel 'by rejecting its ethics of disengagement, even as it builds on its aesthetic of reciprocity by providing Celie with a nearly endless supply of desirable, conversational partners.'[18] While Hurston's novel 'can only imagine a satisfying discursive exchange within a dyadic, female, identificatory, homogeneous, and private public sphere (the back porch),' Walker's novel 'is prepared to celebrate the utopian possibilities of discourse, community, social exchange without [...] reserve and distrust.'[19]

Kaplan suggests that it is because Celie 'learns to fight back, speak for herself, defend other women' that the novel has been identified as a feminist classic.[20] However, she expresses unease with the identification of Celie as being representative of contemporary feminism and wonders whether or not Walker herself lost sight of her own distinctions in the wake of the novel's canonization as feminist Ur-text: 'I want to mark this ascription as vexed, particularly given Walker's own differentiation of "womanist" perspectives from "feminist" ones and her care to mark the alienation and exclusion women of color have often felt from white, mainstream American feminism.' Kaplan continues: 'such distinctions have been ignored and over-ridden (potentially even by Walker herself) in the process of making this novel a feminist "classic." '[21]

CELIE AS FEMINIST HEROINE?

While Kaplan worries that the categorization of Celie as a feminist heroine ignores important distinctions between feminism and woman-ism, Trudier Harris insists that neither term is applicable to Walker's novel. In 'On *The Color Purple*, Stereotypes and Silence,' Harris contends that the novel's canonization has the opposite effect that Walker intended: it poses problems for the black female reader, forcing her into silence. Gloria Steinem anticipated that the novel would unite women across cultures. Harris, however, focuses on the differences between the responses of black and white women to *The Color Purple*. While 'most of the white women with whom [she] talked loved the novel,' the responses of the black women readers she consulted were accompanied by 'a quiet strain of discomfort [...] a quiet tendency to criticize.' Harris suggests that these women readers were reluctant to voice their reservations about *The Color Purple* because they 'were all faced with the idea that to criticize a novel that had been so universally complimented was somehow a desertion of the race and the black woman writer.'[22]

Harris elaborates on these concerns in her later essay, 'From Victimization to Free Enterprise: Alice Walker's *The Color Purple*,' published in *Studies in American Fiction* in 1986. Here she asserts that Celie's survival strategies complicate a feminist reading of the novel: 'Celie, by her own estimation and that of others, is a survivor. *How* she overcomes victimization to survive is the problem' (Harris's italics). Harris points out that '[a]nyone can use her, or say anything to her, or commit violence against her, and she will placidly say something to the effect that she is still here.'[23] Celie's response to abuse and oppression is given 'ironic reinforcement in the novel in the character of [...] Sofia, a black woman who does fight back,' but who is punished for her defiance not only by the white characters in the novel but also by Walker herself: 'Sofia must eventually suppress most of the traits that make her an interesting character, turning from vibrancy to somnambulism.'[24]

Walker's handling of the 'issue of physical beauty' also casts doubt over Celie's feminist credentials. Noting that many black women writers have used fiction to stress the need to 'find an identity and value' beyond the dominant culture's 'narrow-minded conception of physical beauty,' Harris finds Celie's acceptance of this conception 'somewhat anachronistic.'[25] The moment when Celie looks in the mirror and sees no reason for Shug to love her recalls the 'stereotyped notions of looks that black women have been unwarranted heir to for centuries in America.' Moreover, her happiness involves 'no softening of her attitude toward her physical features.' Indeed, '[i]n this area of her life so very vital to self-conception, Celie reflects no evolved state of mind';

Walker's heroine shows 'no substantial change from the majority of her dark-skinned black sisters of the 1930s and 1940s and perhaps a few of those who still devalued themselves early in the 1980s.'[26] For Harris, Celie as 'a representative character [...] presents fewer problems' to the reader than as a fully-fledged, 'progressive' individual subject.[27]

Maroula Joannou counters Harris's reading, insisting that '[t]o criticise [Celie] for passivity is to do so in ignorance of the fear which male violence produces in women.' She observes that the '[y]ears of abuse' suffered by Celie 'may well have weakened [her] spirit, but they have not destroyed it.' While Harris expresses incredulity at Celie's passivity, Joannou finds that '[w]hat is surprising is not that the resistance of victims of domestic violence like Celie is slow to develop, but that it ever develops at all.'[28]

Several critics have made Celie's apparent passivity their focus for feminist readings. Deborah Ellis gives a comparative reading of Walker's novel and the 'Clerk's Tale' from the *Canterbury Tales* (1400) by Geoffrey Chaucer (1343–1400) in her essay '*The Color Purple* and the Patient Griselda' (1987). Usually classified as a moral apologue, the 'Clerk's Tale' tells the story of Walter, a marquis who marries a poor girl named Griselda. For reasons that are not explained in the text, he subjects her to a number of tests, telling her their children have died and threatening to usurp her with a new bride whom she will serve as a maid. Griselda grieves for herself and her children alone but offers no resistance to Walter's plans. At the end of the tale Walter reveals that she has passed all of his tests; her reward is to be embraced as his wife and to live with him for the rest of her days.

Ellis reads Walker's novel as a 'modern analogue' to Chaucer's controversial tale.[29] She takes issue with Trudier Harris's characterization of Celie's passivity, reading her it as an example of 'the covert resistance of a woman forced, like Griselda, to fit into an alien world and to make it her own.'[30] After noting similarities between Celie and Griselda – both 'embody the principle of harmony' and are able to 'impose order on chaos' – Ellis examines the differences:[31] perhaps most importantly, Walker 'transforms [the] impact' of Chaucer's tale by giving Celie the agency to 'interpret[]' its 'themes.'[32] Walker's heroine eventually gains insight into 'the difference between a Griseldian resignation and true acceptance' and recognizes the possibility of achieving true autonomy and empowerment.[33]

The difference between the two heroines emerges through comparisons of the use of clothing in their stories as a 'domestic metaphor[] for self-assertion.'[34] At the end of Chaucer's text, '[a]ll is peace and harmony – and passivity': references to Griselda in the final lines confirm only that she is 'clothed' and guided forward: 'presumably a negatively defined future of not having her clothes snatched away and a broom put in her hand is fulfillment enough.' Celie, on the other hand, has escaped male tyranny and established independence on her own terms, gaining freedom through her pantsmaking enterprise: 'It is Walker's affirmation of women's power through transformation of their homes that finally marks her novel.'[35]

A further exploration of Celie's survival strategies can be found in King-Kok Cheung's comparative reading of Walker's novel and Maxine Hong Kingston's short story cycle, *The Woman Warrior*. In ' "Don't Tell": Imposed Silences in *The Color Purple* and *The Woman Warrior*' (1988) Cheung illuminates how both heroines 'learn to reshape recalcitrant myths glorifying patriarchal values' and progress from silence to articulacy by nurturing their relationships with women and 'taking cues from their mother tongues' in their expression.[36]

This section closes by considering Gina Michelle Collins's essay '*The Color Purple*: What Feminism Can Learn from a Southern Tradition' (1990). Collins reads Celie's passivity as a manifestation of her indifference to patriarchal ideology and her latent independence. Collins notes that Walker uses Celie's passivity as a subversive tool to overturn the negative connotations of images such as 'the mule of the world.' Referring to Walker's essay, 'In Search of Our Mothers' Gardens,' Collins notes that Walker 'embraces rather than denies the identification of women as "mules of the world" in black folklore,' thereby 'shift[ing] our focus from the immediate negative charge carried by the word *mule*' (Collins's italics). Rather, she 'identif[ies] a peculiar strength embodied in the image. A mule after all, while an ugly, comical creature, has one outstanding feature: its ability to survive.' This ability is 'the most often praised attribute of [...] Celie in *The Color Purple*, who throughout the novel is first her father's then her husband's "mule." ' This capacity to survive is one of the attributes which, according to Collins, gives Celie 'potential as a role model for contemporary feminists.'[37]

Owing to black women's exclusion from 'patriarchal power structures,' Walker chooses 'to write almost exclusively about the experience of southern black women.' There is a 'freedom inherent in this position,' which Walker 'us[es] [...] to articulate the unspoken or unspeakable realities of the patriarchal system as a first step toward offering a vision of an alternative social order.'[38] The entrenchment of these power structures manifests itself in the hostile response to this exposure.

Collins refers to Walker's account of the protest led by Mrs. Green against the novel's inclusion on the local school's syllabus. In her response to Mrs. Green, Walker reveals that her mother also took issue with the novel, especially the graphic language of its opening pages. She explains that as she wrote the description of Celie's rape she found herself 'trying to censor' the language. However she refrained from doing so, remembering those children and adults 'who have been sexually abused and who have never been permitted in their own language to tell about it.'[39] Collins observes that both the concerns raised by Mrs. Green and Walker's initial impulse to revise her language 'provide eloquent testimony of the degree to which they, like so many other women, have internalized and are governed by patriarchal structures. This automatic censoring response can be read as one of the patriarchy's most effective repressive tools.'[40]

Collins sees a parallel between Walker's tactics in *The Color Purple* and those of second-wave feminist critic Hélène Cixous, who supported 'the use of repressive, sexist stereotypes in order to "use them up,"' asserting that this would 'rob them of their power over women and prepare the way for a revalorization of the potentially subversive attributes and values that the stereotypes were meant to suppress.' Both Cixous and Walker aim 'to find a voice with which the repressed minority can tell its story, in its own language and from its perspective.' This can only be achieved if one is 'willing to speak what the patriarchy deems unspeakable.' Collins identifies the 'refusal to adopt the values and attitudes of a racist patriarchy, to believe in its stereotypes, along with a recognition of the destructive, limiting effects of adherence to such values,' as the means to 'power' for Walker's heroines. She refers us to the 'distinction' that Walker makes 'between "being a slave and being enslaved"' in her short story 'A Letter of the Times; or, Should This Sado-masochism Be Saved?' from *You Can't Keep a Good Woman Down* (1981). Collins explains: '[a] slave, however limited in terms of physical or material freedoms, can still retain freedom of spirit. The enslaved, however, have succumbed to a far more insidious form of oppression. Those who have been enslaved by their oppressors internalize the values of oppressors.' The enslaved 'identify themselves with the very system that represses them and become its willing, though unwitting allies': Relating this to patriarchy, Collins adds: 'still more serious, should they manage to free themselves sufficiently to attempt to subvert or destroy patriarchal structures, they adopt the very tools of the patriarchy and in so doing, doom themselves to failure.'[41]

In *The Color Purple* this distinction emerges most clearly through a comparison of the survival tactics of Celie and Sofia. Critics who query the novel's politics have been disconcerted by the narrative of Sofia, often identified as a model of female empowerment. In 'Writing the Subject, Reading *The Color Purple*,' bell hooks notes with concern that Sofia 'most radically challenges sexism and racism,' but 'is a tragic figure' and is 'restored to only a semblance of sanity.'[42] Collins offers a different interpretation of Celie's ostensible submission and Sofia's open defiance: one that leads to a refreshing reading of Celie's much-analyzed relationships with other women. Most readings emphasize the wisdom that is passed on from Shug, Nettie, Sofia and Mary Agnes to Celie.

As Collins notes, Celie's role as teacher has been 'overlooked.' Observing that Celie's 'survival' can be attributed to her refusal to absorb the assumptions of patriarchy, Collins goes on to examine how she releases other women from these assumptions. It is Celie who 'teaches the most important lesson of all': it is not until the other women, especially Sofia and Shug, 'have learned to distance themselves from their identification with patriarchal values that they can serve as role models for Celie.' Collins notes that '[a]lthough each of them is remarkably free and independent by comparison with Celie, they are nonetheless enslaved.' These women are 'trapped by their internalization of a patriarchal value system even as they reject the roles it assigns them. Their position may be much like that of many readers of the novel.'[43]

In Collins' reading, Sofia's 'downfall' is attributable to her 'identification with patriarchal values (and repetition of them, by reversal)':[44] while she asserts that she can fight, she 'does not know how to survive' because she has not recognized 'that any attempt to fight the system by its own rules and on its own ground is doomed inevitably to failure.' Celie, on the other hand, 'survives because she has never completely internalized the values and methods of the patriarchy. As she states it so often, she does not know how to fight by their rules.'[45]

Collins also illuminates how patriarchal ideology conditions Shug's perception of the world: 'even though she has rejected her assigned role, she judges Celie according to the same standard,' deriding her physical appearance. It is Celie who teaches Shug about 'sharing, cooperation' and 'love.'[46] Thus, the identification of Shug and Sofia as the novel's feminist characters betrays the extent to which today's readers are informed by patriarchal ideology:

■ The modern feminist all too often shares the plight of a Sofia or a Shug, trapped by her own unconscious internalization of the values of the system she is working to dismantle. Feminist ideology has failed to recognize how completely it identifies with patriarchal values.[47] □

WALKER'S ENGAGEMENT WITH WESTERN REPRESENTATIONS OF WOMEN

This section looks at Christine Froula's groundbreaking essay on *The Color Purple*, 'The Daughter's Seduction: Sexual Violence and Literary History.' First published in the journal *Signs: Journal of Women in Culture and Society* in 1986, it has become one of the most cited feminist readings of the novel. While recognizing Walker's particular contribution to black women's writing, Froula turns our attention to connections between the women of *The Color Purple* and some of the most scrutinized female characters of Western literature and illuminates new ways of reading Celie's silence.

Froula traces a line of descent from *The Color Purple* back to Homer's *Iliad* to demonstrate how Walker rewrites a script created and perpetuated by Western culture which locks women into silence. Froula takes as her starting-point a metaphor crafted by Virginia Woolf (1882–1941) in a speech to the London/National Society for Women's Service in 1931. Woolf represents the woman novelist as a fisherwoman and her imagination as a hook that she drops into 'the world that lies submerged in our unconscious being,' only to have it pulled out. The 'queer knowledge' that the woman novelist has learned concerning 'women's bodies' and their 'passions' must be suppressed until a time when the world can engage with it. Woolf estimates that 'fifty years' will pass before the world is ready for this 'queer knowledge.'[48] Froula examines first the 'literary history implied by Woolf's fisherwoman image' before considering those writers who 'fulfill Woolf's "guess" that women should soon break a very significant silence,' specifically Alice Walker and her contemporary Maya Angelou.[49]

Starting with Helen of Troy's relationship with her father Priam, Froula examines the 'paradigmatic father–daughter dialogue.' By reading it alongside 'Freud's dialogue with the hysterics,' she highlights the entrenchment of what she terms the 'hysterical cultural script: the cultural text that dictates to males and females alike the necessity of silencing woman's speech when it threatens the father's power.'[50] Considering the circumlocutions, silences and omissions in Helen's speeches, Froula finds that the *Iliad* 'suggests that women's silence in culture is neither a natural nor an accidental phenomenon but a cultural achievement, indeed, a constitutive accomplishment of male culture.'[51] One example of this cultural force emerges in Helen's speech to Priam in which her 'reverence' for her father 'frames her expression of her longing for her former life.'[52] Froula sees affinities between the *Iliad*'s treatment of female narratives and Freud's handling of female hysterics: 'As the *Iliad* tells the story of a woman's abduction as a male war story, so Freud turned the hysterics' stories of sexual abuse into a tale to soothe a father's ear.'[53]

Freud's 'seduction theory' posited that 'hysterical symptoms have their origin in sexual abuse suffered in childhood, which is repressed and eventually assimilated to a later sexual experience.'[54] Some feminists have suggested that he rejected this theory in the face of compelling evidence that it was usually the father who carried out the abuse. He does not entirely ignore the daughter's story but 'rewrites it as the story of "femininity," attributing to mothers, nurses and a female "Nature" the damage to female subjectivity and desire wrought by specific historical events' and 'mak[ing] subtle war on woman's desire and on the credibility of her language in order to avert its perceived threat to the father's cultural pre-eminence.'[55]

Froula reads Angelou's celebrated autobiography *I Know Why the Caged Bird Sings* (1970) as a dramatization of 'one woman's emergence from the hysterical cultural text.' *The Color Purple* builds on this dramatization by offering a full revision of this cultural text: '[p]ublished in 1982 (right on schedule with respect to Woolf's prediction), Walker's novel not only portrays a cure of one daughter's hysterical silence but rewrites from the ground up the cultural text that sanctions her violation and dictates her silence.' Walker debunks the 'foundation of the "conventions," social and cultural, that enforce women's silence';[56] she

■ retells the founding story of Western culture from a woman's point of view, and in an important sense, her historical novel – already celebrated as a landmark in the traditions of Black women's, Black, and women's writing – also stands in the tradition inaugurated by Homer and Genesis.[57] □

Celie, Froula argues, is 'a woman reborn to desire and language' and Walker is 'a woman writer whom Woolf might well have considered a hero.'[58]

Froula emphasizes the importance of relationships with women in developing Celie's language and awakening her desire. This development enables Celie to articulate her grievances to Albert after she has discovered Nettie's letters; through Celie's 'powerful speech' Walker is able to 'break down the patriarchal marriage plot that sanctions violence against women.'[59] Celie's curse on Albert opens up the possibility of a nonhierarchical relationship between the genders:

■ Celie's curse, which Walker enhances with epic machinery, is powerful. But unlike the razor which Shug takes out of her hand, it does not return Mr.—'s violence in kind. Instead, the decline of the father's law in Walker's novel creates temporary separate spheres for women and men in which gender hierarchy breaks down in the absence of the 'other,' enabling women and men eventually to share the world again.[60] □

Froula offers insight into the ways that Albert's development in the novel debunks the patriarchal ideology underpinning much Western literature. She illuminates the significance of a minor character introduced in the novel's latter stages and largely neglected by critics: Henrietta, the youngest child of Sofia, who has a blood disease for which she is told to eat yams. The community's liberation from patriarchal ideology manifests itself in its response to Henrietta. Although the identity of Henrietta's father remains unknown, the people of the community, including Albert and Harpo, feel protective of her. As they all strive to invent enticing yam dishes for Henrietta, 'it becomes apparent that, in Walker's recreated universe, the care of children by men and women without respect to proprietary biological parenthood is an important means of undoing the exploitative hierarchy of gender roles.'[61]

This dissolution of 'the gender hierarchy necessitates a rewriting of the Creation myth and a dismantling of the hierarchical concepts of God and authority that underwrite them in Western tradition.' In the 'cosmos' of Walker's novel, 'the monotheistic Western myth of origins gives way to one of multiple, indeed infinite beginnings.'[62] One of the novel's alternative scripts is enacted by Sofia's community of women who follow their own rules. Harpo uses the image of the Amazon warrior to describe this community. In her analysis of the *Iliad*, Froula reads Priam's comparison of Helen to the Amazons as a covert recognition of her resistance to masculine authority; the comparison points to 'repressed fears' of female power on the battlefield.[63] The 'cosmos' depicted in the final pages of *The Color Purple* is a site for Amazonian creativity.

Harpo reveals that he once asked Sofia's mother why she insists on following her own way, and the mother replied: 'you think your way as good as anybody else's. Plus, it's yours.'[64] As the epigraph of the novel testifies, Walker 'fills her historical novel with creators, authorities, beginnings, "others." Like all authors of epic, she collapses transcendence into history.' Froula notes, however, that Walker's 'history differs from that of earlier epics. Originating in a violation of the patriarchal law, it undoes the patriarchal cultural order and builds upon new ground.'[65]

Thus, 'Walker's woman as hero' alerts us to the possibility of 'transformative dialogue between herself and the world, between her story and his': the kind of dialogue 'that Woolf predicted would begin once woman recovered her voice.'[66]

THE COLOR PURPLE AND THE AFRICAN-AMERICAN WOMEN'S CANON

Although she has acknowledged affinities with white women writers, Alice Walker has distanced herself from the feminist tradition. In the title essay of *In Search of Our Mothers' Gardens*, she calls on black women to engage the 'the living creativity some of [their] great-grandmothers were not allowed to know.'[67] In the same essay she describes the artistry of a black woman from Alabama whose quilt of Christ's crucifixion hangs in the Smithsonian Institution. Walker identifies this woman, whose name is unknown, as a foremother who gave expression to her creativity through the only means at her disposal. Quilting is an important part of Walker's creative process and has become a dominant trope for her formal poetics and identity politics. While waiting for the *The Color Purple* to take shape, Walker made progress on her own quilt; as it developed, the characters begin to make connections with each other and their 'medium.' In the novel itself, quilting represents the possibility of connection. When Celie and Sofia bond for the first time, Sofia immediately suggests that they make a quilt from some fragments of curtain material.

Several readings of *The Color Purple* have offered detailed explorations of quilting and its symbolic function in the novel. In 'Alice Walker's American Quilt: *The Color Purple* and the American Tradition' (1999), Priscilla Leder examines how the 'product and process' of quilting 'embody' one of the central characteristics of Walker's work as a whole: 'the ideal of unity in diversity.' The quilt is a metaphor for Walker's engagement with genre in *The Color Purple*, a novel that 'incorporates recognizable pieces of American literary traditions into its own pattern.'[68] A discussion of Judy Elsley's reading, ' "Nothing can be sole or whole that has not been rent": Fragmentation in the Quilt and *The Color Purple*' (1999), can be found in Chapter 4 of this Guide. For Elsley, the quilt symbolizes the possibility of achieving autonomy by embracing fragmentation. In 'Dressing the Spirit: Cloth-Working and Language in *The Color Purple*' (1986), Teresa Tavormina explores the novel's handling of the characters' quest for identity 'as reflected in images of clothing, sewing, and quilting' and considers how these images 'relat[e] to [Walker's] use of such personalized forms of language as dialect and letters.'[69]

Walker's engagement with the literary creativity of her foremothers has generated some of the richest readings of her work. It is her dialogue with Zora Neale Hurston, the writer and anthropologist of the Harlem Renaissance, which has attracted the most critical interest. In his introduction to *Reading Black, Reading Feminist* (1990), Henry Louis Gates, Jr., identifies Hurston as the writer 'whose work and career more than those of any other black woman writer, have become the symbols of a reclaimed literary tradition.'[70] In 'Zora Neale Hurston, Alice Walker and the "Ancient Power" of Black Women' (1985), Marjorie Pryse identifies the publication of Hurston's work as the 'second beginning' and 'first real flowering' of the 'literary tradition of black women's fiction.'[71] Pryse observes that Hurston's engagement with 'folk magic' had a particular impact on Walker's conception of her work and position as an artist. Both writers view their art 'as a form of conjuring': in presenting herself as a 'medium' in *The Color Purple* Walker summons up 'woman's magic' and 'purposely gathers together all the creative force of her black and female forerunners.'[72]

Hurston was for many a controversial figure, derided by some of her contemporaries for her political views. She argued against integration in schools, positing that black children's learning had nothing to do with the presence of white children. In the Civil Rights era she was castigated for her silence on the issue of racism. By the end of her life, her books were out of print. In 'Zora Neale Hurston: A Cautionary Tale and a Partisan View' (1979), Walker recalls feeling 'paralyzed with confusion and fear' upon reading the 'misleading, deliberately belittling, inaccurate and generally irresponsible attacks on [Hurston's] work.'[73] Indeed she notes that critics resist recognition or detailed examination of Hurston's work and choose instead to focus on her politics and her relationships with white women. Walker counters such representations of Hurston, identifying 'racial health' as the defining characteristic of Hurston's work:[74] 'She was so at ease with her blackness it never occurred to her that she should act one way among blacks and another among whites (as her more "sophisticated" black critics apparently did).'[75] In defending herself against criticism of *The Color Purple*'s racial and gender politics, Walker has questioned critics' concern about white readers' responses to the novel.

In the essay 'Looking for Zora,' Walker recounts her journey to Eatonville, Florida – Hurston's birthplace – where she posed as Hurston's niece on her quest for her foremother's grave. In 1979, Walker edited an anthology of Hurston's work, *I Love Myself When I Am Laughing . . . and Then Again When I Am Looking Mean and Impressive: A Zora Neale Hurston Reader*, which would become an invaluable reference point for Hurston scholars. Walker dedicated her collection of short stories, *In Love and Trouble: Stories of Black Women*, to Hurston's memory. The narrator of one story, 'The Revenge of Hannah Kemhuff,' takes a curse directly from Hurston's collection of folklore, *Mules and Men*, in response to the racism of Mrs. Holley.

Many critics have identified Shug Avery as a fictional incarnation of Hurston. In 'Color Me Zora,' Gates observes similarities between Celie's description of Shug's picture – the reader's first sight of Shug – and Walker's description of a photograph of Hurston in 'Zora Neale Hurston: A Cautionary Tale and a Partisan View.' Walker's 'desert island' book is Hurston's most celebrated work, her second novel, *Their Eyes Were Watching God* (1937), which charts narrator-heroine Janie Crawford's search for self-realization. When the novel opens, Janie has returned to her home town of Eatonville, Florida. Here she recounts her life experiences to her friend Pheoby, telling of the influence of her upbringing with her grandmother and her relationships with her three husbands.

A selection of comparative readings of Walker's and Hurston's works can be found in *Alice Walker and Zora Neale Hurston: The Common Bond*

(1980), edited by Lillie P. Howard. This volume includes comparisons of Hurston's first novel *Jonah's Gourd Vine* (1934) and *Their Eyes Were Watching God* with *The Color Purple*. Henry Louis Gates, Jr.'s, examination of Walker's '(re)writing' of Hurston's novel is considered in Chapter 3 of this Guide. The following readings shed new light on Walker's intertextual relationship with Hurston and its impact on her representations of maternity and heterosexuality in *The Color Purple*.

In 'Towards a Map of Mis(sed) Reading: The Presence of Absence in *The Color Purple*' (1992) James C. Hall identifies *The Color Purple* as both a 'novel of black feminist awakening' and 'a model for the reconstruction of a black feminist literary tradition.' Hall argues that established theories of literary influence are inadequate for a discussion of black women's writing. In *The Anxiety of Influence: A Theory of Poetry* (1973), Harold Bloom outlines what Hall terms a 'Freudian ordering of the literary universe, in a succession of anxieties and dissatisfactions in the rupture of communications between fathers and sons': a theory that offers not 'even the briefest contextual outline for a black woman's literary tradition.' Bloom argues that the male poet is so conditioned by the anxiety of influence that he can claim original thought only by 'misreading' his forefathers' work; he must disguise the act of 'misreading' by claiming originality. Hall encourages us to view Walker's work in the context of a tradition of 'mis(sed) reading' rather than 'misreading': Walker, denied access to her literary foremothers, is 'writing/rite-ing within the full emptiness of the page and history.' In *The Color Purple* she has 'textualized' a 'desire' shared by herself and other black women writers such as Paule Marshall: to write books that they themselves 'would have liked to have read.'[76]

Through its 'question[ing]' of 'traditional theological and theocratic structures,' Walker's novel 'subvert[s] the patriarchal and racist dimensions of our *culture of the word*' (Hall's italics). She confronts 'the challenge' facing 'individuals interested in the establishment of a black feminist literary history': 'the necessity of enacting reconstruction and imaginatively identifying new historical categories, constructing theories of influence and theories of individual creation.'[77] For Hall, the discovery of Nettie's letters is the 'radical turning point of the novel': they 'are the powerful connecting metaphor for the reconstruction of a black feminist literary tradition.' As Hall points out, '[t]he text and the tradition have never been missing' but 'have been disguised and sequestered because of the letters' liberating power.'[78]

As Hall notes, Dianne F. Sadoff illuminated the inadequacy of established theories of influence for the black women's literary tradition in her essay 'Black Matrilineage: The Case of Alice Walker and Zora Neale Hurston,' first published in *Signs: Journal of Women and Culture in Society* in 1985. Sadoff scrutinizes the concerns driving Walker's promotion of Hurston's work and draws on Walker's identification of Hurston as literary foremother to sustain her call for a 'revised theory of literary influence': a field so far dominated by two 'models':[79] Bloom's theory of the anxiety of influence and Sandra Gilbert and Susan M. Gubar's feminist revision of Bloom's theory, which suggests that the female writer must 'come to terms with her difference from male writers who (metaphorically) beget the text upon the female muse,' thus 'right[ing] (or rewrit[ing]) the wrongs of literary influence.'[80] Sadoff argues that Gilbert and Gubar's revision serves white, English, nineteenth-century women and that both models of influence pose particular challenges for women of different ethnicities.

Virginia Woolf placed the emphasis firmly on 'maternal literary precedence,' but expressed some 'ambivalence' about her literary foremothers.[81] Sadoff does not detect this ambivalence in Walker's essays on Hurston. Rather, '[r]ace and class oppression intensify the black woman writer's need to discover an untroubled matrilineal heritage.' Therefore, Sadoff argues, 'the contemporary black woman writer covers over more profoundly than does the white writer her ambivalence about matrilineage, her own misreading of precursors, and her link to an oral as well as a written tradition'.

Sadoff observes that Walker elevates Hurston to the place of 'originator' rather than 'predecessor':[82] an elevation which, Sadoff argues, betrays a concern with her own sense of marginality: 'Walker's enthusiastic battle to restore both Hurston and her work to the Afro-American literary canon, however, masks an underlying anxiety about the black woman writer's singularity in white America.'[83] Sadoff finds evidence of this anxiety, 'although disguised, in Walker's fiction.' She suggests that Walker '[n]eed[s] a precursor to validate her own enterprise as a writer' and therefore 'virtually invents Hurston before she defines herself as indebted to Hurston's example.' In Sadoff's view, 'Walker's essays on and editorship of Hurston designate the Renaissance writer precursor and obscure the Second Renaissance writer's fear of her cultural marginality, her own deep need for a foremother.'[84]

Sadoff goes on to argue that these female precursors 'facilitate misreading by their daughters': 'doubly culturally jeopardized by gender and race, the black woman writer will necessarily represent herself even more ambiguously in her texts than do white women writers.' While the literary daughters of black women writers may 'idealize' their foremothers in order to mask their anxiety, they may also use their fictional texts to 'expose this process of misreading, this idealized matriliny that covers over the troubling history of black women's motherhood.'

Sadoff finds evidence of such strategies in the writing of Hurston as the foremother and Walker as the literary daughter. She delivers a detailed reading of the 'scars of disguise or concealment' in Hurston's writing and explores Walker's engagement with them in *The Color Purple*.[85] Walker herself has recognized these 'scars' in her reading of Hurston's much-maligned autobiography *Dust Tracks on a Road* (1942). Sadoff finds that Hurston's ambivalence toward her own roots emerges most clearly in *Dust Tracks* and feeds into her representation of family in her first novel, *Jonah's Gourd Vine*. In *Dust Tracks*, Sadoff detects a false note in Hurston's expressed 'feelings about her mother's death' and an avoidance of her 'oedipal jealousy of her stepmother.' While Hurston 'sought a surrogate family in "godmother" Mason and "Papa" Franz Boas, her patroness and anthropology teacher,' she suppressed the 'jealous and solitary girl' in her autobiography, presenting instead the 'acceptable story of black girlhood and woman-hood.'[86]

Further strategies of displacement surface in Hurston's dramatization of heterosexual love in *Their Eyes Were Watching God*. Sadoff argues that Hurston's handling of 'subversive material' has prompted 'literary critics and daughters' to misinterpret her as a 'celebrator of liberated heterosexual love':[87] however, the reading of the narrative as one of a 'woman [who] liberates her sexuality by taking as her third husband a man dedicated not to domination but to equality' is sustained only by the novel's 'surface.'[88] Hurston repeatedly 'arouses our suspicions about' Janie's third husband's 'dedication to sexual equality.' Tea Cake 'begins physically to abuse his wife and so to resemble Jody Starks [Janie's second husband], the manipulator of male power and privilege.' Sadoff concludes from Hurston's depiction of marriage in *Their Eyes Were Watching God* that she 'profoundly distrusts heterosexual relationships because she thinks them based on male dominance and willing female submissions; yet such inequality appears necessary to the institution of marriage.'

Sadoff reads the ending of *Their Eyes Were Watching God* as a covert expression of Hurston's hostility to patriarchal oppression: when a flood hits the town, a mad dog bites Janie's husband Tea Cake. In his insanity he tries to shoot Janie but she shoots him first in 'self-defense.' Although 'plot and language manipulate events so that the heroine kills off her man metaphorically or unintentionally, Janie is clearly a dangerous woman.'[89]

In her reading of *The Color Purple*, Sadoff illuminates Walker's engagement with the 'subversive' elements of Hurston's texts. The rhetoric deployed by Walker in her essays on Hurston betrays no recognition of her foremother's 'subterranean thematic concern to punish dominating males in *Their Eyes* nor to idealize mothers while vilifying mother substitutes in *Dust Tracks* and *Jonah's Gourd Vine*.' However, Walker's novels tell a different story: 'while celebrating matrilineage in her essays, Walker subverts that celebration on the margins of her own fictional texts.'[90]

In *The Color Purple*, Walker engages the 'subversive' elements of Hurston's depiction of heterosexuality in *Their Eyes* by having Celie learn to battle oppressive gender ideology. Hurston's ambivalence toward mother figures, covertly dramatized in *Jonah's Gourd Vine*, also emerges in *The Color Purple*. Mothers in *The Color Purple* either die or lose their role to 'sisters.' Walker engages Hurston's ambivalence toward mothers and 'distrust of heterosexuality' by 'idealizing sisterhood and economic progress.' In Walker's novel, '[w]omen gain strength by feminizing their men and creating a community of women and men who affirm female values of loving equality.'

Nettie and Celie 'independently imagine a God, neither man nor woman, who loves "everything"; this God metaphorically calls Nettie home from Africa so the reunited sisters may inherit their rightful estate and become merchants.' For Sadoff, this constitutes a 'misread[ing]' of *Their Eyes*. It is through her 'romanticized female economics' that Walker, Sadoff contends, 'misreads Hurston's analysis in which class aspiration and male dominance – [...] cooperate to oppress the black woman.'[91]

In her reading of *The Color Purple* as a romance, Molly Hite responds to Sadoff's claims, recognizing her characterisation of *Their Eyes Were Watching God* as a 'celebration of heterosexual love that is undercut by Hurston's own ambivalence over the compatibility of marriage and the creative "voice" that produces fiction.'[92] However, she sees in Sadoff's reading of Hurston's novel some of the assumptions that informed early reviews of *The Color Purple*: in his review of Walker's novel, Robert Towers 'presumes' that she had aimed to write a realist novel. The same assumption underpins Sadoff's reading of Hurston's *Their Eyes Were Watching God*, which she reads within the context of 'the heterosexual romance plot' of 'so many European and American novels about women in the eighteenth and nineteenth centuries.'[93]

Hite offers a different perspective from Sadoff on the representations of mothering in both novels. Sadoff 'perceives [...] an unacknowledged theme of failed mothering within the two novels'; both texts work to 'suppress or overtly repudiate traditional mothering.'[94] For Hite, however, 'the issue is less one of the failure of mothering than of a redefinition, in which mothering is present as a wholly relational activity.'[95] In Walker's novel, women who have not given birth can take on the role of mother; in *Their Eyes* 'mothering is intimately allied with production of a powerful narrative that enjoins a world view and a series of prescriptions about how to live.' Janie 'replac[es]' her grandmother's 'story about sexual oppression with an alternative story about sexual love that paradoxically enables her to live independently and alone.' In doing this she 'in effect takes on the maternal function, in company of course with her listener, Pheoby.'[96] Both novels suggest that 'mothering is a slippery and even reversible relationship.'

Hite argues that '[i]n casting Hurston as Shug, Walker revises theories of influence as they apply to black women' and that '[i]n recreating her relationship to Hurston as a reciprocal and interactive one, Walker dramatizes Hurston's literary role as the undoer of inessential and divisive hierarchies.' The discourse on maternity not only links *Their Eyes Were Watching God* and *The Color Purple* but also holds a mirror up to the model of 'literary motherhood' particular to the black female literary tradition.[97]

This chapter has focused on issues surrounding the positioning of *The Color Purple* in the feminist and African-American women's canon. Clearly, for some critics Walker's novel remains the quintessential feminist text, engaging women readers across cultural boundaries. Other critics have cast doubt on this categorization, either because they share Walker's reservations about feminism's marginalization of the experiences of black women or because they contest the very notion that the novel presents a positive message for its women readers.

The issues covered in this chapter also pertain to the following one, which turns to one of the most contested dimensions of the novel: its representation of African-American men and its treatment of male and female sexuality.

CHAPTER EIGHT

Gender and Sexuality in *The Color Purple*

The final chapter of this Guide explores criticism that addresses some of the most contentious dimensions of *The Color Purple*: its gender and sexual politics. There is no aspect of *The Color Purple* that has provoked as much controversy and debate as Walker's treatment of black masculinity. Her representation of black men in her most famous novel has fuelled some of the most vitriolic criticism of her work. In his reading of the novel, 'Sisterhood as Salvation: Black Male Characterization in Alice Walker's *The Color Purple*' (1986), Ralph D. Story states that 'no other black woman writer has sought or gained so much retrospective retribution from black males *exclusively* as Walker has in this work' (Story's italics).[1] The first sections of this chapter present interpretations that reflect or respond to prevalent concerns about the representation of black masculinity in *The Color Purple*. The final section presents readings that examine the novel's representation and handling of lesbian sexuality.

THE COLOR PURPLE AND BLACK MASCULINITY

Much of the concern about Walker's treatment of black masculinity in *The Color Purple* stems from the notion that it legitimizes racist and sexist stereotypes embedded in white culture. In her review of Spielberg's film, Pauline Kael accuses Walker of 'rampant female chauvinism' and suggests that she 'gets by with' this 'because it's put in the mouth of her battered fourteen-year-old heroine.'[2]

In his initial review of the novel, Mel Watkins identifies 'the role of male domination in the frustration of black women's struggle for independence' as its major theme, but does not offer direct criticism of Walker's representation of men.[3] After the release of Spielberg's film, Watkins revisited the novel. In an article for the *New York Times*, 'Sexism, Racism and Black Women Writers' (1986), he castigates Walker and other black women writers for 'target[ing]' black men in their fiction and thereby 'put[ting] themselves at odds with what seems to be an unspoken but almost universally accepted covenant among Black writers.'[4] This sense of betrayal identified by Watkins emerges in many critiques of the novel's gender politics.

One of Walker's most vocal and persistent critics is novelist, poet and critic Ishmael Reed (b. 1938). He has criticized Walker for being in league with white feminists who, he claims, have systematically conspired to denigrate black men. Several critics, including Reed, found verification of their reservations about *The Color Purple* in Steven Spielberg's film adaptation. Reed has repeatedly voiced his concern about the representation of black men in the novel and the film in his essays and has used his fiction to give further expression to his animosity toward Walker. In the essay 'Steven Spielberg Plays Howard Beach' (1998), he writes that the film, placed in the hands of white men, legitimizes 'all of the myths that have been directed at black men since the Europeans entered Africa.' He also notes that, while 'defenders' of the novel will 'argue that these creations were merely one woman's story, critics in the media [use] both the book and the movie to indict all black men.'[5]

Ralph D. Story's essay addresses several of the concerns that have been raised by Walker's treatment of masculinity in *The Color Purple*. In a rather sweeping evaluation of the novel, he declares that Walker gives her main male characters no redeeming features: 'from Walker's story-hook on the first page to the last page of her epistolary novel, not one primary black male character of any worth makes an appearance in this work.'[6] He goes on to complain that the character of Shug Avery and the depiction of her relationship with the heroine is so well developed that they render the men redundant, leaving no room in the novel's world for healthy relationships between the genders. Walker's representation of Shug is 'so marvelously crafted – so whole – that the black male characters become flat and increasingly insignificant':[7]

■ It is through Shug Avery that Celie is finally fulfilled, experiences rapid intellectual growth, gets stronger and eventually achieves her womanhood. In contrast, the [...] male characters in the novel are rendered in such a way that they are mere obstacles and/or impediments to the females' self-fulfillment and self-realization. Thus, a kind of retrospective feminism is imposed on Afro-American social history which would have us believe black women, great black women, were denied their self-actualization by virtually all the black men with whom they were intimate.[8] □

Story also objects that the novel's secondary male characters are portrayed in a negative light, citing Albert's brother as an example. He makes no mention of Celie's father or Jack, the husband of Sofia's sister Odessa, noted by Celie for the respect he shows his wife. While Samuel has 'positive traits,' Story argues they can be attributed to his 'reli-giosity.' Samuel merely fulfils another stereotype: 'he is the dedicated, selfless, and *sexless* "Good Negro" black preacher' (Story's italics). More-over, his 'wisdom and intellectual growth are achieved outside of the U.S., while he is in Africa. Walker would have black men go a *long way* figuratively and spiritually to gain their righteousness and treat women accordingly' (Story's italics).[9]

While some critics perceive in Walker's gender politics complicity with white feminism, others perceive in such accusations the inter-nalization of the misogyny of white society. Gloria Steinem, writing before the publication of *The Color Purple*, observes that 'a dispropor-tionate number of [Walker's] negative reviews have been by black men' who 'seem[] to be reviewing their own conviction that black men should have everything white men have had, including dominance over women, or reflecting their fear that black women's truth telling would be misused by a racist society.'[10] In his review of the novel and the film Carl Dix notes:

■ it is quite revealing of the depths of male supremacy in society that many Black men, who being themselves oppressed have every reason to oppose *any* form of oppression this system dishes out, check out *The Color Purple* and end up complaining about the male images it portrays (Dix's italics).[11] □

Moreover, Dix insists that the novel makes it clear that 'there is hope for these men – if they can *stop* being oppressors of women' (Dix's italics).[12] In Chapter 1 of this Guide we saw how Tony Brown expressed concern about the representation of black men in the film of *The Color Purple*. In her riposte to Brown, Anita Jones declares:

■ *The Color Purple* is not a story against black men: it is a story about black women. [...] Walker chose a particular feminist theme and dealt with it, which resulted in many black men protesting and licking their wounded egos. All too often, it is with such dispatch that black men come to the defense of their egos that they fail to realize that they are not the issue at hand.[13] □

Walker agrees. In *The Same River Twice* she reveals that '[o]f all the accu-sations' levelled at her after the publication of *The Color Purple*, 'it was hardest to tolerate the charge that [she] hated black men.'[14] She has expressed bewilderment at the critical preoccupation with masculine cruelty in the novel, wondering why so few critics have chosen to focus on her dramatization of redemption. In her essay 'In the Closet of the Soul,' Walker expresses disappointment that so many black men who responded to her earlier novels *The Third Life of Grange Copeland* and *Meridian* seemed incapable of 'empathiz[ing] with black women's suffering under sexism' and 'refus[ed] even to acknowledge [their] struggles.' She regrets that the book and film of *The Color Purple* 'became the opportunity by which many black men drew attention to themselves.' This reaction, Walker argues, was not indicative of 'an effort to rid themselves of the desire or tendency to oppress women and children'; it was rather 'to claim that inasmuch as a "negative" picture of them was presented to the world, they were, in fact, the ones *being* oppressed' (Walker's italics).[15] Walker argues that the novel clearly demonstrates the causes of Albert's initial behaviour toward Celie and attributes the lack of understanding of his character to the

> ■ deep, painful refusal to accept the fact that we are not only descendants of slaves, but we are also the descendants of slave *owners*. And that just as we have had to struggle to rid ourselves of slavish behavior, we must as ruthlessly eradicate any desire to be mistress or 'master' (Walker's italics).[16] □

While Walker acknowledges that she has not encountered 'all the negative reviews of Mister's character and its implications for blacks in America,' she has noted 'the absence of any analysis of who, in fact, Mister is. Nobody, no critic, that is, has asked this character, "Boy, who your peoples?" '[17]

She has asserted that both the novel and the film make it 'clear that Mister's father is part white,' and that Old Mister's attitudes toward 'women and children' are inherited from his father, a white slave owner. Old Mister is filled with 'self-hatred, particularly of his black "part," the "slave" part' – a hatred that manifests itself in his 'contempt' for Shug Avery. Walker has also expressed regret that few critics have given Albert credit for changing and points out that it is Albert's 'ability to love Shug' that signals the possibility of 'loving himself' in a way that his father cannot.[18] It is certainly the case that critiques of the novel's representations of black men tend to ignore the latter half of the novel. In his evaluation of Albert, Story gives no consideration to this character's transformation into Celie's supportive, nurturing friend.

In his assessment of the controversy surrounding the novel, '*The Color Purple* Debate: Reading Between the Lines' (1986), Richard Wesley (b. 1945) identifies himself as one of the few black male critics who 'found little that was offensive' in the novel and film's dramatizations of black men. He adds, however, that he was 'disappointed' that Walker's novel did not offer positive representations of black men from the rural South because such representations would not fit her political agenda and that 'there were times [he] did think, "Alice Walker doth protest too much." '[19] Wesley also argues that the ideologies fuelling anger toward

Walker are inherently sexist: while he declares his 'respect' for those who 'have enormous problems with' the novel and the film, he condemns the responses of those who 'have taken it upon themselves to be guardians of the black image.' He adds: 'A symposium is held to discuss the film and suddenly these "guardians" start popping up, and before you know it, the symposium has turned into an "image tribunal." '

Wesley traces the anger that has been expressed toward Walker back to the politics of the 1960s: 'These image tribunes are most often black males, usually in their thirties and older. They almost always seem to base their attacks on political concepts developed in the community during the turbulent days of the 1960s.' Wesley observes that '[f]or these men, the Black Power ideology of that time has remained sacrosanct and is in no need of revision. Part of that ideology requires black men and women to pull together.' Welsey notes that in this model of 'unity' between the genders, 'the man *leads*' and the woman 'must always defer to her man and subjugate her will to his.' Wesley argues that this ideology informs some of the criticism of gender politics in *The Color Purple*:

■ Few black men in their right minds will come out and couch their objections to Walker's novel in those terms, but you can hear echoes of those sentiments in much of their criticism of her: Walker is airing dirty linen in public. She is reminding many of us men of our own failures. She is reminding women of *their* failures as well. She is saying that Black is Beautiful, but not necessarily always *right*. A lot of people do not want to hear that (Wesley's italics).[20] □

In 'Who's Afraid of Alice Walker?' Calvin C. Hernton places Walker in the company of other black women writers such as Gloria Naylor and Zora Neale Hurston, but singles out *The Color Purple* for 'the depth and scope' with which it explores 'the subject of sexual oppression within the black race.'[21] Hernton argues that Walker's novel and Spielberg's adaptation 'go beyond the stock excuse for female abuse as isolated incidents committed by misguided men who are frustrated by the economic and political injustices of American racism, which prevent them from realizing their manhood.'[22] His reading argues that Walker's engagement with the generic premises of the slave narrative informs her representations of gender and sexuality:

■ Traditional narratives portray how personal behavior of masters and the personal life of slaves are located in a social context governed by the ideology of slavery and racism, which permeates every situation in the environment. They show, moreover, how the ideology of slavery and racism is supported and perpetuated by an ongoing Power Structure of *roles* and *offices*. Similarly, Alice Walker shows how sexist beliefs, ideas, attitudes and practices inhabit all spheres and aspects of life. In short, the ideology of sexism structures, institutionalizes, constitutes, and empowers itself both *as* patriarchy and *in* patriarchy (Hernton's italics).[23] □

This power structure manifests itself in the relationship between Albert and his son Harpo: 'In *The Color Purple*, a gerontocracy obtains and a pecking order is established, with older males characteristically possessing the most power and the younger ones having less power, but always aspiring to possess more.' Hernton observes that 'in all patriarchies, so-called strong males dominate and serve as role models for so-called weaker ones,' and that '[w]ith women supposedly completely out of the picture, patriarchy fosters an ongoing stepladder (hierarchy) between males possessing varying amounts and qualities of power.' Hernton sees the operation of this hierarchy in the relationship 'between Albert and his father [...] Harpo and Albert; and, of course, between black men and white.'[24]

Hernton notes '[o]wnership [...] is an essential ingredient of power' and is therefore forbidden to the women in *The Color Purple*.[25] He identifies one moment as the 'apex of patriarchal arrogance' in the novel: Albert's demand that Celie shave him. Hernton's reading of this moment sustains Walker's assertion that masculine brutality in the novel is a manifestation of the legacy of slavery. Hernton notes that, '[i]n slavery, the feelings of the slave do not matter to the all-powerful master.' Walker's Albert has such 'power over Celie that he puts a razor in her hand and gives no thought as to whether she will shave his face or cut his throat, because in patriarchy, the man is lord and master.'[26]

Some critics have argued that the controversy surrounding the novel's gender politics misses Walker's point: in *The Color Purple* she presents gender boundaries only to debunk them. Liesbeth Brouwer's reading of the novel features in the volume *Women's Studies and Culture: A Feminist Introduction* (1995), edited by Anneke Smelik and Rosemarie Buikema. The book explores a wide range of cultural issues from a feminist perspective using *The Color Purple* as a case study. In 'The Colour of the Sign: Feminist Semiotics,' Liesbeth Brouwer contends that 'gender is ultimately meaningless' in Walker's novel. Hegemonic gender ideology has no currency in this world: 'Together, Celie and Mr.—discover what life is about: every person – of whatever gender or status – should come to terms with life, should learn to love and to forgive and should learn to appreciate the beauty of nature.'[27]

THE REDEMPTION OF MEN IN *THE COLOR PURPLE*

Another objection commonly raised by critics of Walker's gender politics is her offering of feminization as the only means of redemption for her male characters. Maryemma Graham found this aspect of the novel 'disturbing': 'Walker's relatively narrow view of the source of black women's oppression results in all men coming across either as leeches or predators who stalk the earth, from whom no mother or daughter is safe.' In the world of the novel, 'Walker's black men must and do undergo a conversion experience' before they can be ' "accepted" by their wives and daughters.'[28]

In his essay 'Womanist Fiction and Male Characters' (1985), George Stade reads in the tenets of Walker's womanism the pernicious implication of female superiority: while feminism is 'based on the reasonable premise that since women are as good as men in fact, they should be equal to them under the law,' womanism is 'based on invidious comparisons between the sexes.'[29] Stade takes an opposing view of Walker's womanism to Sherley Anne Williams, who reads in its 'commmit[ment] to the survival and wholeness of entire people' the inclusion of men and women. Stade objects to the womanism that underpins *The Color Purple*, a novel which, rather than positing 'the equality of the sexes,' presents 'the virtues of women and the vices of men.'[30] He contends that the novel offers no explanation for these vices. While Walker has insisted that the novel dramatizes the effects of racist oppression on its male characters, Stade sees no such recognition. He notes that 'men are just as awful' in Africa as they are in rural Georgia, and that the only way that the male characters can be saved is 'by giving them the courage to be women, by releasing the woman already in them': Harpo and Albert are 'redeem[ed]' by taking up traditionally female activities such as cooking and sewing. Masculinity in the novel, then, is 'radical evil, irreducible, the causeless cause of all that's wrong in the world.'[31]

King-Kok Cheung counters Stade's reading, arguing that Albert's sewing signifies his movement beyond gender binaries:

■ Celie and Albert, sewing amicably together, are not engaged in a 'feminine' and therefore (unmanly) activity. Although they envy Shug and Sofia's aggressiveness, they do not consider it unwomanly or specifically masculine – or intrinsically superior. Both sexes are allowed to craft their different lives, fashion their own destinies.[32] □

In response to Stade's suggestion that Walker is 'releasing the woman already in them' Cheung writes: 'Quite the contrary, Albert and Harpo are now free to be their own men.'[33] Lean'tin Bracks agrees. While noting that the novel 'explores the very real tension between female growth and male dominance in the black community' and demonstrates 'male anxiety over women's knowledge' she insists that 'Walker's model of human growth embraces men, too,' and that the male characters have the opportunity to see beyond the narrow terms of hegemonic gender ideology.[34]

Lisa Maria Hogeland, in her book *Feminism and Its Fictions* (1998), reads *The Color Purple* as a form of consciousness-raising novel. This genre, dominated by white writers, came to the fore in the 1970s and became a powerful vehicle for the anti-pornography movement. Hogeland identifies several aspects of Walker's novel that account for this classification, including its 'focus on sexuality as a site of women's oppression and [...] as a privileged site of women's self-determination.' While 'incest is the site of Celie's oppression,' her 'site of freedom' is 'lesbianism.'[35] Walker's novel 'engages the anti-porn movement's emphasis on sexual victimage while still maintaining a vision of sexual self-determination that is not wholly privative.'

Concerning the 'controversy' surrounding the novel's treatment of men, Hogeland notes the absence of engagement with the 'history of similar debates surrounding white feminists' depictions of men.' Marilyn French's representation of men in her novel *The Women's Room* (1977) gave rise to similar questions as *The Color Purple*. Responses to *The Color Purple*, however, 'replayed these debates in ways that were specifically racialized [...] most critics of Walker's depiction of her men characters argued that critiques of black men's behavior formed a political rhetoric that divided the (presumably unified African-American community).' Therefore, 'a black feminist could not be responding to gendered divisions and problems within the black community'; she 'could only be creating those divisions and problems – and, moreover, could only be doing so in ways that were inevitably complicitous with white racism.'[36]

While Hogeland observes that these kinds of critiques of Walker's gender politics 'managed to overlook both the novel's and the film's insistence on the recuperation of black men characters,' she also recognizes their concerns that redemption for these characters involves, in the words of bell hooks, becoming 'desexualized.'[37] After all, Albert's transformation differs significantly from those of the women characters who achieve autonomy. Hogeland argues that this kind of transformation points to 'the novel's engagement with notions of male sexuality constructed by the anti-porn movement in the late 1970s.' While the presentation of 'desexualization as recuperation' may 'appeal to feminist readers,' it can also 'be taken far too comfortably by white readers and viewers as confirmation' of stereotypes of black male sexuality.[38]

RE-READING GENDER POLITICS IN *THE COLOR PURPLE*

This subchapter focuses on Candice M. Jenkins's twenty-first-century reading, 'Queering Black Patriarchy: The Salvific Wish and Masculine

Possibility in Alice Walker's *The Color Purple*' (2002). Jenkins presents a persuasive reading of the novel and the criticism arising from its gender politics. She sheds new light on the hostility directed toward Walker's treatment of black masculinity, attributing it to the novel's 'transformative revision' of domestic paradigms that validate masculine authority. This revision 'accomplishes no less than the emptying of "black masculinity" as a term, insofar as that term has been dependent upon an assumption of black men's authoritative role in the family sphere.'

According to Jenkins, then, 'Walker's refashioning of the black family "queers" the very notion of the potent black patriarch.' It is this 'queering' of 'patriarchal fantasies' that has provoked such resistance toward the novel's representation of men. In the family portrayed in the final scenes of the novel, there is a 'possibility' more subversive and 'bewildering' than the missing father: a father who is *present*, but nonetheless no longer dominant or even interested in domination' (Jenkins's italics). Jenkins therefore expresses little surprise that critics have condemned the novel as 'an affront to black community wholeness': *The Color Purple* 'both posits a community without a (male) leader' and 'a masculinity without even the desire for what has traditionally been understood as masculinity's hallmark: power.'[39]

Jenkins's reading sustains Walker's argument that the novel recognizes the impact of white codes on the behaviour of Albert and his father. She notes that it is in the 'domestic sphere,' the place where the 'traditional patriarch wields unchecked power,' that the novel's aggressive men assert their supremacy over women, children and more vulnerable men.[40] Celie reads Harpo's fear of his father in his 'sad and thoughtful' eyes, and immediately reports: 'his face begin to look like a woman face.'[41] This comparison to a woman's face 'points out the ways that all those subordinate to a family patriarch are feminized, because they are all subject to the same hierarchical relationship.' The novel also delivers moments of 'joy' during which characters 'counter[] gendered expectation,' such as Harpo's 'pride' in Sofia's defiance of his efforts to assert his control in the home.[42]

Jenkins compares Walker's representations of father–son relations to those of African-American writer Richard Wright. Both writers present father figures who seek a sense of masculinity 'through the recreation of a violent (white) patriarchy in their own homes.' Jenkins refers to David Marriott's reading of Wright's work, which states that Wright's 'autobiographical universe posits a straightforwardly mimetic relationship between black and white masculinity.'[43] She notes that Walker's novel 'masks the actual interactions that black men have with white.' However, she agrees with Walker that the *influence* of these interactions is made clear in the novel: 'the violent relationship that exists between black and white men in *The Color Purple*'s southern rural setting is never far from the surface in the text.' It manifests itself in the use of the name

'Mister,' a 'subtle reminder of white controls over black life.' Marriott notes that in the South white men were called 'Mister' and black men were expected to answer to 'boy.' The black men in *The Color Purple* 'are scripted into a pattern of titular naming that even without direct reference to whiteness is informed by racial hierarchies.'[44]

Jenkins uses the term 'salvific' to signify the 'aspiration, most often but not only middle-class and female, to save or rescue the black community from white racist accusations of sexual and domestic pathology, through the embrace of conventional bourgeois propriety.'[45] Jenkins suggest that this wish has been adopted as 'a response to [...] the stigma of deviance that has been attached to African-American sexual identity' and identifies one dimension of this wish as the 'insistence that women in particular suppress their own desires (sexual or otherwise) and surrender passively to patriarchal control.'[46] Jenkins notes a difference between the motivations of men and women who have adopted the 'salvific wish.' While both genders 'hope to control the appearance and actuality of the domestic sphere for the sake of propriety,' it is the women who 'link this control to the idea of recuperation or rescue for the community,' while the men in the novel 'seem to desire control for its own sake – to make a statement about their own capacity to rule in the private sphere.'[47] Albert and Harpo forbid Celie and Sofia from attending the juke joint, but see no problem with attending themselves. Masculine 'articulations' of the salvific wish 'eschew the project of communal recuperation in favor of self-aggrandizement.' However, it is through the 'alignment' of 'masculine articulations' and 'feminine gestures' that Walker indicates the 'pitfalls of the ostensibly feminine salvific wish, that drive to protect the community through self-control and sacrifice':

■ When voiced through the bodies of male characters, these ostensibly noble behaviors become something disturbingly close to tyranny, creating not community safety but a hyper-powerful masculinity that lays down the law of propriety solely in pursuit of the authority to enforce that law. And it is this patriarchal authority, so spotlighted in early portions of Walker's narrative, which subsequently becomes the object of not only critique but creative and queer revision in the latter part of the text.[48] □

Jenkins goes on to deliver the kind of reading of Albert's transformation that Walker hoped for: his development from 'traditional patriarch' to 'philosophical friend and companion' to his former wife and mistress.[49] Jenkins's reading is particularly useful in illuminating the dangerous influence of the salvific wish on other readings of the novel. Jenkins notes that Mel Watkins cites W. E. B. Du Bois's essay

'The Talented Tenth' (1903) to support his criticism of Walker's capitulation to 'politics and propaganda.'[50] Du Bois predicts that '[t]he Negro race, like all races, is going to be saved by its exceptional men'; only by 'developing' the talented tenth can 'the Mass' be 'elevated.'[51] Jenkins notes the 'irony' of Watkins's reaction to Walker and other black feminists by noting that the 'middle-class blacks such as the ones Du Bois describes in his famous essay were the originators of the salvific wish' and that '[a] blind determination to "present positive images of blacks" is certainly as political and as propagandistic as any other artistic choice.'[52]

Jenkins also engages with one of Trudier Harris's objections to the novel, raised in her essay 'On *The Color Purple*: Stereotypes and Silence.' Harris argues that *The Color Purple* perpetuates stereotypes of black sexuality by suggesting that '[b]lack males and females form units without the benefit of marriage.'[53] Jenkins sees in this reading 'underlying investments in domestic and sexual orthodoxy highly similar to those supported by the salvific wish.'[54] She wonders why Harris includes in her essay an 'alarmingly misogynist' response from a student to the representation of Jack, the devoted husband of Odessa. The student characterizes Jack as 'middle-aged and henpecked,' and observes that his 'only goal in life seems to be to please his wife (because she can beat him up?).'[55] Puzzled as to why Harris presents this view without questioning it in any detail, Jenkins does so herself. She perceives in this student's response the entrenchment of hegemonic notions of masculinity. Jenkins argues that Jack 'stays loyal' to Odessa 'not from a stoic sense of duty [...] but out of simple devotion' to his wife 'and a single-minded willingness to please her.' The student reads this 'devotion' as 'cowardice or weakness, indicating the extent to which traditional "manliness" or masculinity has in this view been divorced from emotional vulnerability.'[56]

Jenkins concludes her analysis by assessing Walker's utopian vision at the end of the novel. The innovation of her reading lies in her illumination of the plurality of options available to Walker's men in the novel's final scenes: '[t]he radical symmetry between genders that this vision implies is certainly inspiring, though if Walker's critics are to be believed, it is also deeply frightening, verging on impossible to contemplate.' In *The Color Purple* 'Walker demands an entirely new way of defining and understanding gender and male–female interaction, one which begins with men who are men *in spite of* patriarchal power, not because of it' (Walker's italics). Jenkins observes that the novel 'remains a bit enigmatic about the role that men can or should play in the "new" black family' but that Walker 'leaves several possibilities open, as evidenced, for example, by the difference between Jack's quiet confidence, Harpo's grudging acquiescence, and Mr.—'s philosophical companionship.'[57]

SEXUALITY IN *THE COLOR PURPLE*: QUEER READINGS

The readings in this final subchapter address issues arising from the sexual politics of *The Color Purple*, focusing particularly on Walker's representation of lesbian sexuality. In an essay published in 1984, Barbara Christian noted a growing trend in black women's literature: more writers were placing 'black lesbian experience' at the heart of their texts.[58] She compared representations of this experience in four texts published in 1982: *Sassafras, Cypress and Indigo* by Ntozake Shange (b. 1948), *The Women of Brewster Place* by Gloria Naylor (b. 1950), *Zami* by Audre Lorde (1934–92) and Alice Walker's *The Color Purple*. Placing an emphasis on the variety of experiences explored in these texts, Christian focuses primarily on the differences between their treatment of black lesbian relationships.

Unlike her contemporaries, Walker presents lesbian characters who 'do not have contact with other lesbians' but whose 'relationship enhances their entire community, male or female.'[59] Christian argues that Walker's 'characterization of the sexual love between Celie and Shug is conditioned by two themes that overlap and are both expressed in metaphors of familial relationships.' These themes are 'the natural bonding between women' and 'the sexism that men direct against women unless women generate relationships among themselves and create their own community.'[60] For Christian, then, Walker's exploration of lesbian love is part of her 'feminis[t]' project: '[b]y being sexually independent of men, lesbians, by their very existence, call into question society's definition of woman at its deepest level.' Walker, along with Shange, Naylor and Lorde, declares 'the importance of this truth': she 'challenge[s] society's definition by presenting women's communities that are sexually and economically independent of men, though not separate from them' and shows us 'how sisterhood among women benefits the entire black community.'[61]

As we have seen, many reviewers and critics have taken exception to this challenge. Upon the novel's publication, some critics launched a direct attack on Walker's depiction of lesbian sexuality, while others chose simply to ignore it. Many of the critics who attacked Walker's depiction of men viewed Celie and Shug's relationship as further evidence of Walker's sexism and refused to consider it on its own terms. Much of the hostility toward Walker's treatment of black masculinity stems from her privileging and celebration of female relationships. As Walker herself notes: 'it is not the depiction of the brutal behavior of a black male character that is the problem for the critics.' She believes that:

■ it is the behavior of the women characters that is objectionable; because whatever else is happening in the novel and the film (and as is true more and more in real life), women have their own agenda, and it does not include knuckling under to abusive men.[62] □

In his article for the *Carolina Peacemaker*, 'Blacks Need to Love One Another,' Tony Brown delivers a defiant dismissal of the novel's lesbian narrative, declaring: 'lesbian affairs will never replace the passion and beauty of a free black man and a free black woman.' He adds that Walker's fictional world, where 'emotional and sexual salvation for women is found in other women' does not represent 'the real world, as some black women, out of frustration, seem to want to believe.'[63] In 'Scars of Indifference' Anita Jones balks at Brown's audacity in 'conclud[ing] without an ounce of evidence, not to mention openmindedness, that a woman can never love a woman with the "passion and beauty of a free black man and a free black woman,"' and she accuses Brown of 'attempt[ing] to slander the basic principle upon which feminism and humanitarianism are built [...] personal freedom – the right to choose.'[64] She encourages him to '[t]ake a good look around' and open his eyes to the many configurations which love continues to take in the 'real world.'[65]

In her review of the novel, 'Sexual Oppression Unmasked' (1984), Barbara Smith writes that Walker's positive depiction of women's sexuality, and '[l]esbian sexuality in particular' in *The Color Purple* 'places the novel in a class by itself within Black mainstream literature.'[66] Maryemma Graham, however, airs some reservations about Celie and Shug's sexual relationship, feeling compelled to ask if it should be viewed as 'an extension or the logical consequence of the theme of female bonding?' and to speculate: 'Wouldn't it have been sufficient to treat this theme without the lesbian overlays, which tend to muddy the water?'[67] For Elliott Butler-Evans, however, 'lesbianism' in *The Color Purple* 'becomes an essential aspect of "womanist" theory and praxis.'[68] He warns against reductive readings of Celie and Shug's relationship:

■ Any limited focus on the homoerotic aspect of the involvement between the two women runs the risk of downplaying the complexity of Shug's representational status and its broad symbolic implications. In her chosen career as a blues singer, her refusal to settle for a life of domesticity, and her insistence on enjoying all the sexual freedoms generally limited to men, Shug becomes the embodiment of feminist existential freedom.[69] □

Linda Abbandonato delivers a detailed reading of the novel's sexual politics in her essay ' "A View from Elsewhere": Subversive Sexuality and the Rewriting of the Heroine's Story in *The Color Purple'* (1991). Abbandonato illustrates how Walker uses 'the story of that most marginalized of heroines the black lesbian' to 'challenge[] patriarchal constructions of female subjectivity and sexuality.'[70] Walker poses this challenge through her elaboration of two narratives rendered 'taboo' by psychoanalytical theory: incest and homosexuality. Abbandonato proposes that 'the great twentieth-century cultural narratives of sexuality and socialization, Freud's oedipal theory and Lévi-Strauss's theory of kinship systems and the exchange of women are played out in the drama of Celie's life.' Both 'center on the incest taboo' and 'have been used to reinforce [] our system of "compulsory heterosexuality,"' a term coined by Gayle Rubin in the essay 'The Traffic in Women (1975).'[71]

In *The Elementary Structures of Kinship* (1969), Claude Lévi-Strauss (1908–2009) sees what Abbandonato terms 'the exchange of women' as 'the system of binding men together.' This system functions as 'a means of reinforcing male power through the circulation of women.'[72] Abbandonato observes: '[c]ompulsory heterosexuality thus becomes the basis on which society operates and the exchange of women the condition whereby the patriarchy flourishes.' In this society '[w]omen are prevented from becoming subjects in an economy where they are exchanged as objects, and homosexual desire becomes taboo, like incest, because it disrupts the terms of the social contract.'[73] Abbandato points out that '[p]sychoanalytic accounts of enculturation also rest on the prohibition of incest, as enforced through the castration complex; in the oedipal plot the phallus becomes the coveted marker of sexual difference and desire.' However, this plot 'predicates female sexuality on a masculine paradigm, thus effacing the very subject of femininity it claims to investigate.' Thus '[w]omen are effectively excluded from being desiring subjects or from having their sexuality theorized except through a distorting masculine lens. Consequently the lesbian remains outside the framework of representation.'

In *The Color Purple*, Walker considers the implications of violating this particular taboo: she asks what would occur if women rejected 'compulsory heterosexuality' by 'refus[ing] in effect to become objects of exchange between men?' The novel 'reduces the system of compulsory heterosexuality to its basic level, making it abstract.'[74] Abbandonato finds the revelation that 'Pa' is not Celie's real father a 'puzzling moment in the text' and argues that 'suggestions of incest recur too insistently' for us to disregard the novel's engagement with this taboo: suggestions such as the marriage between Nettie and Samuel, who refer to each other as 'Sister' and 'Brother'; the union between 'sisters' Celie and Shug; and Shug and the boy with whom she has a sexual relationship and whom she compares to a son or grandson. Abbandonato offers a new reading of the function of these recurring inferences, suggesting that the 'focus on incest is an honest and courageous attempt to situate sexuality where it belongs: in the heart of the family.' She adds: 'If the family is the site of sexual repression and taboo, it is also the place where sexuality is engendered, in the fullest sense.' Nettie's revelation that 'Pa' is not their real father presents Celie with a further 'contradiction': 'The Pa who is not Pa is yet – irrevocably – Pa. Her history has been shattered, and she cannot connect with the revised version sent by sister Nettie.' It is only her love for Shug that 'enables her to bury her sad double narrative of paternal origins' and liberate herself from 'patriarchal law.'[75]

Abbandonato notes the significance of maternal imagery in the depiction of Shug and Celie's initial sexual contact. Shug's lips recall one of the babies that Celie lost, causing her to 'act like a little lost baby too':[76] Abbandonato reads this reponse as 'a symbolic return to the pre-oedipal stage, an idealized state of innocent eroticism.'[77] Thus Celie violates 'the taboo against homosexuality' and 'symbolically exits the masternarrative of female sexuality and abandons the position ascribed to her within the symbolic order.'[78]

According to Abbandonato, Celie's sexual awakening debunks some of the myths about homosexuality and female sexuality initiated by Freud:

▇ If homosexuality involves narcissism, as Freud believes, we see its positive and empowering effect on Celie. In loving Shug, Celie becomes a desiring subject, and in being loved by Shug, she is made visible to herself as an object of desire. In contrast to the repression that Celie has experienced in accepting her social position as a 'mature' woman in a phallocentric culture, her 'infantile regression' is an act of radical rebellion. □

Furthermore, Celie's moment of sexual awakening undermines Freud's hierarchical evaluation of female orgasms which presents clitoral orgasm as inferior to its vaginal counterpart – a misconception that, Abbandonato notes, prevails in our 'compulsorily heterosexual society' today because 'it is a necessary myth.' Abbandonato suggests that the reason for this is that it secures the position of the man as pleasure-giver: '[t]he erotic zone of the clitoris *has* to be censored in social constructions of sexuality, since its mapping on the female body would allow women to "just say no" to the coveted male organ' (Abbandonato's italics). Celie's awakening to clitoral stimulation marks the beginning of 'a whole range of other discoveries that relegate man to the margins of a world he has always dominated.'[79]

For some critics the novel fails to capitalize on the subversive possibilities of Celie's sexual relationship with Shug. For example, bell hooks finds that although sexuality is 'graphically and explicitly discussed' in *The Color Purple*, it is 'ignored' as a 'key narrative pattern.' According to hooks, Walker is at least partly responsible for this. hooks refers us to Rosalind Coward's essay 'The True Story of How I Became My Own

Person,' from her collection *Female Desire* (1985). Coward 'warns against the reproduction of an ideology where female identity is constructed solely in relationship to sexuality.'[80] hooks argues that *The Color Purple* sustains this ideology. 'Homophobia does not exist' in Walker's novel because Celie's sexuality is seen as having no bearing on the world beyond personal relationships. We need look no further than Albert's ready acceptance of Celie's lesbianism for evidence of this. While the novel recognizes that 'sexual desire can disrupt and subvert oppressive social structures because it does not necessarily conform to social prescription [...] this realization is undermined by the refusal to acknowledge it as threatening – dangerous.'[81]

For hooks, the novel's ostensibly 'womanist' ending only confirms the patriarchal premise that male–female relationships are integral to women's happiness. She claims that Walker makes a number of U-turns in the novel and sells out to hegemonic sexual politics. The revelation that Alphonso is not Nettie and Celie's father further deflates the novel's revolutionary potential. hooks finds that '[t]he tragedy and trauma of incest is trivialized': '[p]resented in retrospect as though it was all an absurd drama, the horror of Celie's early sexual experience and the pleasure of her sexual awakening assume the quality of spectacle.'

Walker mutes the potent sexuality of Shug, whom she writes back into heterosexual romance. Indeed '[s]exual desire' ultimately serves only as 'a means to an end but not an end in itself.' Indeed, it is love for Shug that brings Celie and Albert together, enabling Walker to 'uphold[] the promise of an intact heterosexual bond.'[82] The subversive potential of the novel's sexual politics is further compromised by Shug's desire for a young man, which hooks interprets as 'a disempowering force, one that exposes [Shug's] vulnerability and weakness.' Finally, the novel's 'ideal world of true love and commitment' is devoid of 'erotic tension.'[83]

For hooks, the 'transformation' of Albert confirms that Walker is '[u]nable to reconcile sexuality and power': 'Since sexuality and power are so closely linked to politics of domination, Mr. Albert must be completely desexualized as part of the transformative process.'[84] However, Albert's desexualization does not impact on the wider context of the novel. After all, the 'phallocentric social order which exists outside the domain of private relationships remains intact.' Unlike many other critics, hooks sees Celie's folkspants as a form of affirmation of the hegemony of 'the phallus' rather than 'a radical revisioning of gender.' The 'vision' embodied by Celie's product is one of 'inclusion that enables women to access power via symbolic phallic representation.'[85]

In her essay 'Heterosexual Screening: Lesbian Studies' (1995), Renée C. Hoogland considers whether or not *The Color Purple* qualifies as a 'lesbian novel.' Hoogland opens her essay by tracing the development of lesbian studies across the 1980s and 1990s: 'lesbian scholarship has evolved into a distinct mode of practice and theory in which lesbianism functions as an interpretative framework that encompasses more than questions of (lesbian) sexuality *per se*.'[86] Hoogland notes that from its title onward – the shades violet and lavender have had 'association[s] with lesbianism' since '600 BC' – Walker's novel calls attention to Celie's sexuality. Noting that feminist readings of the novel have argued that its 'plot is [...] triggered off by Celie's discovery of her sexuality regardless of its orientation,' Hoogland argues that 'the protagonist's moment of "awakening" is emphatically rendered as a non-normatively "female,″ i.e., a *lesbian* moment of self-discovery' (Hoogland's italics).

Hoogland points out that 'the force of Celie's same-sex desire for Shug is frequently, explicitly remarked upon' and that '[t]he overtly physical nature of their relationship highlights the experience of lesbian sex at the core of the heroine's burgeoning subjectivity.' To sustain this reading she draws attention to 'the interconnected meanings of the novel's title':

■ The colour purple literally refers to a field of flowers that comes to symbolise the protagonist's rejection of a God as a white male authority and his transformation into a non-Christian, depersonalised spiritual force. On a metaphorical level, however, the colour purple, with its long-standing tradition of associations, signifies sex between Celie and Shug, and lesbianism generally. It is thus suggested that it is only as a lesbian, in her emotional, intellectual *and* sexual independence from men, that Celie can become an autonomous subject, the author of her own perceptions, and, ultimately, of her own discourse (Hoogland's italics).[87] □

Hoogland considers how a 'queer' reading might address issues such as the novel's 'relative neglect of questions of "race."' She states that, '[s]een from a lesbian perspective, this is not necessarily a political flaw, but rather an indication that "race" does not stand, or at least not exclusively, at the novel's centre.' Moreover, 'Celie's "inexplicable" mildness toward Mr.— at the end of the story' can be accounted for if we remind ourselves that 'it is Shug, another woman, who constitutes the object of Celie's desires, and who, in the course of time, becomes the "significant other" to the heroine's self.'

Nevertheless, Hoogland 'hesitate[s] to call *The Color Purple* a lesbian text,' owing to the 'manner in which the lesbian subject is dealt with, especially in the latter half of the novel.'[88] She concurs with hooks's evaluation of the lesbian narrative, noting that Celie's 'sexuality does not obtain in a social context' and is 'reduc[ed] to a matter of private preference.' This suggests to Hoogland 'that Celie's sexuality has no significance beyond the walls of the bedroom in which she and Shug perform their perverse practices.' This explains why when Shug re-enters 'the normal order of (unhappy) heterosexuality, Celie does not merely stop having sex, she stops being a sexual subject altogether. Lacking any collective sense of lesbian identity, Shug's betrayal means the end of the lesbian performance as a whole.'[89]

For Hoogland, Celie's folkspants are the 'only remaining marker of her subversive sexuality.' The novel 'conclusively neutralis[es] her "abnormal" desire by eventually implying its integration into love of kin, in particular for her sister Nettie.' In the end, '[t]he potentially disruptive force of the heroine's sexual self is thus contained within the traditional family structure – however strangely assorted a group the members of Celie's "family" in the novel's closing section may be.' The novel's credentials as a 'lesbian' text are undermined by Shug's 'heterosexualization' and the absence of any 'narrative critique' thereof. While some critics have dismissed the novel 'for being more of a romantic fairy tale than a critical piece of realist fiction,' Hoogland, '[a]s a lesbian reader,' is 'perhaps primarily disappointed with the novel for precisely *not* being that: a romantic fairy tale' (Hoogland's italics). She explains:

> ■ Fairy tales have of old offered both readers and writers opportunities to range freely the never-never land of their wildest fantasies. *The Color Purple* precludes such possibilities. In my imaginary, ideal lesbian fairy tale, the fantastic, alluring, and unregenerately lesbian lovers would not be stripped of their life-giving force so as to be brought back into a very real, heterosexual order: they would, quite extraordinarily, end up living happily ever after. But that, of course, is another story.[90] □

We have seen in this chapter how Walker's handling of sexuality and gender politics has provoked fierce debate. Looking at the breadth of responses on issues such as Walker's representation of black masculinity and her portrayal of lesbian sexuality, it again becomes clear that critics and readers disagree fundamentally over the issue of what the novel is about. There can be little doubt that this question will continue to perplex and inspire readers in the twenty-first century.

Conclusion

Championed for its radicalism and rejected for its conservatism, *The Color Purple* divided critics from the start. Early criticism opened up lines of enquiry into the novel's generic identity, its formal and narrative strategies and its handling of race, gender and class. The late eighties and early nineties brought queer readings and psychoanalytical explorations of Celie's development. Critics began to focus on issues pertaining to the reception of the novel, its canonization and its pedagogical potential.

Critics continue to home in on particular dimensions of *The Color Purple* in order to locate its meaning and to explain its broad and enduring appeal. While they seem to have reached a consensus on the lyricism of Celie's voice, they agree on little else. In particular, the generic identity of the novel remains up for debate: should the novel be read as a feminist utopia, a neo-slave narrative, a folk tale, a piece of social realism or liberal humanism?

Walker herself has identified one avenue of enquiry that, she feels, merits further pursuit. In the preface to the twenty-fifth anniversary edition of the novel, she returns to what she views as its central theme. She considers the consequences of oppression for the spiritual health of African-American people who were living 'among demons' but would remember their own 'Gods [] and Goddesses' and realize that 'the one God/Goddess that had proved sturdy enough to be in Africa with them, on the slave ship, and also with them in Mississippi and New York, was Nature.'[1] Twenty-five years on, she wonders why the novel is 'so infrequently discussed as a book about God.'[2] In this Guide we have explored several readings that take the novel's theological dimension into account but there is perhaps scope for more detailed investigation into this subject.

Critics and readers alike continue to recognize and assert the novel's cross-cultural appeal, despite the controversy surrounding its reception and canonization. The comments that fill the opening pages of the twenty-fifth anniversary edition testify to this appeal. Critics, writers and readers from a range of professional fields and cultures share their personal responses to Celie's story. Praise from poet Benjamin Zephaniah (b. 1958) and journalist and author Yasmi Alibhai-Brown (b. 1949) sits alongside comments from comedian Lenny Henry (b. 1958) and singer-songwriter Corinne Bailey Rae (b. 1979). Zephaniah echoes Steinem's early review, emphasizing the novel's universalism:

■ This book works on all levels, the political, the historical, the personal, the emotional, the spiritual . . . If you are not touched by this book you can't be touched. Not a word is wasted, every breath is accounted for. We all know that this is one of the greatest books of all time. It's a no-brainer. □

Alibhai-Brown speaks for many readers when she reveals that the novel deeply affected her personal view of familial relationships:

■ I was afraid and insecure when I read this book. Families are not always sanctuaries. This book and a couple of others came at the right time to make me see it was possible to be strong and not choked up with self-pity.[3] □

The Color Purple was the novel that secured Alice Walker the status of international best-selling author. To date, she has written three novels and numerous collections of short stories, essays and poems since its publication, yet it remains her most studied and debated text. In the popular media her name is usually prefaced by the phrase '*Color Purple* author.' Biographical accounts often pay more attention to Walker's involvement in Spielberg's cinematic adaptation of *The Color Purple* than to her other works of fiction.

Clearly, the plaudits and accusations that followed the novel's publication have had a lasting impact on Walker's personal and professional lives. *The Same River Twice* charts the personal cost of writing the novel: Walker became 'the object of literary stalking' as a 'black male writer attacked [her] obsessively in lecture, interview and book for over a decade';[4] her local newspaper in San Francisco joined the attack, forcing her to escape to Mexico; she had to 'work[] hard to reassure' her male relatives and friends that she was not the 'monster they saw being projected.'[5]

While Walker has expressed reservations about the fame that accompanied the success of the novel, she has also recognized the artistic licence that its popularity afforded her as a writer. In an interview for the *Guardian* in 2007, Walker reflects on the novel's impact on her life. She observes that the success of the novel enabled her to write the narratives that she 'wants to write.' Her abiding sense of the autonomy of her characters remains as strong as ever. Twenty-five years after the novel's publication, she continues to position herself as a 'medium': she views the success of the novel, which has 'taken care of' her, as evidence of her ancestors' care and recognition of the way that she represented their lives in the novel.[6]

It is the responses of readers around the world to Celie's story that have most pleased Walker over the years. *The Same River Twice* includes letters from readers who express their gratitude to Walker for creating characters they can identify with. Walker recognizes the positive impact of Celie's story on victims of oppression:

■ I have been glad to see how the issues of incest and domestic violence were opened up by the book, and more widely by the film. In letters and on visits women and men all over the world have expressed to me the power and transformation they've received from both.[7] □

In an interview with Holly Near, Walker expresses her sense of satisfaction that one of her primary aims in writing the novel was achieved: to breach the gap between 'the literary' and 'the popular.' In writing this novel, she aimed 'to reach [...] the supermarket crowd.' The most rewarding aspect of the novel's commercial success was the discovery that she had achieved this goal:

■ The high point of this whole business with *Purple* was not when they told me about the awards but when they told me the people on the IRT [the New York City subway line] were reading it. That was the first time I felt I had connected with my audience.[8] □

As the novel's success became impossible to ignore, critics began to turn to the issue of reception. Reading interpretations of *The Color Purple*, one is often struck by the close engagement with the views of readers from a range of cultures. In particular, the research of Jacqueline Bobo, Trudier Harris, Alison Light and Cora Kaplan offers valuable insight into the ways in which readers with different cultural backgrounds have responded to the novel. There is certainly scope for further research into the responses of 'the supermarket crowd.' Given the endurance of the novel's popularity, a study of twenty-first-century readers' responses might be particularly fruitful. What is it that makes *The Color Purple* one of the five most re-read books in America? The novel's international reputation also merits further exploration. In *The Same River Twice*, Walker notes that responses to *The Color Purple* have generally been more favourable in 'Africa, China, Cuba and other parts of the world' than in America. Readers and critics outside America have, she feels, shown a greater 'understanding of the historical, racial and sexual politics of the work' than their American and African-American counterparts.[9]

In the twenty-first century, Celie's story of survival remains as lucrative as ever. In 2007, the *Guardian* reported that the novel can now be read in twenty-five languages. Audiences of the musical have spent more than $5 million on '*The Color Purple* souvenirs.'[10] In addition to the twenty-fifth anniversary edition, the novel was reissued in 2006 as a 'musical tie-in.' The official website for the musical adaptation provides links to 'The Color Purple Store' and 'The Color Purple Community.'

Online, people continue to claim identification with Celie and to assert the universality of her story. The musical's official website features a link entitled 'The Color Purple Touches Everyone.' Here, a short video clip presents a review of the musical by critic Greg Moody, who defines *The Color Purple* as 'the story of characters both transformed and redeemed in their lives and in their relationships and in their very culture.' He adds: 'It's not just the characters who change: it's everyone inside the theatre.'[11]

Debate over tensions between the novel's public and private discourses have underpinned many critical readings. However, these tensions have been all but erased in the public's embrace of Celie's story. The 'Sights and Sounds' link on the musical's website leads to short video clips of viewers from a variety of cultures expressing their identification with Celie's narrative. The clips present responses to some of the most resonant lines from the novel. Characters repeat Sofia's 'Hell no,' and Celie's 'I'm here' before explaining their interpretations of these lines: clearly, these audience members feel that this story is about them. The musical closed on Broadway in 2008; critics identified one factor in this decision as the departure of *American Idol* winner Fantasia, who played Celie to great acclaim. Since her departure, there have been rumours that a cinematic version of the musical, starring Fantasia, is set to appear.[12]

Attitudes toward Spielberg's adaptation of *The Color Purple* seem to be changing. In 2003, the film was reissued in America as a Special Edition DVD set. It includes documentaries on the adaptation process and an interview with Walker herself. Reviews of the DVD suggest that twenty-first-century reactions to the film are generally more positive than initial responses. Today, the adaptation is evaluated on its own merits and the controversy surrounding the choice of Spielberg as director is present only as a footnote, if at all.

While the public continues to embrace Celie's story, critical attention to the novel has diminished considerably in the first decade of the twenty-first century. Perhaps we can attribute this waning of critical interest to the widespread awareness that a wealth of readings immediately followed the novel's publication. The controversy that prompted many critics to voice their concerns or spring to the novel's defence has certainly diminished over the past decade. Often, new readings of a literary text will emerge from a wider consideration of the writer's oeuvre as a whole; the publication of later texts will prompt critics to return to the writer's earlier work. However, *The Color Purple* remains Walker's most popular and critically acclaimed work; her later novels have attracted fewer critical readings.

It is therefore fascinating to reflect on the possible directions that critical reception of *The Color Purple* might take in the future. Will there be a shift in emphasis? Will Celie's financial prosperity continue to confound critics? Will the novel's sexual politics prove as unpalatable to new critics and readers as it did for some in the 1980s? In the age of 'post-feminism' will the label of 'feminist Ur-text' have as much currency? Will Walker's novel have the same sort of legacy as Hurston's *Their Eyes Were Watching God*?

It will be interesting to observe what kinds of comparative readings will emerge if new writers choose to claim a position in the Hurston and Walker line of descent. In her examination of Walker's womanism, Lovalerie King states that Walker's 'acknowledged debt to certain foremothers [...] is as apparent as is her own influence on a growing body of women's literature and criticism worldwide.'[13] In 'Coming of Age in the African-American Novel,' Claudine Raynaud offers an example of this, noting the intertextual references to *The Color Purple* in the novel *Push* (1996) by African-American poet Sapphire (b. 1950). Raynaud observes that Sapphire's first novel 'explicitly cites *The Color Purple*' and points out similarities in plot structure and characterization: '*Push* [...] tells of the gradual awakening to literacy and to a better self-integration of Precious Jones, a young girl of sixteen raped by her father, a crack addict.' She adds: 'Precious and her class comrades are Celie and Nettie's sisters.'[14]

Reviewing the welter of readings of this novel, it is striking how critics approaching it through a variety of frameworks fixate on the same moments or lines of dialogue to sustain their interpretations. Naturally, the novel is remembered primarily for its main characters and central relationships, but some of the narratives of minor characters leave much scope for new readers and critics. It is safe to assume that *The Color Purple* and its various reworkings will continue to generate vigorous debate for many years to come.

Notes

INTRODUCTION: *THE COLOR PURPLE*

1 Peter S. Prescott, 'A Long Road to Liberation,' *Newsweek*, 99.25 (21 June 1982), p. 67.

2 Elliott Butler-Evans, *Race, Gender and Desire: Narrative Strategies in the Fiction of Toni Cade Bambara, Toni Morrison and Alice Walker* (Philadelphia, PA: Temple University Press, 1991), p. 163.

3 bell hooks, 'Writing the Subject: Reading *The Color Purple*,' in Harold Bloom (ed.), *Alice Walker*, Modern Critical Views (New York: Chelsea House, 1988), p. 215.

4 Liesbeth Brouwer, 'The Color of the Sign: Feminist Semiotics,' in Anneke Smelik and Rosemary Buikema (eds), *Women's Studies and Culture: A Feminist Introduction* (New York: St. Martin's Press, 1995), p. 158.

5 David Bradley, 'Novelist Alice Walker: Telling the Black Woman's Story,' *New York Times* (8 Jan. 1984), p. 31.

6 Henry Louis Gates, Jr., 'Color Me Zora,' in Henry Louis Gates, Jr., and Kwame Anthony Appiah (eds), *Alice Walker: Critical Perspectives Past and Present*, Amistad Library Series (New York: Amistad Press, 1993), p. 244.

7 Alice Walker, 'In Search of Our Mothers' Gardens,' in *In Search of Our Mothers' Gardens: Womanist Prose* (London: Women's Press, 1984), p. 240.

8 Alice Walker, 'From an Interview,' in *In Search*, p. 244. All quotations from this source originally come from the interview with John O'Brien, first published in his book *Interviews with Black Writers* (New York: Liveright, 1973).

9 Gloria Steinem, 'Alice Walker: Do You Know This Woman? She Knows You,' *Ms.* (June 1982), in *Outrageous Acts and Everyday Rebellions*, 2nd edn (New York: Owl-Holt, 1995), p. 295.

10 Krista Brewer, 'Writing to Survive: An Interview with Alice Walker,' *Southern Exposure*, 9.2 (1981), p. 14.

11 Brewer (1981), p. 15.

12 Alice Walker, 'From an Interview,' p. 250.

13 Claudia Tate, 'Alice Walker,' *Black Women Writers at Work* (New York: Continuum, 1983), p. 176.

14 Tate (1983), p. 176.

15 Tate (1983), p. 177.

16 Alice Walker, *In Search* (1984), xi.

17 Steinem (1995), p. 288.

18 Maria Lauret, '*The Color Purple*,' *Alice Walker* (London: Macmillan, 2000), p. 91.

19 Molly Hite, 'Romance, Marginality, and Matrilineage: *The Color Purple* and *Their Eyes Were Watching God*' in Henry Louis Gates, Jr. (ed.), *Reading Black, Reading Feminist* (New York: Meridian, 1990), p. 431.

20 Alice Walker, *The Same River Twice: Honoring the Difficult: A Meditation on Life, Spirit, Art and the Making of the Film, The Color Purple, Ten Years Later* (London: Women's Press, 1996), p. 38.

21 Alice Walker, 'Tsunamis and Hurricanes: Twenty-Five Years After Publishing *The Color Purple*,' Foreword to *The Color Purple*, 25th Anniversary Edition (London: Weidenfeld and Nicolson, 2007), p. 15.

CHAPTER ONE

1   Alice Walker, 'Writing *The Color Purple*,' *In Search of our Mothers' Gardens* (London: Women's Press, 1984), p. 355.
2   Walker, 'Writing,' *In Search* (1984), p. 356.
3   Walker, *The Color Purple* (London: Women's Press, 1983) np., p. 245.
4   *Alice Walker: Omnibus.* Dir. Samira Osman. Prod. Leslie Megahey and Alan Yentob. BBC (1986).
5   Sharon Wilson, 'A Conversation with Alice Walker,' in Henry Louis Gates, Jr., and Kwame Anthony Appiah (eds), *Alice Walker: Critical Perspectives Past and Present*, Amistad Library Series (New York: Amistad Press, 1993), p. 325.
6   Walker, *The Same River Twice: Honoring the Difficult* (New York: Scribner, 1996), p. 163.
7   Gloria Steinem, 'Alice Walker: Do You Know This Woman? She Knows You,' *Ms.* (June 1982) in *Outrageous Acts and Everyday Rebellions*, 2nd edn (New York: Owl-Holt, 1995), p. 292.
8   Steinem (1982), p. 291.
9   Robert Towers, 'Good Men Are Hard to Find,' review of *The Terrible Twos* by Ishmael Reed and *The Color Purple* by Alice Walker, *New York Review of Books* 29.13 (12 Aug. 1982), p. 36.
10 Steinem (1982), p. 289.
11 Steinem (1982), pp. 289–90.
12 Dinitia Smith, 'Celie, You A Tree!' review of *The Color Purple*, *The Nation* 235.6 (4 Sept. 1982), 181–3 in Gates and Appiah (1993), p. 21.
13 Towers (1982), p. 36.
14 Steinem (1982), p. 291.
15 Towers (1982), p. 36.
16 Smith (1982), p. 20.
17 Smith (1982), p. 21.
18 Walker, *Purple* (1983), p. 76.
19 Smith (1982), p. 20.
20 Mel Watkins, 'Some Letters Went to God,' review of *The Color Purple*, *The New York Times Book Review* 87 (25 July 1982), p. 7, in Gates and Appiah (1993), pp. 17, 18.
21 Watkins (1982), p. 18.
22 Maryemma Graham, 'Alice Walker; Skillful but Disturbing Novel,' *Freedomways* (1983), Vol. 23, p. 278.
23 Graham (1983), p. 280.
24 Graham (1983), pp. 279–80.
25 Graham (1983), p. 280.
26 Gerald L. Early, '*The Color Purple* as Everybody's Protest Art,' *Antioch Review* 44 (Summer 1986), p. 265.
27 Early (1986), p. 273.
28 Early (1986), pp. 273–4.
29 Wilson (1993), p. 321.
30 Trudier Harris, 'On *The Color Purple*, Stereotypes and Silence,' *Black American Literature Forum* 18.4 (1984), p. 157.
31 Harris (1984), p. 155.
32 Harris (1984), p. 156.
33 Steinem (1982), p. 290.
34 Harris (1984), p. 156.
35 Tamar Katz, ' "Show Me How to Do Like You": Didacticism and Epistolary Form in *The Color Purple*,' in Bloom, *Alice Walker* (1988), p. 187.
36 bell hooks, 'Writing the Subject: Reading *The Color Purple*' in Bloom, *Alice Walker* (1988), p. 215.

37   Steven C. Weisenburger, 'Errant Narrative and *The Color Purple*,' *Journal of Narrative Technique* (1989), pp. 258, 257.

38   Weisenburger (1989), p. 258.

39   Weisenburger (1989), p. 259.

40   Walker, 'Writing,' pp. 359–60, quoted in Weisenburger (1989), p. 261.

41   Weisenburger (1989), p. 264.

42   Weisenburger (1989), pp. 264–5.

43   Weisenburger (1989), p. 265.

44   Bettye J. Parker-Smith, 'Alice Walker's Women: In Search of Peace of Mind' in Mari Evans (ed.), *Black Women Writers: A Critical Evaluation* (Garden City, NY: Anchor Books, 1984), 478–93.

45   Weisenburger (1989), pp. 265–6.

46   Weisenburger (1989), p. 266.

47   Weisenburger (1989), pp. 266–7.

48   In his conference paper on Walker's novel, Alan Sinfield notes that 'in Shug's theology, conventional Christianity is replaced [...] by a privatised essentialist humanism' whereby 'all possibilities of meaning are, simultaneously, collapsed back into the individual consciousness and projected out onto a supposedly universal human condition,' and he finds in the novel's central philosophy 'a revival of sixties counter-cultural religiosity (pp. 117, 118).' He finds this 'disappointing,' noting that this religiosity 'proves all too easily re-absorbable into American mainstream capitalist ideology' (p. 117). He notes, however, that 'we should not be surprised or upset to find a mixture of progressive and regressive attitudes' in *The Color Purple*, adding that the novel 'should not be expected to spring, miraculously, out of the conditions of its historical production, into political truth' but 'is constructed, like other texts, from elements available in the prevailing culture' (p. 119). See Alan Sinfield, 'Problems of the Progressive Text: *The Color Purple* by Alice Walker,' in Helen Taylor (ed.), *Literature Teaching Politics 1985 – Conference Papers* (Bristol: Bristol Polytechnic, 1985).

49   Weisenburger (1989), p. 269.

50   Weisenburger (1989), p. 270.

51   Joan Digby, 'From Walker to Spielberg: Transformations of *The Color Purple*,' in Peter Reynolds (ed.), *Novel Images: Literature in Performance* (London: Routledge, 1993), p. 162.

52   Walker, *Same* (1996), p. 285.

53   Walker, *Same* (1996), p. 286.

54   Walker, *Omnibus* (1986).

55   Susan Dworkin, 'The Strange and Wonderful Story of the Making of *The Color Purple*,' *Ms.* (Dec. 1985), in Walker, *Same River*, p. 175.

56   Walker included her script for the film in her book *The Same River Twice: Honoring the Difficult* (1996). See pp. 60–149.

57   Pauline Kael, '*The Color Purple*,' *New Yorker* magazine 61 (30 Dec. 1985), p. 69.

58   Jacqueline Bobo, 'Sifting Through the Controversy,' *Callaloo* 39 (Spring 1989), p. 332.

59   Digby, p. 173.

60   Vincent Canby, 'From a Palette of Clichés Comes '*The Color Purple*,' *The New York Times* (5 Jan. 1986), p. 17.

61   Tony Brown, 'Tony Brown's Comments: Blacks Need to Love One Another,' *Carolina Peacemaker* (4 Jan. 1986), in Walker, *Same River* (1996), p. 224.

62   Anita Jones, 'Scars of Indifference,' *Carolina Peacemaker* (4 Jan. 1986), *Same River*, p. 226.

63   In the essay '*The Color Purple*: Black Women as Cultural Readers' (1988), Jacqueline Bobo notes that Brown's quotation was read out on *The Phil Donahue Show*, 25 April 1986, when Brown appeared on a panel to discuss the film. When a woman in the audience suggested that Brown had not seen the film, he neither confirmed nor denied this.

64   John Simon, 'Black and White in Purple,' *National Review* 38.2 (14 Feb. 1986,) p. 56.
65   David Ansen, 'We Shall Overcome: Spielberg Takes on Rural, Matriarchal, Black Life,' review of *The Color Purple, Newsweek* (30 Dec. 1986), p. 59.
66   Early (1986), p. 267.
67   David Denby, 'Purple People-Eater,' review of *The Color Purple, New York* magazine 19.2 (13 Jan. 1986), p. 56.
68   Bobo (1989), p. 333.
69   Bobo (1989), p. 333.
70   Bobo (1988), p. 101.
71   Bobo (1988), p. 102.
72   Bobo (1989), p. 336.
73   Wayne C. McMullen and Martha Solomon, 'The Politics of Adaptation: Steven Spielberg's Appropriation of *The Color Purple,' Text and Performance Quarterly* 14 (1994), p. 158.
74   McMullen (1994), p. 160.
75   McMullen (1994), p. 163.
76   McMullen (1994), p. 164.
77   McMullen (1994), p. 165.
78   McMullen (1994), p. 167.
79   McMullen (1994), p. 168.
80   McMullen (1994), p. 169.
81   McMullen (1994), p. 170.
82   Walker, *Same* (1996), p. 160.
83   Walker, *Same* (1996), p. 153.
84   Walker, *Same* (1996), p. 161.
85   Walker, *Omnibus* (1986).
86   Marcus Crowder, 'How *The Color Purple* Found Its Stage Voice' (1 Nov. 2008), http://www.sacbee.com/crowder/story.
87   'About the Production.' http://www.thecolorpurple.com.
88   Wendell Brook, 'Shades of "Purple" from Book to Stage' (9 July 2008), http://www.accessatlanta.com/arts/content/arts/stories.
89   Jeremy McCarter, 'Metropolitan Oprah,' *New York* magazine (4 Dec. 2005), http://nymag.com.nymetro/arts/theater/reviews/15230.
90   Ben Brantley, 'One Woman's Awakening, in Double Time,' (2 Dec. 2005), http://theater2.nytimes.com/2005/12/02/theater/reviews.

CHAPTER TWO

1   Alastair Fowler, 'Transformations of Genre,' in David Duff (ed.), *Modern Genre Theory* (Harlow: Longman, 2000), p. 232.
2   bell hooks, *'Writing the Subject: Reading The Color Purple,'* in Harold Bloom (ed.), *Alice Walker* (New York: Chelsea House, 1988), p. 215.
3   Maria Lauret, *'The Color Purple,' Alice Walker* (London: Macmillan, 2000), p. 96.
4   Maroula Joannou, *'To The Color Purple,' Contemporary Women's Writing: from The Golden Notebook to The Color Purple* (Manchester: Manchester University Press, 2000), p. 175.
5   Keith Byerman, ' "Dear Everything": Alice Walker's *The Color Purple* as Womanist Utopia,' in Arno Heller et al. (eds), *Utopian Thought in American Literature* (Tübingen: Gunter Narr Verlag, 1988), p. 171.
6   Byerman, 'Womanist Utopia' (1988), p. 172.
7   Jean Pfaelzer, 'The Impact of Political Theory on Narrative Structures,' in Kenneth Roemer (ed.) *America as Utopia* (New York: Franklin, 1981), p. 119, quoted in Byerman (1988), p. 172.

8 Byerman, 'Womanist Utopia' (1988), p. 172.

9 Byerman, 'Womanist Utopia' (1988), p. 176.

10 Byerman, 'Womanist Utopia' (1988), p. 177.

11 Byerman, 'Womanist Utopia' (1988), pp. 177–8.

12 Byerman, 'Womanist Utopia' (1988), p. 181.

13 Byerman, 'Womanist Utopia' (1988), p. 182.

14 Margaret Walsh, 'The Enchanted World of *The Color Purple*,' *Southern Quarterly* 25 (Winter 1987), p. 182.

15 Walsh (1987), p. 95.

16 Walsh (1987), p. 99.

17 Walsh (1987), p. 96.

18 Walsh (1987), pp. 96–7.

19 Walsh (1987), p. 97.

20 Walsh (1987), p. 100.

21 Thomas F. Marvin, ' "Preachin' the Blues": Bessie Smith's Secular Religion and Alice Walker's *The Color Purple*,' *African American Review* 28.3 (1994), p. 411.

22 Keith Byerman, 'Walker's Blues,' in Harold Bloom (ed.), *Alice Walker*, Modern Critical Views (New York: Chelsea House, 1988), pp. 59–60.

23 Byerman, 'Blues' (1988), p. 59.

24 Byerman, 'Blues' (1988), p. 60.

25 Byerman, 'Blues' (1988), p. 62.

26 Byerman, 'Blues' (1988), p. 63.

27 Byerman, 'Blues' (1988), p. 64.

28 Byerman, 'Blues' (1988), p. 65.

29 Byerman, 'Blues' (1988), p. 66.

30 Marvin (1994), p. 411.

31 Marvin (1994), p. 412.

32 Marvin (1994), p. 411.

33 Diane Gabrielsen Scholl, 'With Ears to Hear and Eyes to See: Alice Walker's Parable *The Color Purple*,' in Harold Bloom (ed.), *Alice Walker's The Color Purple*, Modern Critical Interpretations (Philadelphia: Chelsea House, 2000), pp. 107, 107–8. [Essay originally issued 1991.]

34 Scholl (2000), p. 111.

35 Scholl (2000), p. 114.

36 Molly Hite, 'Romance, Marginality, and Matrilineage: *The Color Purple* and *Their Eyes Were Watching God*,' in Henry Louis Gates, Jr. (ed.), *Reading Black, Reading Feminist* (New York: Meridian, 1990), p. 434.

37 Hite (1990), pp. 434–5, 435.

38 Frank Kermode, 'Introduction,' in William Shakespeare, *The Tempest* (London: Methuen, 1954), p. lix.

39 Hite (1990), p. 435.

40 Hite (1990), p. 436.

41 Kermode (1954), p. liv, quoted in Hite (1990), p. 436.

42 Hite (1990), p. 436.

43 Northrop Frye, *A Natural Perspective: The Development of Shakespearean Comedy and Romance* (New York: Columbia University Press, 1965), pp. 123–4, quoted in Hite (1990), p. 437.

44 Hite (1990), p. 437.

45 Frye (1965), pp. 142–3.

46 Hite (1990), p. 438.

47 Hite (1990), p. 439.

48 Calvin C. Hernton, 'Who's Afraid of Alice Walker?' in *The Sexual Mountain and Black Women Writers: Sex, Literature and Real Life* (New York: Anchor-Doubleday, 1987), p. 1.

49   Henry Louis Gates, Jr., 'Color Me Zora,' in Henry Louis Gates, Jr., and Kwame Anthony Appiah (eds), *Alice Walker: Critical Perspectives Past and Present*, Amistad Library Series (New York: Amistad Press, 1993), p. 243.

50   Hernton (1987), p. 5.

51   Hernton (1987), pp. 5–6.

52   Hernton (1987), p. 9.

53   Hernton (1987), p. 6.

54   Hernton (1987), p. 29.

55   Hernton (1987), pp. 29, 29–30.

56   Hernton (1987), p. 30.

57   bell hooks, 'Writing the Subject: Reading *The Color Purple*,' in Bloom, *Alice Walker* (1988), p. 223.

58   hooks (1988), p. 224.

59   hooks (1988), p. 225.

60   Scholl (2000), p. 109.

61   Tamar Katz, ' "Show Me How to Do Like You": Didacticism and Epistolary Form in *The Color Purple*,' in Bloom, *Alice Walker* (1988), p. 187.

62   Marjorie Pryse, 'Introduction: Zora Neale Hurston, Alice Walker, and the "Ancient Power" of Black Women,' in Marjorie Pryse and Hortense Spillers (eds), *Conjuring: Black Women, Fiction, and Literary Tradition* (Bloomington, IN: Indiana University Press, 1985), p. 1.

63   Linda S. Kauffman, 'Constructing Otherness: Struggles of Representation in *The Color Purple*,' *Special Delivery: Epistolary Modes in Modern Fiction*, Women in Culture and Society (Chicago: University of Chicago Press, 1992), p. 195.

64   Kauffman (1992), p. 203.

65   Kauffman (1992), pp. 186–7.

66   Kauffman (1992), p. 187.

67   Kauffman (1992), pp. 187, 188. Héloïse d'Argenteuil (1101–64) was a French scholar who had a tragic love affair with Pierre Abélard (1079–1142), a teacher and philosopher. Once separated, the two intellectuals communicated their passion and sense of loss through letters. Kauffman refers her to the heroines of the *Heroides* by Ovid (43 BCE–17/18 CE). This text is composed of letters written by mythological female figures such as Penelope, Medea and Dido to their lost loves.

68   Kauffman (1992), p. 195.

69   Kauffman (1992), p. 188.

70   Kauffman (1992), p. 191.

71   Kauffman (1992), p. 192.

72   Kauffman (1992), p. 207.

73   Mae G. Henderson, '*The Color Purple*: Revisions and Definitions,' in Bloom, *Alice Walker* (1988), p. 67.

74   Henderson (1988), p. 70.

75   Henderson (1988), p. 68.

76   Henderson (1988), p. 80.

77   Lauret (2000), p. 98.

78   Lauret (2000), p. 99.

79   Lauret (2000), p. 100.

80   Claudine Raynaud, 'Coming of Age in the African American Novel,' in Maryemma Graham (ed.), *The Cambridge Companion to the African American Novel* (Cambridge: Cambridge University Press, 1988), p. 115.

81   Carolyn Williams, ' "Trying to Do Without God": The Revision of Epistolary Address in *The Color Purple*,' in Elizabeth C. Goldsmith (ed.), *Writing the Female Voice: Essays on Epistolary Literature* (Boston: Northeastern University Press, 1988), p. 275.

82   Williams points to pp. 13–46 of Janet Gurkin Altman, *Epistolarity: Approaches to a Form* (Columbus: Ohio State UP, 1982).

83   Williams (1988), p. 276.
84   Williams (1988), pp. 276–7.
85   Williams (1988), p. 277.
86   Williams (1988), p. 281.
87   Williams (1988), p. 283.
88   Williams (1988), pp. 283–4, 284.
89   Williams (1988), p. 284.

CHAPTER THREE

 1   Gloria Steinem, 'Alice Walker: Do You Know This Woman? She Knows You,' *Ms.* (June 1982), in *Outrageous Acts and Everyday Rebellions*, 2nd edn (New York: Owl-Holt, 1995), p. 293.
 2   Trudier Harris, 'On *The Color Purple*, Stereotypes and Silence,' *Black American Literature Forum* 18.4 (1984), p. 156.
 3   Dinitia Smith, 'Celie, You A Tree!' review of *The Color Purple*, *The Nation* 235.6 (4 Sept. 1982), in Henry Louis Gates, Jr., and Kwame Anthony Appiah (eds), *Alice Walker: Critical Perspectives Past and Present*, Amistad Library Series (New York: Amsitad Press, 1993), p. 21.
 4   Towers (1982), 'Good Men Are Hard to Find,' review of *The Terrible Twos* by Ishmael Reed and *The Color Purple* by Alice Walker, *New York Review of Books* 29.13 (12 Aug. 1982), p. 36.
 5   Steinem reports that Walker uses the term 'black folk English' in reference to her characters' speech, rather than 'dialect,' a term that 'has been used in a condescending, often racist way,' p. 289.
 6   Walker, 'Coming in from the Cold: Welcoming the Old, Funny-Talking Ancient Ones into the Warm Room of Present Consciousness, or Natty Dread Rides Again!' *Living by the Word: Selected Essays and Writings* (New York: Harvest – Harcourt, Brace, Jovanovich, 1988), p. 55.
 7   Walker, 'Coming' (1988), p. 63.
 8   Walker, 'Coming' (1988), p. 64.
 9   Henry Louis Gates, Jr., 'The Trope of the Talking Book' in *The Signifying Monkey: A Theory of Afro-American Literary Criticism* (New York: Oxford University Press, 1988), p. 131.
10   Henry Louis Gates, Jr., 'Color Me Zora,' in Henry Louis Gates, Jr., and Kwame Anthony Appiah (eds), *Alice Walker: Critical Perspectives Past and Present*, Amistad Library Series (New York: Amistad Press, 1993), p. 239.
11   King-Kok Cheung, ' "Don't Tell": Imposed Silences in *The Color Purple* and *The Woman Warrior*,' *PMLA* 103 (1988), p. 162.
12   Maroula Joannou, 'To *The Color Purple*,' *Contemporary Women's Writing: from The Golden Notebook to The Color Purple* (Manchester: Manchester University Press, 2000), p. 176.
13   Elizabeth Fifer, 'The Dialect and Letters of *The Color Purple*' in Catherine Rainwater and William J. Scheick (eds), *Contemporary American Women Writers: Narrative Strategies* (Lexington: University Press of Kentucky, 1985), p. 160.
14   Fifer (1985), p. 157.
15   Fifer (1985), p. 160.
16   bell hooks, 'Writing the Subject: Reading *The Color Purple*,' in Harold Bloom (ed.), *Alice Walker*, Modern Critical Views (New York: Chelsea House, 1988), p. 225.
17   Maria Lauret, *Alice Walker*, Modern Novelists (London: Macmillan, 2000), p. 101, pp. 101–2.
18   Lauret (2000), p. 102.
19   Lauret (2000), pp. 101, 103.

20 Linda S. Kauffman 'Constructing Otherness: Struggles of Representation in *The Color Purple*,' *Special Delivery: Epistolary Modes in Modern Fiction*, Women in Culture and Society (Chicago: University of Chicago Press, 1992), p. 192.

21 Kauffman (1992), p. 193.

22 Kauffman (1992), p. 194.

23 Valerie Babb, '*The Color Purple*: Writing to Undo What Writing Has Done,' *Phylon* 47 (1986), p. 110.

24 Babb (1986), p. 111.

25 Babb (1986), p. 112.

26 Fifer (1985), p. 163.

27 Fifer (1985), p. 164.

28 Fifer (1985), p. 155.

29 Fifer (1985), p. 158.

30 Fifer (1985), p. 159.

31 Linda Abbandonato, ' "A View from Elsewhere": Subversive Sexuality and the Rewriting of the Heroine's Story in *The Color Purple*,' *PMLA* 106.5 (Oct. 1991), p. 1108.

32 Teresa de Lauretis, *Technologies of Gender: Essays on Theory, Film, and Fiction* (Bloomington: Indiana University Press, 1984), p. 125, quoted in Abbandonato, p. 1108.

33 Abbandonato (1984), p. 1108.

34 Babb (1986), p. 112.

35 Walker, 'From an Interview,' *In Search of Our Mothers' Gardens: Womanist Prose* (London: Women's Press, 1984), p. 251.

36 Walker, 'In Search of Our Mothers' Gardens,' *In Search* (1984), p. 234, quoted in Babb (1986), p. 108.

37 Babb (1986), p. 108.

38 Walker, *The Color Purple* (London: Women's Press, 1983), p. 9, quoted in Babb (1986), p. 109.

39 Babb (1986), p. 109.

40 Babb (1986), p. 112.

41 Babb (1986), pp. 112–13.

42 Babb (1986), p. 113.

43 Babb (1986), p. 114.

44 Babb (1986), p. 115.

45 Babb (1986), pp. 115–16.

46 Dorrit Cohn, *Transparent Minds: Narrative Modes for Presenting Consciousness in Fiction* (Princeton, NJ: Princeton University Press, 1983), p. 100.

47 Shlomith Rimmon-Kenan, *Narrative Fiction: Contemporary Poetics*, New Accents, (London: Routledge, 1983) p. 113.

48 Gates, 'Color Me Zora,' p. 239.

49 Gates, 'Zora Neale Hurston and the Speakerly Text,' *The Signifying Monkey* (1988), p. 181.

50 Gates, 'Zora Neale' (1988), pp. 191, 192.

51 Gates, 'Color Me Zora' (1988), p. 240.

52 Gates, 'Color Me Zora' (1988), p. 244.

53 Gates, 'Color Me Zora' (1988), p. 246.

54 Gates, 'Color Me Zora' (1988), p. 247.

55 Gates, 'Color Me Zora' (1988), p. 249.

56 Gates, 'Color Me Zora' (1988), p. 250.

57 Walker, *Purple*, p. 216, quoted in Gates, 'Color Me Zora (1988), p. 251.

58 Gates, 'Color Me Zora' (1988), p. 251.

59 Gates, 'Color Me Zora' (1988), pp. 251–2, 252.

CHAPTER FOUR

1 Maryemma Graham, 'Alice Walker; Skillful but Disturbing Novel,' review of *The Color Purple*, by Alice Walker, *Freedomways* (1983), p. 278.

2 Thadious M. Davis, 'Alice Walker's Celebration of Self in Southern Generations,' in Peggy Whitman Prenshaw (ed.), *Women Writers of the Contemporary South* (Jackson: University Press of Mississippi, 1984), p. 50.

3 Thadious M. Davis (1984), p. 51.

4 Alice Walker, *The Color Purple*, (London: Women's Press, 1983), p. 176, Davis (1984), p. 51.

5 Langston Hughes, 'Final Fear,' in *Simple Speaks His Mind* (New York: Simon and Schuster, 1950), pp. 112–13. Quoted in Davis (1984), p. 51.

6 Davis (1984), p. 52.

7 Wall points us to Mary Daly, *Gyn/Ecology: A Metaethics of Radical Reminism* (Boston: Beacon Press, 1978), pp. 110, 155–78.

8 Wall, 'Lettered Bodies and Corporeal Texts,' in Henry Louis Gates, Jr., and Kwame Anthony Appiah (eds), *Alice Walker: Critical Perspectives Past and Present*, Amistad Library Series (New York: Amistad Press, 1993), p. 261.

9 Wall (1993), p. 262.

10 Wall (1993), p. 263.

11 Wall (1993), p. 264.

12 Wall (1993), p. 265.

13 Wall (1993), p. 268.

14 Wall (1993), p. 270.

15 W. E. B. Du Bois, 'The Souls of Black Folk,' in Nathan Huggins (ed.), *Writings* (New York: Library of American College, 1986), p. 364.

16 Wall (1993), p. 270.

17 Walker, *Purple* (1983), pp. 224, 224–5.

18 Walker, *Purple* (1983), pp. 225, 225, 225–6.

19 Wall (1993), p. 270.

20 Judy Elsley, ' "Nothing can be sole or whole that has not been rent": Fragmentation in the Quilt and *The Color Purple*,' in Ikenna Dieke (ed.), *Critical Essays on Alice Walker* (Westport, CT: Greenwood, 1999), p. 164.

21 Elsley (1999), p. 163.

22 Walker, *Purple*, p. 3.

23 Elsley (1993), pp. 164, 164–5.

24 Elsley (1993), p. 165.

25 Elsley (1993), p. 167.

26 Luce Irigaray, *This Sex Which Is Not One* (Ithaca: Cornell University Press, 1985), p. 30.

27 Elsley (1993), pp. 167–8.

28 See Jacques Lacan, *Ecrits: A Selection*, translated by Alan Sheridan (New York; Norton, 1977).

29 Walker, *Purple* (1983), pp. 69, 69, 70.

30 Daniel W. Ross, 'Celie in the Looking Glass: The Desire for Selfhood in *The Color Purple*,' *Modern Fiction Studies* 34.1 (Spring 1988), p. 70.

31 Ross (1988), p. 73.

32 Ross (1988), p. 74.

33 Sharon Hymer, 'Narcissistic Friendships,' *Psychoanalytic Review* 71 (1984), p. 433, quoted in Ross, p. 75.

34 Ross (1988), p. 75.

35 Ross (1988), pp. 75–6.

36 Ross (1988), p. 76.

37 Ross (1988), p. 77.

38 Ross (1988), p. 78.

39   Sigmund Freud, 'Material and Sources of Dreams,' *The Interpretation of Dreams*, translated by James Strachey (Middlesex: Penguin, 1980), p. 364.

40   Ross (1988), p. 78.

41   Ross (1988), pp. 78–9. Freud uses these terms in his essay 'On Narcissism: An Introduction,' *The Standard Edition of the Complete Works of Sigmund Freud*, Vol. 22, translated and edited by James Strachey (London: Hogarth Press, 1957), pp. 87–9.

42   Ross (1988), p. 79.

43   Ross (1988), p. 81. For Freud's thoughts on sewing see 'Femininity,' *Standard Edition*, Vol. 22 (1957), p. 132.

44   Ross (1988), p. 81.

45   Ross (1988), p. 82.

46   Charles L. Proudfit, 'Celie's Search for Identity: A Psychoanalytic Developmental Reading of Alice Walker's *The Color Purple*,' *Contemporary Literature* 32.1 (Spring 1991), p. 13.

47   Proudfit (1991), p. 14.

48   Proudfit (1991), pp. 15–16. For further discussion of Winnicott's terms see D. W. Winnicott, *The Maturational Processes and the Facilitating Environment* (New York: International Universities, 1965), pp. 44, 50, 86, 118, 145, and *Playing and Reality* (London: Tavistock, 1971), p. 10.

49   Proudfit (1991), p. 16. See Winnicott (1971), p. 112.

50   Proudfit (1991), p. 19.

51   Leonard Shengold, *Soul Murder: The Effects of Childhood Abuse and Deprivation* (New Haven: Yale University Press, 1989), pp. 24–5.

52   Proudfit (1991), p. 20.

53   Proudfit (1991), p. 21.

54   Proudfit (1991), p. 22.

55   Proudfit (1991), p. 23.

56   Proudfit (1991), p. 26.

57   Proudfit (1991), p. 29.

58   Proudfit (1991), p. 31.

59   Proudfit (1991), p. 32.

60   Proudfit (1991), p. 34.

61   Proudfit (1991), p. 33.

62   Proudfit (1991), p. 34.

CHAPTER FIVE

1   Alice Walker, 'The Black Writer and the Southern Experience,' *In Search of Our Mothers' Gardens: Womanist Prose* (London: Women's Press, 1984), p. 19.

2   bell hooks, 'Writing the Subject, Reading *The Color Purple*,' in Harold Bloom (ed.), *Alice Walker*, Modern Critical Views (New York: Chelsea House, 1988), p. 224.

3   Elliott Butler-Evans, *Race, Gender and Desire: Narrative Strategies in the Fiction of Toni Cade Bambara, Toni Morrison and Alice Walker* (Philadelphia, PA: Temple University Press, 1991), p. 166.

4   Keith Byerman, ' "Dear Everything": Alice Walker's *The Color Purple* as Womanist Utopia,' in Arno Heller et al. (eds.) *Utopian Thought in American Literature* (Tübingen: Gunter Narr Verlag, 1988), p. 178.

5   Cora Kaplan, 'Keeping the Color in *The Color Purple*,' *Sea Changes: Culture and Feminism*, Questions for Feminism (London: Verso-New Left, 1986), p. 178.

6   Kaplan (1986), p. 182.

7   Kaplan (1986), pp. 187, 178.

8   Kaplan (1986), p. 183.

9   Kaplan (1986), p. 185.

10 Alison Light, 'Fear of the Happy Ending: *The Color Purple*, Reading and Racism,' in Linda Anderson (ed.), *Plotting Change: Contemporary Women's Fiction* (London: Arnold, 1990), pp. 89, 88, 89.

11 Light (1990), p. 89.

12 Light (1990), p. 90.

13 Light (1990), p. 91.

14 Light (1990), p. 90.

15 Lauren Berlant, 'Race, Gender, and Nation in *The Color Purple*,' in Henry Louis Gates, Jr., and Kwame Anthony Appiah (eds.), *Alice Walker: Critical Perspectives, Past and Present*, Amistad Library Series (New York: Amistad Press, 1993), p. 213.

16 Walker, *The Color Purple* (London: Women's Press, 1983), p. 11.

17 Berlant (1993), p. 213.

18 Berlant (1993), p. 221.

19 Berlant (1993), p. 217.

20 Berlant (1993), p. 218.

21 Walker, *Purple* (1983), p. 148.

22 Berlant (1993), pp. 221, 219.

23 Walker, *Purple* (1983), p. 76, quoted in Berlant, p. 219.

24 Berlant (1993), p. 219.

25 Berlant (1993), pp. 219–20.

26 Berlant (1993), p. 220.

27 Berlant (1993), p. 229.

28 Walker, *Purple* (1983), p. 243, quoted in Berlant, p. 230.

29 Berlant (1993), p. 231.

30 Berlant (1993), pp. 231–2.

31 Berlant (1993), p. 232.

32 Berlant (1993), p. 233.

33 Carl Dix, 'Thoughts on The Color Purple,' *The Revolutionary Worker* (1985), in Alice Walker, *The Same River Twice: A Meditation on Life, Spirit, Art and the Making of the Film, The Color Purple, Ten Years Later* (New York: Scribner, 1996), p. 196.

34 Melissa Walker, *Down from the Mountaintop: Black Women's Novels in the Wake of the Civil Rights Movement 1966–1989* (New Haven: Yale University Press, 1991), p. 64.

35 Walker, *Purple* (1983), p. 90, quoted in Melissa Walker (1991), p. 65.

36 Melissa Walker (1991), p. 65.

37 Walker, *Purple* (1983), p. 115, quoted in Melissa Walker (1991), p. 66.

38 Melissa Walker (1991), p. 66.

39 Melissa Walker (1991), p. 66.

40 Melissa Walker (1991), p. 67.

41 Lean'tin Bracks, 'Alice Walker's *The Color Purple*: Racism, Sexism, and Kinship in the Process of Self-Actualization,' *Writings on Black Women of the Diaspora: History, Language and Identity* (New York: Garland, 1998), p. 83.

42 Bracks (1998), p. 84.

43 Bracks (1998), pp. 84, 84, 84–5,85.

44 Bracks (1998), pp. 89, 88.

45 Bracks (1998), p. 91.

46 Bracks (1998), p. 85.

47 Bracks (1998), pp. 85, 85–6.

48 Bracks (1998), p. 86.

49 Gloria Steinem, 'Alice Walker: Do You Know This Woman? She Knows You,' *Ms.* (June 1982), in *Outrageous Acts and Everyday Rebellions*, 2nd edn (New York: Owl-Holt, 1995), p. 298.

50 Graham (1983), p. 279.

51 Bracks (1998), p. 87.

52 Bracks (1998), p. 86.

53   Bracks (1998), pp. 86–7.

54   Bracks (1998), p. 87.

55   Berlant (1993), pp. 222, 222–3.

56   Berlant (1993), p. 223.

57   Berlant (1993), p. 224.

58   Berlant (1993), p. 225.

59   Berlant (1993), p. 226.

60   Linda Selzer, 'Race and Domesticity in *The Color Purple*,' *African American Review* 29.1 (1995), p. 68.

61   Selzer (1995), p. 69.

62   Walker, *Purple* (1983), p. 102, quoted in Selzer, p. 68.

63   Selzer (1995), p. 68.

64   Selzer (1995), p. 69.

65   Walker, *Purple* (1983), pp. 232–3, quoted in Selzer, p. 69.

66   Selzer (1995), p. 69.

67   Selzer (1995), pp. 69–70.

68   Selzer (1995), p. 70.

69   Selzer (1995), p. 71.

70   Walker, *Purple* (1983), p. 195, quoted in Selzer, p. 71.

71   Selzer (1995), p. 71.

72   Selzer (1995), p. 72.

73   Walker, *Purple* (1983), p. 117, quoted in Selzer (1995), p. 72.

74   Selzer (1995), p. 72.

75   Walker, *Purple* (1983), p. 200, quoted in Selzer (1995), p. 72.

76   Selzer (1995), p. 72.

77   Selzer (1995), p. 73.

78   Selzer (1995), p. 74.

79   Selzer (1995), p. 75.

80   Walker, *Purple* (1983), p. 226, quoted in Selzer (1995), p. 75.

81   Selzer (1995), p. 75.

82   Selzer (1995), p. 76.

83   Selzer (1995), p. 77.

84   Walker, *Purple* (1983), p. 211, quoted in Selzer (1995), p. 78.

85   Selzer (1995), p. 78.

CHAPTER SIX

1   Alice Walker, *Color Purple* (London: Women's Press, 1983), p. 170.

2   Alice Walker, *Purple* (1983), p. 183.

3   Maryemma Graham, 'Alice Walker; Skillful but Disturbing Novel,' review of *The Color Purple*, by Alice Walker, *Freedomways* (1983), p. 280.

4   See Karl Marx, *A Contribution to the Critique of Political Economy*, translated S. W. Ryanzanskaya (Moscow: Progress Publishers, 1859).

5   Claudia Tate, 'Alice Walker,' *Black Women Writers at Work* (New York: Continuum, 1983), p. 185.

6   Alice Walker, 'In the Closet of the Soul' (1987), *Living by the Word: Selected Writings 1973–1987* (New York: Harvest – Harcourt, Brace, Jovanovich, 1988), p. 92.

7   Carl Dix, 'Thoughts on *The Color Purple*,' The Revolutionary Worker (1985), in Alice Walker, *The Same River Twice: A Meditation on Life, Spirit, Art and the Making of the Film, The Color Purple, Ten Years Later* (New York: Scribner, 1996), p. 195.

8   Walker, 'Closet' (1987), p. 92.

9   Walker, 'Closet' (1987), p. 92. Walker has identified the year of Celie's father's death as 1903. See *Same River* (1996), p. 50.

10 Walker, 'Closet' (1987), p. 92.

11 Cynthia Hamilton, 'Alice Walker's Politics, or the Politics of *The Color Purple*,' *Journal of Black Studies*, 18.3 (Mar. 1988), p. 386.

12 Hamilton (1988), p. 380.

13 Hamilton (1988), pp. 383, 382.

14 Hamilton (1988), p. 386.

15 Hamilton (1988), p. 387.

16 Hamilton (1988), p. 388.

17 Hamilton (1988), p. 389.

18 Du Bois, 'Criteria of Negro Art,' Nathan Huggins (ed.), *Writings* (New York: Library of American College, 1986), p. 998.

19 Hamilton (1988), pp. 390–1.

20 Hamilton (1988), p. 391.

21 Melissa Walker, *Down from the Mountaintop: Black Women's Novels in the Wake of the Civil Rights Movement, 1966–1989* (New Haven: Yale University Press, 1991), p. 62.

22 Toni Morrison, *The Bluest Eye* (London: Picador-Macmillan, 1990), pp. 12, 11.

23 Melissa Walker (1991), p. 60.

24 Melissa Walker (1991), p. 61.

25 Melissa Walker (1991), p. 69.

26 Melissa Walker (1991), p. 72.

27 Melissa Walker (1991), pp. 72–3, 73.

28 Susan Willis, 'I Shop Therefore I Am: Is There a Place for Afro-American Culture in Commodity Culture?' in Cheryl Wall (ed.), *Changing Our Own Words: Essays on Criticism, Theory, and Writing by Black Women* (New Brunswick: Rutgers University Press, 1989), p. 184.

29 Willis (1989), p. 184.

30 See bell hooks, 'Overcoming White Supremacy,' *Zeta* (Jan. 1988), p. 24, quoted in Willis (1989), p. 184.

31 Willis (1989), p. 184.

32 Willis (1989), p. 195.

33 Hamilton (1988), p. 381.

34 Maroula Joannou, 'To The Color Purple,' *Contemporary Women's Writing: from The Golden Notebook to The Color Purple* (Manchester: Manchester University Press, 2000), p. 181.

35 Walker, *Purple* (1983), p. 155, quoted in Byerman, ' "Dear Everything": Alice Walker's *The Color Purple* as Womanist Utopia,' in Arno Heller et al. (eds), *Utopian Thought in American Literature* (Tübingen: Gunter Narr Verlag, 1988), p. 175.

36 Byerman, 'Womanist' (1988) p. 176.

37 Byerman, 'Womanist' (1988), p. 177.

38 Byerman, 'Womanist' (1988), pp. 177–8.

39 Byerman, 'Womanist' (1988), p. 181.

40 Lauren Berlant, 'Race, Gender, and Nation in *The Color Purple*,' in Henry Louis Gates, Jr., and Kwame Anthony Appiah (eds), *Alice Walker: Critical Perspectives, Past and Present*, Amistad Library Series (New York: Amistad Press, 1993), p. 213.

41 Berlant (1993), p. 218.

42 Walker, *Purple* (1983), p. 148, quoted in Berlant (1993), p. 217.

43 Berlant (1993), p. 218.

44 Berlant (1993), p. 228.

45 Berlant (1993), p. 229.

46 Berlant (1993), p. 232.

47 Berlant (1993), p. 233.

48 Peter Kerry Powers, ' "Pa Is Not Our Pa": Sacred History and Political Imagination in *The Color Purple*,' *South Atlantic Review* 60.2 (May 1995), p. 81.

49 Powers (1995), p. 82.

50 Powers (1995), p. 83.

51 Powers (1995), p. 84.
52 Powers (1995), p. 85.
53 Powers (1995), p. 87.

CHAPTER SEVEN

1 Henry Louis Gates, Jr., *Loose Canons: Notes on the Culture Wars* (New York: Oxford University Press, 1992), p. 91.
2 Alison Light, 'Fear of the Happy Ending: *The Color Purple*, Reading and Racism,' in Linda Anderson (ed.), *Plotting Change: Contemporary Women's Fiction* (London: Arnold, 1990), p. 93.
3 Judy Elsley, ' "Nothing can be sole or whole that has not been rent": Fragmentation in the Quilt and *The Color Purple*,' in Ikenna Dieke (ed.), *Critical Essays on Alice Walker* (Westport, CT: Greenwood, 1999), pp. 169–70.
4 Maggie Humm (ed.), *Feminisms: A Reader* (New York: Prentice-Hall/Harvester Wheatsheaf, 1992), p. 12.
5 Krista Brewer, 'Writing to Survive: An Interview with Alice Walker,' *Southern Exposure*, 9.2 (1981), p. 12.
6 David Bradley, 'Novelist Alice Walker: Telling the Black Woman's Story,' *New York Times* (8 Jan. 1984), p. 35.
7 Sherley Anne Williams, 'Some Implications of Womanist Theory,' in Henry Louis Gates, Jr. (ed.), *Reading Black, Reading Feminist* (New York: Meridian, 1990), p. 70. Williams refers here to the concerns expressed by Deborah E. McDowell in 'New Directions for Black Feminist Criticism,' in Elaine Showalter (ed.), *The New Feminist Criticism: Essays on Women, Literature and Theory* (New York: Pantheon, 1985), p. 196.
8 Jita Tuzyline Allan, '*The Color Purple*: A Study of Walker's Womanist Gospel,' in Harold Bloom (ed.), *Alice Walker's The Color Purple*, Modern Critical Interpretations (Philadelphia: Chelsea House, 2000), p. 136.
9 Allan (2000), p. 137.
10 Elliott Butler-Evans, *Race, Gender and Desire: Narrative Strategies in the Fiction of Toni Cade Bambara, Toni Morrison and Alice Walker* (Philadelphia: Temple University Press, 1991), pp. 12–13.
11 Butler-Evans (1991), p. 13.
12 Butler-Evans (1991), pp. 162, 162, 162–3.
13 Maroula Joannou, 'To The Color Purple,' *Contemporary Women's Writing: from The Golden Notebook to The Color Purple* (Manchester: Manchester University Press, 2000), pp. 176, 176–7.
14 Lovalerie King, 'African-American Womanism: from Nora Zeale Hurston to Alice Walker,' in Maryemma Graham (ed.), *The Cambridge Companion to the African-American Novel* (Cambridge: Cambridge University Press, 2004), p. 236.
15 Lovalerie (2004), pp. 236, 236, 245.
16 Carla Kaplan, *The Erotics of Talk: Women's Writing and Feminist Paradigms* (New York: Oxford University Press, 1996), pp. 141, 14.
17 Kaplan (1996), p. 15.
18 Kaplan (1996), p. 125.
19 Kaplan (1996), p. 123.
20 Kaplan (1996), p. 124.
21 Kaplan (1996), p. 196, n.6.
22 Trudier Harris, 'On *The Color Purple*, Stereotypes and Silence,' *Black American Literature Forum* 18.4 (1984), p. 155.
23 Trudier Harris, 'From Victimization to Free Enterprise: Alice Walker's *The Color Purple*,' *Studies in American Fiction* 14.1 (1986), p. 7.
24 Harris (1986), pp. 7, 8.

25 Harris (1986), p. 10.

26 Harris (1986), p. 12.

27 Harris (1986), pp. 14, 15.

28 Joannou (2000), p. 183.

29 Deborah Ellis, 'The Color Purple and the Patient Griselda,' College English 49.2 (1987), p. 188.

30 Ellis (1987), p. 189.

31 Ellis (1987), p. 190.

32 Ellis (1987), p. 192.

33 Ellis (1987), p. 193.

34 Ellis (1987), p. 198.

35 Ellis (1987), p. 200.

36 King-Kok Cheung, ' "Don't Tell": Imposed Silences in The Color Purple and The Woman Warrior,' PMLA 103 (1988), pp. 163, 170.

37 Gina Michelle Collins, 'What Feminism Can Learn from a Southern Tradition,' in Jefferson Humphries (ed.), Southern Literature and Literary Theory (Athens, GA: University of Georgia Press, 1990), p. 75. For Walker's observations on the stereotyping that black women have been subjected to, see 'In Search of Our Mothers' Gardens,' in Alice Walker, In Search of Our Mothers' Gardens (London: Women's Press, 1983), p. 237.

38 Collins (1990), p. 76.

39 Walker, 'Finding Celie's Voice,' Ms. (Dec. 1985), p. 71, quoted in Collins (1990), p. 77.

40 Collins (1990), p. 77.

41 Collins (1990), p. 78. See Alice Walker, 'A Letter of the Times: or, Should This Sado-masochism Be Saved?' in You Can't Keep a Good Woman Down (New York: Harcourt Brace Jovanovich, 1981), p. 120.

42 bell hooks, 'Writing the Subject, Reading The Color Purple,' in Harold Bloom (ed.), Alice Walker, Modern Critical Views (New York: Chelsea House, 1988), p. 222.

43 Collins (1990), p. 79.

44 Collins (1990). p. 80.

45 Collins (1990), p. 81.

46 Collins (1990), p. 84.

47 Collins (1990), p. 86.

48 Virginia Woolf, The Pargiters: The Novel-Essay Portion of the Years, Mitchell Leaska (ed.), (New York: Harvest – Harcourt, Brace, Jovanovich 1978), pp. xxxviii–xxxix, quoted in Christine Froula, 'The Daughter's Seduction: Sexual Violence and Literary History,' Signs 11 (1986), pp. 621, 622.

49 Froula (1986), p. 622.

50 Froula (1986), p. 623.

51 Froula (1986), p. 628.

52 Froula (1986), p. 624.

53 Froula (1986), p. 628.

54 Froula (1986), p. 629. For Freud's seduction theory, Froula points us to Sigmund Freud, New Introductory Lectures on Psychoanalysis, in Standard Edition of the Complete Psychological Works, translated and edited by James Strachey, Vol. 22 (London: Hogarth Press, 1953–1974).

55 Froula (1986), p. 632.

56 Froula (1986), p. 637.

57 Froula (1996), pp. 637–8.

58 Froula (1996), p. 638.

59 Froula (1986), p. 639.

60 Froula (1986), p. 640.

61 Froula (1986), pp. 641–2.

62 Froula (1986), p. 642.

63   Froula (1986), p. 628.

64   Walker, *Purple* (1983), p. 186, quoted in Froula (1986), p. 643.

65   Froula (1986), p. 643.

66   Froula (1986), p. 644.

67   Walker, 'In Search of Our Mothers' Gardens,' *In Search of Our Mothers' Gardens: Womanist Prose* (London: Women's Press, 1984), p. 237.

68   Priscilla Leder, 'Alice Walker's American Quilt: *The Color Purple* and American Literary Tradition,' in Dieke (1999), p. 141.

69   Teresa M. Tavormina, 'Dressing the Spirit: Cloth-Working and Language in *The Color Purple*,' *Journal of Narrative Technique* 16.3 (Fall 1986), p. 220.

70   Gates, 'Introduction,' *Reading* (1990), p. 9.

71   Marjorie Pryse, 'Introduction: Zora Neale Hurston, Alice Walker, and the "Ancient Power" of Black Women,' in *Conjuring: Black Women, Fiction, and Literary Tradition* (Bloomington, IN: Indiana University Press, 1985), p. 12.

72   Pryse (1985), p. 2.

73   Walker, 'Zora Neale Hurston: A Cautionary Tale and a Partisan View' (1979), in *In Search* (1984), p. 86.

74   Walker, 'Zora Neale,' (1979), in *In Search* (1984), p. 85.

75   Walker, 'From an Interview' (1973), in *In Search* (1984), p. 261.

76   James C. Hall, 'Towards a Map of Mis(sed) Reading: The Presence of Absence in *The Color Purple*,' *African American Review*, 26.1 (1992), p. 89.

77   Hall (1992), p. 96.

78   Hall (1992), p. 93.

79   Sadoff, Dianne F., 'Black Matrilineage: The Case of Alice Walker and Zora Neale Hurston,' in Bloom, *Alice Walker* (1988), p. 116.

80   Sadoff (1988), p. 115.

81   Sadoff (1988), p. 116.

82   Sadoff (1988), p. 118.

83   Sadoff (1988), pp. 117–18.

84   Sadoff (1988), p. 118.

85   Sadoff (1988), p. 127.

86   Sadoff (1988), p. 128.

87   Sadoff (1988), p. 131.

88   Sadoff (1988), p. 129.

89   Sadoff (1988), p. 130.

90   Sadoff (1988), p. 131.

91   Sadoff (1988), p. 133.

92   Molly Hite, 'Romance, Marginality, and Matrilineage: *The Color Purple* and *Their Eyes Were Watching God*,' in Gates, *Reading* (1990), p. 433.

93   Hite (1990), p. 434.

94   Hite (1990), p. 447.

95   Hite (1990), pp. 447–8.

96   Hite (1990), p. 448.

97   Hite (1990), p. 449.

CHAPTER EIGHT

1   Ralph D. Story, 'Sisterhood as Salvation: Black Male Characterization in Alice Walker's *The Color Purple*,' *Journal of Popular Literature* 2.2 (1986), p. 12.

2   Pauline Kael, '*The Color Purple*,' *The New Yorker* 61 (30 Dec. 1985), p. 69.

3   Mel Watkins, 'Some Letters Went to God,' review of *The Color Purple*, *New York Times Book Review* 87 (25 July 1982), p. 7, in Henry Louis Gates, Jr., and Kwame Anthony Appiah (eds.), *Alice Walker: Critical Perspectives, Past and Present*, Amistad Library Series (New York: Amistad Press, 1993), p. 17.

4   Mel Watkins, 'Sexism, Racism and Black Women Writers,' *New York Times Book Review* 5 June 1986), p. 36.

5   Ishmael Reed, 'Steven Spielberg Plays Howard Beach,' *Writin' and Fightin': Thirty-Seven Years of Boxing on Paper* (New York: Atheneum, 1998), pp. 145–6.

6   Story (1986), p. 3.

7   Story (1986), p. 8.

8   Story (1986), pp. 8–9.

9   Story (1986), p. 11.

10   Gloria Steinem, 'Alice Walker: Do You Know This Woman? She Knows You,' *Ms.* (June 1982) in *Outrageous Acts and Everyday Rebellions*, 2nd edn (New York: Owl-Holt, 1995), p. 286.

11   Carl Dix, 'Thoughts on *The Color Purple*,' *The Revolutionary Worker* (1985), in Alice Walker, *The Same River Twice: A Meditation on Life, Spirit, Art and the Making of the Film, The Color Purple, Ten Years Later* (New York: Scribner, 1996), p. 195.

12   Dix (1985), *Same River*, p. 198.

13   Anita Jones, 'Scars of Indifference,' *Carolina Peacemaker* (4 Jan. 1986), *Same River*, p. 226.

14   Alice Walker, *Same River* (1996), p. 23.

15   Alice Walker, 'In the Closet of the Soul' (1987), *Living by the Word: Selected Writings 1973–1987* (New York: Harvest – Harcourt, Brace, Jovanovich, 1988), p. 79.

16   Walker, 'Closet' (1987), *Living*, p. 80.

17   Walker, 'Closet' (1987), *Living*, pp. 80, 81.

18   Walker, 'Closet' (1987), *Living*, p. 81.

19   Richard Wesley, '*The Color Purple* Debate: Reading Between the Lines,' *Ms.* 15.3 (Sept. 1986), p. 62.

20   Wesley (1986), p. 90.

21   Calvin C. Hernton, 'Who's Afraid of Alice Walker?' *The Sexual Mountain and Black Women Writers: Sex, Literature and Real Life* (New York: Anchor-Doubleday, 1987), p. 18.

22   Hernton (1987), p. 11.

23   Hernton (1987), pp. 11–12.

24   Hernton (1987), p. 12.

25   Hernton (1987), p. 13.

26   Hernton (1987), p. 14.

27   Liesbeth Brouwer, 'The Colour of the Sign: Feminist Semiotics,' in Anneke Smelik and Rosemarie Buikema (eds), *Women's Studies and Culture: A Feminist Introduction* (New York: St. Martin's Press, 1995), p. 160.

28   Maryemma Graham, 'Alice Walker; Skillful but Disturbing Novel,' review of *The Color Purple*, by Alice Walker, *Freedomways* (1983), p. 279.

29   George Stade, 'Womanist Fiction and Male Characters,' *Partisan Review* 52.3 (1985), p. 264.

30   Stade (1985), pp. 264–5, 265.

31   Stade (1985), p. 266.

32   King-Kok Cheung, ' "Don't Tell": Imposed Silences in *The Color Purple* and *The Woman Warrior*,' *PMLA* 103 (1988), p. 171.

33   Cheung (1988), p. 173, n.14.

34   Lean'tin Bracks, 'Alice Walker's *The Color Purple*: Racism, Sexism, and Kinship in the Process of Self-Actualization,' *Writings on Black Women of the Diaspora: History, Language and Identity* (New York: Garland, 1998), pp. 93, 94, 98, 98.

35   Lisa Maria Hogeland, *Feminism and Its Fictions: The Consciousness-Raising Novel and the Women's Liberation Movement* (Philadelphia: University of Pennsylvania Press, 1998), p. 96.

36   Hogeland (1998), p. 97.

37   Hogeland (1998), p. 97. See hooks, 'Writing the Subject: Reading *The Color Purple*,' in Harold Bloom (ed.), *Alice Walker*, Modern Critical Views (New York: Chelsea House, 1988), p. 220; quoted in Hogeland (1998), p. 97.

38   Hogeland (1998), p. 98.

39   Candice M. Jenkins, 'Queering Black Patriarchy: The Salvific Wish and Masculine Possibility in Alice Walker's *The Color Purple*,' *Modern Fiction Studies* 48.4 (2002), p. 972.

40   Jenkins (2002), p. 977.

41   Alice Walker, *The Color Purple* (London: Women's Press, 1983), p. 27, quoted in Jenkins (2002), p. 978.

42   Jenkins (2002), p. 979.

43   Jenkins (2002), p. 980.

44   Jenkins (2002), p. 981. See David Marriott, *On Black Men* (New York: Columbia University Press, 2000). In the TV interview for *Omnibus*, Walker talks about this issue of naming in the South.

45   Jenkins (2002), p. 973.

46   Jenkins (2002), p. 974.

47   Jenkins (2002), p. 982.

48   Jenkins (2002), p. 983.

49   Jenkins (2002), p. 984.

50   Watkins, 'Sexism (1985), p. 35, quoted in Jenkins (2002), p. 989.

51   Du Bois, 'The Talented Tenth,' in Nathan Huggins (ed.), *Writings* (New York: Library of American College 1986), p. 842.

52   Jenkins (2002), p. 989.

53   Harris, 'On *The Color Purple*, Stereotypes and Silence,' *Black American Literature Forum* 18.4 (1984), p. 157, quoted in Jenkins (2002), p. 990.

54   Jenkins (2002), p. 990.

55   Harris, 'Stereotypes' (1984), p. 158, quoted in Jenkins, p. 991.

56   Jenkins (2002), pp. 991, 991–2.

57   Jenkins (2002), p. 994.

58   Barbara Christian, 'No More Buried Lives: The Theme of Lesbianism in Audre Lorde's *Zami*, Gloria Naylor's *The Women of Brewster Place*, Ntozake Shange's *Sassafras, Cypress and Indigo*, and Alice Walker's *The Color Purple*,' *Black Feminist Criticism: Perspectives on Black Women Writers* (New York: Pergamon Press, 1985), p. 187.

59   Christian (1985), p. 192.

60   Christian (1985), p. 194.

61   Christian (1985), p. 199.

62   Walker, 'Closet' (1987), *Living* p. 91.

63   Tony Brown, 'Blacks Need to Love One Another,' *Carolina Peacemaker* (4 Jan. 1986), in Walker, *Same River*, p. 224.

64   Jones, 'Scars' (1986), in Walker, *Same River*, p. 225.

65   Jones, 'Scars' (1986), in Walker, *Same River*, p. 226.

66   Barbara Smith, 'Sexual Oppression Unmasked,' review of *The Color Purple*, *Callaloo*, 22 (Autumn 1984), p. 174.

67   Graham (1983), p. 280.

68   Butler-Evans (1991), p. 169.

69   Butler-Evans (1991), p. 168.

70   Linda Abbandonato ' "A View from Elsewhere": Subversive Sexuality and the Rewriting of the Heroine's Story in *The Color Purple*,' *PMLA* 106.5 (Oct. 1991), p. 1106.

71   Abbandonato (1991), p. 1109. See Rubin's 'The Traffic in Women,' in Rayna R. Reiter (ed.), *Toward an Anthropology of Women* (New York: Monthly Review, 1975), pp. 157–210.

72   Claude Lévi-Strauss, *The Elementary Structures of Kinship*, translated by James Hurle Bell et al., 2nd edn (Oxford: Beacon Press, 1969), p. 481.

73   Abbandonato (1991), pp. 1109, 1109–10.

74 Abbandonato (1991), p. 1110.
75 Abbandonato (1991), p. 1111.
76 Walker, *The Color Purple* (London: Women's, 1983), p. 97, quoted in Abbandonato (1991), p. 1111.
77 Abbandonato (1991), p. 1111.
78 Abbandonato (1991), pp. 1111, 1111–12.
79 Abbandonato (1991), p. 1112.
80 hooks (1988), p. 216.
81 hooks (1988), p. 217.
82 hooks (1988), pp. 218, 217.
83 hooks (1988), p. 218.
84 hooks (1988), p. 220.
85 hooks (1988), p. 222.
86 Renée C. Hoogland, 'Heterosexual Screening: Lesbian Studies,' in Smelik and Buikema (1995), p. 119.
87 Hoogland (1995), p. 130.
88 Hoogland (1995), p. 131.
89 Hoogland (1995), p. 132.
90 Hoogland (1995), p. 133.

CONCLUSION

1 Walker, 'Tsunamis and Hurricanes: Twenty-five Years After Publishing *The Color Purple*,' *The Color Purple*, 25th Anniversary Edition (London: Weidenfeld and Nicolson, 2007), p. xi.
2 Walker, 'Tsunamis' (2007), p. xiv.
3 Alice Walker, *The Color Purple* (2007), np.
4 Walker, *The Same River Twice: Honoring the Difficult: A Meditation on Life, Spirit, Art and the Making of the Film, The Color Purple, Ten Years Later* (New York: Scribner, 1996), p. 22.
5 Walker, *Same River*, p. 23.
6 Aida Edemariam, 'Free Spirit,' interview with Alice Walker, *Guardian* 23 June 2007, p. 20.
7 Walker, *Same River* (1996), p. 41.
8 Walker, *Same River* (1996), p. 205.
9 Walker, *Same River* (1996), p. 270.
10 Edemariam (2007), *Aida*, 'Free Spirit.' Interview with Alice Walker, *Guardian* (23 June 2007), p. 20.
11 Greg Moody, review of *The Color Purple*, National Tour, Buell Theatre (3 Jan. 2009), http://cbs4denver.com/video/?id+51245@kcnc.dayport.com.
12 See Garth Bardsley, '*The Color Purple* Ends Broadway Run Weeks After Fantasia's Exit; Movie Version May Be on the Way' (25 Jan. 2008), http://www.mtv.com/movies/news/articles.
13 Lovalerie King, 'African-American Womanism: from Nora Zeale Hurston to Alice Walker,' in Maryemma Graham (ed.), *The Cambridge Companion to the African-American Novel* (Cambridge: Cambridge University Press, 2004), p. 235.
14 Claudine Raynaud, 'Coming of Age in the African-American Novel,' in Graham, *Cambridge*, p. 115.

Select Bibliography

EDITIONS OF *THE COLOR PURPLE*

Walker, Alice, *The Color Purple* (London: Women's Press, 1983; preface, Alice Walker, 1992).
Walker, Alice, *The Color Purple*, 25th Anniversary Edition (London: Women's Press, 1983; Weidenfeld & Nicolson, 2007).

SELECTED BOOKS BY ALICE WALKER

Walker, Alice, *In Search of Our Mothers' Gardens: Womanist Prose* (London: Women's Press 1984).
Walker, Alice, *Living by the Word: Selected Writings 1973–1987* (New York: Harvest – Harcourt, Brace, Jovanovich, 1988).
Walker, Alice, *The Same River Twice: Honoring the Difficult: A Meditation on Life, Spirit, Art and the Making of the Film, The Color Purple, Ten Years Later* (New York: Scribner, 1996).

ESSAYS BY ALICE WALKER

Walker, Alice, 'Beyond the Peacock: The Reconstruction of Flannery O'Connor' (1975), in *In Search*, pp. 42–59.
Walker, Alice, 'The Black Writer and the Southern Experience' (1970), *In Search*, pp. 15–21.
Walker, Alice, '*The Color Purple*: Preface written for the 10th Anniversary Edition,' *The Color Purple* (1992), pp. ix–x.
Walker, Alice, 'Coming in from the Cold: Welcoming the Old, Funny-Talking Ancient Ones into the Warm Room of Present Consciousness, or Natty Dread Rides Again!' (1984), *Living*, pp. 54–68.
Walker, Alice, 'Finding Celie's Voice,' *Ms.* (Dec. 1985), p. 71.
Walker, Alice, 'In Search of Our Mothers' Gardens' (1974), *In Search*, pp. 231–43.
Walker, Alice, 'In the Closet of the Soul' (1987), *Living*, pp. 78–92.
Walker, Alice, 'Looking for Zora' (1975), *In Search*, pp. 93–116.
Walker, Alice, 'Tsunamis and Hurricanes: Twenty-five Years After Publishing *The Color Purple*,' *The Color Purple* (2007), pp. ix–xv.
Walker, Alice, 'Writing *The Color Purple*' (1982), in *In Search*, pp. 355–60.
Walker, Alice, 'Zora Neale Hurston: A Cautionary Tale and a Partisan View' (1977), in *In Search*, pp. 83–92.

INTERVIEWS WITH ALICE WALKER

Alice Walker: Omnibus. Directed by Samira Osman. Produced by Leslie Megahey and Alan Yentob, BBC, 1986.
Brewer, Krista, 'Writing to Survive: An Interview with Alice Walker,' *Southern Exposure* 9.2 (1981), pp. 12–16.
Edemariam, Aida, 'Free Spirit,' interview with Alice Walker, *Guardian* (23 June 2007), p. 20.
Near, Holly with Amy Bank, 'Alice Walker on the Movie *The Color Purple*,' *Voices* (1985), in Walker, *Same River*, pp. 202–5.
Tate, Claidia, 'Alice Walker,' *Black Woman Writers at Work* (New York: Continuum, 1983), pp. 175–87.

Walker, Alice, 'From an Interview,' interview with John O'Brien, in *In Search*, pp. 244–72.

Wilson, Sharon, 'A Conversation with Alice Walker,' in Gates and Appiah, pp. 319–25.

REVIEWS OF *THE COLOR PURPLE*

Bradley, David, 'Novelist Alice Walker: Telling the Black Woman's Story,' *New York Times* (8 Jan. 1984), pp. 24–37.

Brown, Tony, 'Tony Brown's Comments: Blacks Need to Love One Another,' *Carolina Peacemaker* (4 Jan. 1986), in Walker, *Same River*, pp. 223–5.

Graham, Maryemma, 'Alice Walker; Skillful but Disturbing Novel,' review of *The Color Purple*, by Alice Walker, *Freedomways* 23 (1983), pp. 278–80.

Jones, Anita, 'Scars of Indifference,' *Carolina Peacemaker* (4 Jan. 1986), in Walker, *Same River*, pp. 225–8.

Prescott, Peter S., 'A Long Road to Liberation,' review of *The Color Purple*, by Alice Walker, *Newsweek* 99.25 (21 June 1982), pp. 67–8.

Smith, Barbara, 'Sexual Oppression Unmasked,' review of *The Color Purple*, by Alice Walker, *Callaloo* 22 (Autumn 1984), pp. 170–6.

Smith, Dinitia, 'Celie, You A Tree!' review of *The Color Purple*, by Alice Walker, *The Nation*, 235.6 (4 Sept. 1982), pp. 181–3, in Gates and Appiah, pp. 19–20.

Steinem, Gloria, 'Alice Walker: Do You Know This Woman? She Knows You,' *Ms.* (June 1982), *Outrageous Acts and Everyday Rebellions*, 2nd edn (New York: Owl-Holt, 1995), pp. 283–300.

Towers, Robert, 'Good Men Are Hard to Find,' review of *The Terrible Twos*, by Ishmael Reed and *The Color Purple*, by Alice Walker, *New York Review of Books* 29.13 (12 Aug. 1982), pp. 35–6.

Watkins, Mel, 'Sexism, Racism and Black Women Writers,' review of *The Color Purple*, by Alice Walker, *New York Times Book Review* (15 June 1986), pp. 35–7.

Watkins, Mel, 'Some Letters Went to God,' review of *The Color Purple*, by Alice Walker, *New York Times Book Review* 87 (25 July 1982), p. 7, in Gates and Appiah, pp. 16–18.

Wesley, Richard, '*The Color Purple* Debate: Reading Between the Lines,' *Ms.* 15.3. (Sept. 1986), pp. 62, 90–2.

CRITICISM OF *THE COLOR PURPLE*

Conception and Reception of *The Color Purple*

Bloom, Harold, *Alice Walker*, Modern Critical Views (New York: Chelsea House, 1988).

Bobo, Jacqueline, '*The Color Purple*: Black Women as Cultural Readers,' in Deidre Pribram (ed.), *Female Spectators: Looking at Film and Television* (London: Verso Books, 1988), pp. 90–109.

Bobo, Jacqueline, 'Sifting Through the Controversy,' *Callaloo* 39 (Spring 1989), pp. 332–42. Gates, Henry Louis, Jr., and Kwame Anthony Appiah (eds), *Alice Walker: Critical Perspectives Past and Present*, Amistad Library Series (New York: Amistad Press, 1993).

Harris, Trudier, 'On *The Color Purple*, Stereotypes and Silence,' *Black American Literature Forum* 18.4 (1984), pp. 155–61.

hooks, bell, 'Writing the Subject: Reading *The Color Purple*,' in Bloom, *Alice Walker*, pp. 215–28.

Weisenburger, Steven C., 'Errant Narrative and *The Color Purple*,' *Journal of Narrative Technique* 3 (1989), pp. 257–75.

Defining *The Color Purple*: The Question of Genre

Bloom, Harold, *Alice Walker's The Color Purple*, Modern Critical Interpretations (Philadelphia: Chelsea House, 2000).

Byerman, Keith, ' "Dear Everything": Alice Walker's *The Color Purple* as Womanist Utopia,' in Arno Heller et al. (eds), *Utopian Thought in American Literature* (Tübingen: Gunter Narr Verlag, 1988), pp. 171–83.

Byerman, Keith, 'Walker's Blues,' in Bloom, *Alice Walker*, pp. 59–66.

Graham, Maryemma (ed.), *The Cambridge Companion to the African-American Novel* (Cambridge: Cambridge University Press, 2004).

Henderson, Mae G., '*The Color Purple*: Revisions and Definitions,' in Bloom, *Alice Walker*, pp. 67–80.

Hernton, Calvin, C., 'Who's Afraid of Alice Walker?' *The Sexual Mountain and Black Women Writers: Sex, Literature and Real Life* (New York: Anchor-Doubleday, 1987), pp. 1–36.

Hite, Molly, 'Romance, Marginality, and Matrilineage: *The Color Purple* and *Their Eyes Were Watching God*,' in Gates, *Reading*, pp. 431–53.

hooks, bell, 'Writing the Subject: Reading *The Color Purple*,' in Bloom, *Alice Walker*, pp. 215–28.

Joannou, Maroula, '*To The Color Purple*,' *Contemporary Women's Writing: from The Golden Notebook to The Color Purple* (Manchester: Manchester University Press, 2000), pp. 164–87.

Katz, Tamar, ' "Show Me How to Do Like You": Didacticism and Epistolary Form in *The Color Purple*,' in Bloom, *Alice Walker*, pp. 185–93.

Kauffman, Linda S., 'Constructing Otherness; Struggles of Representation in *The Color Purple*,' *Special Delivery: Epistolary Modes in Modern Fiction*, Women in Culture and Society (Chicago: University of Chicago Press, 1992), pp. 183–220.

Kermode, Frank, 'Introduction,' *The Tempest*, by William Shakespeare (London: Methuen, 1954), pp. xi–lxxxviii.

Lauret, Maria, *Alice Walker*, Modern Novelists (London: Macmillan, 2000).

Marvin, Thomas F., ' "Preachin' the Blues": Bessie Smith's Secular Religion and Alice Walker's *The Color Purple*,' *African American Review* 28.3 (1994), pp. 411–21.

Parker-Smith, Bettye, 'Alice Walker's Women: In Search of Some Peace of Mind,' in Mari Evans (ed.), *Black Women Writers: A Critical Evaluation* (Garden City, NY: Anchor Books, 1984), pp. 478–93.

Raynaud, Claudine, 'Coming of Age in the African-American Novel,' in Graham, *Cambridge*, pp. 106–21.

Scholl, Diane Gabrielsen, 'With Ears to Hear and Eyes to See: Alice Walker's Parable *The Color Purple*,' in Bloom, *Alice Walker's The Color Purple*, pp. 107–18.

Sinfield, Alan, 'Problems of the Progressive Text: *The Color Purple* by Alice Walker,' *Literature Teaching Politics: 1985 Conference Papers* (Bristol: Bristol Polytechnic, 1985).

Walsh, Margaret, 'The Enchanted World of *The Color Purple*,' *Southern Quarterly* 25(Winter 1987), pp. 89–101.

Williams, Carolyn, ' "Trying to Do Without God": The Revision of Epistolary Address in *The Color Purple*,' in Elizabeth C. Goldsmith (ed.), *Writing the Female Voice: Essays on Epistolary Literature* (Boston: Northeastern University Press, 1988), pp. 273–85.

Language and Narrative Poetics in *The Color Purple*

Babb, Valerie, '*The Color Purple*: Writing to Undo What Writing Has Done,' *Phylon* 47 (1986), pp. 107–16.

Fifer, Elizabeth, 'The Dialect and Letters of *The Color Purple*,' in Catherine Rainwater and William J. Scheick (eds), *Contemporary American Women Writers: Narrative Strategies* (Lexington: University Press of Kentucky, 1985), pp. 155–71.

Gates, Henry Louis, Jr., 'Color Me Zora,' in Gates and Appiah (1993), pp. 239–60.

Gates, Henry Louis, Jr., *The Signifying Monkey: A Theory of Afro-American Literary Criticism* (New York: Oxford University Press, 1988).

Gates, Henry Louis, Jr., 'Zora Neale Hurston and the Speakerly Text,' *Signifying*, pp. 170–216.

Harris, Trudier, 'On *The Color Purple*, Stereotypes and Silence,' *Black American Literature Forum* 18.4 (1984), pp. 155–61.

hooks, bell, 'Writing the Subject: Reading *The Color Purple*,' in Bloom, *Alice Walker*, pp. 215–28.

Lauret, Maria, *Alice Walker*, Modern Novelists (London: Macmillan, 2000).

Wall, Wendy, 'Lettered Bodies and Corporeal Texts,' in Gates and Appiah, pp. 261–74.

Language and Subjectivity in *The Color Purple*

Davis, Thadious M., 'Alice Walker's Celebration of Self in Southern Generations,' in Peggy Whitman Prenshaw (ed.), *Women Writers of the Contemporary South* (Jackson: University Press of Mississippi, 1984), pp. 38–53.

Dieke, Ikenna (ed.), *Critical Essays on Alice Walker*, Contributions in Afro-American and African Studies (Westport, CT: Greenwood, 1999).

Proudfit, Charles L., 'Celie's Search for Identity: A Psychoanalytic Developmental Reading of Alice Walker's *The Color Purple*,' *Contemporary Literature* 32.1 (Spring 1991), pp. 12–37.

Ross, Daniel W., 'Celie in the Looking Glass: The Desire for Selfhood in *The Color Purple*,' *Modern Fiction Studies* 34.1 (Spring 1988), pp. 69–84.

Reading Race in *The Color Purple*

Berlant, Lauren, 'Race, Gender, and Nation in *The Color Purple*,' in Gates and Appiah, pp. 211–38.

Bracks, Lean'tin, 'Alice Walker's *The Color Purple*: Racism, Sexism, and Kinship in the Process of Self-Actualization,' *Writings on Black Women of the Diaspora: History, Language and Identity* (New York: Garland, 1998), pp. 83–103.

Butler-Evans, Elliott, *Race, Gender and Desire: Narrative Strategies in the Fiction of Toni Cade Bambara, Toni Morrison and Alice Walker* (Philadelphia, PA: Temple University Press, 1991).

Dix, Carl, 'Thoughts on *The Color Purple*' (1985), *The Revolutionary Worker*, in Walker, *Same River*, pp. 191–8.

hooks, bell, 'Writing the Subject: Reading *The Color Purple*,' in Bloom, *Alice Walker*, pp. 215–28.

Kaplan, Cora, 'Keeping the Color in *The Color Purple*,' *Sea Changes: Culture and Feminism*, Questions for Feminism (London: Verso-New Left, 1986), pp. 177–87.

Light, Alison, 'Fear of the Happy Ending: *The Color Purple*, Reading and Racism,' in Linda Anderson (ed.), *Plotting Change: Contemporary Women's Fiction* (London: Arnold, 1990), pp. 85–96.

Selzer, Linda, 'Race and Domesticity in *The Color Purple*,' *African American Review* 29.1 (1995), pp. 67–82.

Walker, Melissa, *Down from the Mountaintop: Black Women's Novels in the Wake of the Civil Rights Movement 1966–1989* (New Haven: Yale University Press, 1991).

Reading Class and Consumerism in *The Color Purple*

Berlant, Lauren, 'Race, Gender, and Nation in *The Color Purple*,' in Gates and Appiah, pp. 211–38.

Byerman, Keith, ' "Dear Everything": Alice Walker's *The Color Purple* as Womanist Utopia,' in Arno Heller et al. (eds), *Utopian Thought in American Literature* (Tübingen: Gunter Narr Verlag, 1988), pp. 171–83.

Dix, Carl, 'Thoughts on *The Color Purple*' (1985), *The Revolutionary Worker*, in Walker, *Same River*, pp. 191–8.

Hamilton, Cynthia, 'Alice Walker's Politics, or the Politics of *The Color Purple*,' *Journal of Black Studies* 18.3 (Mar. 1988), pp. 379–91.

Joannou, Maroula, 'To The Color Purple,' Contemporary Women's Writing: from The Golden Notebook to The Color Purple (Manchester: Manchester University Press, 2000), pp. 164–87.

Powers, Peter Kerry, ' "Pa Is Not Our Pa": Sacred History and Political Imagination in The Color Purple,' South Atlantic Review 60.2 (May 1995), pp. 69–92.

Walker, Melissa, Down from the Mountaintop: Black Women's Novels in the Wake of the Civil Rights Movement 1966–1989 (New Haven: Yale University Press, 1991).

Willis, Susan, 'I Shop Therefore I Am: Is There a Place for Afro-American Culture in Commodity Culture?' in Cheryl Wall (ed.), Changing Our Own Words: Essays on Criticism, Theory, and Writing by Black Women (New Brunswick: Rutgers University Press, 1989), pp. 173–95.

The Color Purple: Feminist Text?

Allan, Tuzyline Jita, 'The Color Purple: A Study of Walker's Womanist Gospel,' in Bloom, Alice Walker's The Color Purple, pp. 119–38.

Brouwer, Liesbeth, 'The Colour of the Sign: Feminist Semiotics,' in Smelik and Buikema, pp. 148–61.

Butler-Evans, Elliott, Race, Gender and Desire: Narrative Strategies in the Fiction of Toni Cade Bambara, Toni Morrison and Alice Walker (Philadelphia, PA: Temple University Press, 1991).

Collins, Gina Michelle, 'What Feminism Can Learn from a Southern Tradition,' in Jefferson Humphries (ed.), Southern Literature and Literary Theory (Athens, GA: University of Georgia Press, 1990), pp. 75–87.

Ellis, Deborah, 'The Color Purple and the Patient Griselda,' College English 49.2 (1987), pp. 188–201.

Elsley, Judy, ' "Nothing can be sole or whole that has not been rent": Fragmentation in the Quilt and The Color Purple,' in Dieke, pp. 163–70.

Froula, Christine, 'The Daughter's Seduction: Sexual Violence and Literary History,' Signs 11 (1986), pp. 621–44.

Hall, James C., 'Towards a Map of Mis(sed) Reading: The Presence of Absence in The Color Purple,' African American Review 26.1 (1992), pp. 89–97.

Harris, Trudier, 'From Victimization to Free Enterprise: Alice Walker's The Color Purple,' Studies in American Fiction 14.1 (1986), pp. 1–17.

Harris, Trudier, 'On The Color Purple, Stereotypes and Silence,' Black American Literature Forum 18.4 (1984), pp. 155–61.

Hite, Molly, 'Romance, Marginality, and Matrilineage: The Color Purple and Their Eyes Were Watching God,' in Gates, Reading, pp. 431–53.

Hogeland, Lisa Maria, Feminism and Its Fictions: The Consciousness-Raising Novel and the Women's Liberation Movement (Philadelphia: University of Pennsylvania Press, 1998).

hooks, bell, 'Writing the Subject: Reading The Color Purple,' in Bloom, Alice Walker, pp. 215–28.

Howard, Lillie P., Alice Walker and Zora Neale Hurston: A Common Bond (Boston: Twayne, 1980).

Joannou, Maroula, 'To The Color Purple,' Contemporary Women's Writing: from The Golden Notebook to The Color Purple (Manchester: Manchester University Press, 2000), pp. 164–87.

Kaplan, Carla, ' "Somebody I Can Talk To": Teaching Feminism Through The Color Purple,' The Erotics of Talk: Women's Writing and Feminist Paradigms (New York: Oxford University Press, 1996), pp. 123–43.

King, Lovalerie, 'African-American Womanism: from Nora Zeale Hurston to Alice Walker,' in Graham, Cambridge, pp. 233–52.

Leder, Priscilla, 'Alice Walker's American Quilt: The Color Purple and American Literary Tradition,' in Dieke, pp. 141–51.

Pryse, Marjorie, 'Introduction: Zora Neale Hurston, Alice Walker, and the "Ancient Power" of Black Women,' in Pryse and Spillers, pp. 1–24.

Pryse, Marjorie and Hortense Spillers (eds), *Conjuring: Black Women, Fiction, and Literary Tradition* (Bloomington, IN: Indiana University Press), 1985.

Sadoff, Dianne F., 'Black Matrilineage: The Case of Alice Walker and Zora Neale Hurston,' in Bloom, *Alice Walker*, pp. 115–34.

Tavormina, Teresa M., 'Dressing the Spirit: Cloth-Working and Language in *The Color Purple*,' *Journal of Narrative Technique* 16.3 (Fall 1986), pp. 220–30.

Gender and Sexuality in *The Color Purple*

Abbandonato, Linda, ' "A View from Elsewhere": Subversive Sexuality and the Rewriting of the Heroine's Story in *The Color Purple*,' *PMLA* 106.5 (Oct. 1991), pp. 1106–15.

Butler-Evans, Elliott, *Race, Gender and Desire: Narrative Strategies in the Fiction of Toni Cade Bambara, Toni Morrison and Alice Walker* (Philadelphia, PA: Temple University Press, 1991).

Cheung, King-Kok, ' "Don't Tell": Imposed Silences in *The Color Purple* and *The Woman Warrior*,' *PMLA* 103 (1988), pp. 162–74.

Christian, Barbara, 'No More Buried Lives: The Theme of Lesbianism in Audre Lorde's *Zami*, Gloria Naylor's *The Women of Brewster Place*, Ntozake Shange's *Sassafras, Cypress and Indigo*, and Alice Walker's *The Color Purple*,' *Black Feminist Criticism: Perspectives on Black Women Writers* (New York: Pergamon Press, 1985), pp. 187–204.

Dix, Carl, 'Thoughts on *The Color Purple*' (1985), *The Revolutionary Worker*, in Walker, *Same River*, pp. 191–8.

Early, Gerald, L., '*The Color Purple* as Everybody's Protest Art,' *Antioch Review* 44 (Summer 1986), pp. 261–75.

Harris, Trudier, 'On *The Color Purple*, Stereotypes and Silence,' *Black American Literature Forum* 18.4 (1984), pp. 155–61.

Hernton, Calvin, C., 'Who's Afraid of Alice Walker?' *The Sexual Mountain and Black Women Writers: Sex, Literature and Real Life* (New York: Anchor-Doubleday, 1987), pp. 1–36.

Hoogland, Renée C., 'Heterosexual Screening: Lesbian Studies,' in Smelik and Buikema, pp. 119–34.

hooks, bell, 'Writing the Subject: Reading *The Color Purple*,' in Bloom, *Alice Walker*, pp. 215–28.

Jenkins, Candice M., 'Queering Black Patriarchy: The Salvific Wish and Masculine Possibility in Alice Walker's *The Color Purple*,' *Modern Fiction Studies* 48.4 (2002), pp. 969–1000.

Smelik, Anneke, and Rosemarie Buikema (eds), *Women's Studies and Culture: A Feminist Introduction* (New York: St. Martin's, 1995).

Stade, George, 'Womanist Fiction and Male Characters,' *Partisan Review* 52.3 (1985), pp. 264–70.

Story, Ralph D., 'Sisterhood as Salvation: Black Male Characterization in Alice Walker's *The Color Purple*,' *Journal of Popular Literature* 2.2 (1986), pp. 1–15.

ADAPTATIONS OF *THE COLOR PURPLE*

The Color Purple. Directed by Steven Spielberg. With Whoopi Goldberg, Danny Glover, Oprah Winfrey and Margaret Avery. Produced by Steven Spielberg, Quincy Jones, Kathleen Kennedy and Frank Marshall. Adapted screenplay by Menno Meyjes. Warner Brothers, 1985.

The Color Purple. Musical. Directed by Gary Griffin. Produced by Roy Furman, Quincy Jones, Scott Sanders and Oprah Winfrey, 2005.

ADAPTATIONS OF *THE COLOR PURPLE*: ARTICLES AND REVIEWS

'About the Production' (4 Apr. 2009), http://www.colorpurple.com.

Ansen, David, 'We Shall Overcome: Spielberg Takes on Rural, Matriarchal, Black Life,' review of *The Color Purple*, *Newsweek* (30 Dec. 1986), pp. 59–60.

Bardsley, Garth, 'The Color Purple Ends Broadway Run Weeks After Fantasia's Exit; Movie Version May Be On the Way' (25 Jan. 2008), http://www.mtv.com/movies/news/articles.

Brantley, Ben, 'One Woman's Awakening, in Double Time,' review of The Color Purple (2 Dec. 2005), http://theater2.nytimes.com/2005/12/02/theater/reviews.

Brook, Wendell, 'Shades of Purple from Book to Stage' (9 July 2008), http://www. accessatlanta.com/arts/content/arts/stories.

Canby, Vincent, 'From a Palette of Clichés Comes The Color Purple,' review of film version of The Color Purple, New York Times (5 Jan. 1986), Section 2, p. 17.

Crowder, Marcus. 'How The Color Purple Found Its Stage Voice' (1 Nov. 2008), http://www. sacbee.com/crowder/story.

Denby, David, 'Purple People-Eater,' review of the film version of The Color Purple, New York 19.2 (13 Jan. 1986), pp. 56–7.

Digby, Joan, 'From Walker to Spielberg: Transformations of The Color Purple,' in Peter Reynolds (ed.), Novel Images: Literature in Performance (London: Routledge, 1993), pp. 157–74.

Dworkin, Susan, 'The Strange and Wonderful Story of the Making of The Color Purple,' Ms. 14.6 (Dec. 1985), pp. 66–70, in Walker, Same River, pp. 174–82.

Kael, Pauline, 'The Color Purple,' New Yorker 61 (30 Dec. 1985), pp. 68–70.

McCarter, Jeremy, 'Metropolitan Oprah,' New York (4 Dec. 2005), http://nymag.com. nymetro/arts/theater/reviews/15230.

McMullen, Wayne C. and Martha Solomon, 'The Politics of Adaptation: Steven Spielberg's Appropriation of The Color Purple,' Text and Performance Quarterly 14 (1994), pp. 158–74.

Moody, Greg, review of the musical theatre version of The Color Purple, National Tour, Buell Theatre (3 Jan. 2009), http://cbs4denver.com/video/?id+51245@kcnc.dayport.com.

'Oprah Winfrey Presents The Color Purple: The Musical About Love' (13 Apr. 2009), http://www.colorpurple.com.

Reed, Ishmael, 'Steven Spielberg Plays Howard Beach,' Writin' and Fightin': Thirty-Seven Years of Boxing on Paper (New York: Atheneum, 1988), pp. 145–6.

Simon, John, 'Black and White in Purple,' review of film version of The Color Purple, National Review 38.2 (14 Feb. 1986), pp. 56–9.

MISCELLANEOUS WORKS CITED

Cohn, Dorrit, Transparent Minds: Narrative Modes for Presenting Consciousness in Fiction, (Princeton, NJ: Princeton University Press, 1978; reprinted 1983).

De Lauretis, Teresa, Technologies of Gender: Essays on Theory, Film, and Fiction (Bloomington: Indiana University Press, 1984).

Du Bois, W. E. B., 'Criteria of Negro Art,' in Writings, pp. 993–1002.

Du Bois, W. E. B., The Souls of Black Folk, in Writings, pp. 357–547.

Du Bois, W. E. B., 'The Talented Tenth,' in Writings, pp. 842–61.

Du Bois, W. E. B., Writings, Nathan Huggins (ed.) (New York: Library of American College, 1986).

Fowler, Alastair, 'Transformations of Genre,' in David Duff (ed.), Modern Genre Theory (Harlow: Longman, 2000), pp. 232–49.

Freud, Sigmund, 'Femininity,' The Standard Edition of the Complete Works of Sigmund Freud, Vol. 22, translated and edited by James Strachey (London: Hogarth Press, 1957), pp. 112–35.

Freud, Sigmund, 'Material and Sources of Dreams,' The Interpretation of Dreams, translated by James Strachey (Middlesex: Penguin, 1980), pp. 247–380.

Freud, Sigmund, 'On Narcissism: An Introduction,' Standard Edition, Vol. 14, pp. 73–102.

Frye, Northrop, A Natural Perspective: The Development of Shakespearean Comedy and Romance (New York: Columbia University Press), 1965.

Gates, Henry Louis, Jr., 'Introduction,' in Reading, pp. 1–17.

Gates, Henry Louis, Jr., *Loose Canons: Notes on the Culture Wars* (New York: Oxford University Press, 1992.

Gates, Henry Louis, Jr. (ed.), *Reading Black, Reading Feminist* (New York: Meridian, 1990).

Gates, Henry Louis, Jr., 'The Trope of the Talking Book,' *Signifying*, pp. 127–69.

Gurkin Altman, Janet, *Epistolarity: Approaches to a Form* (Columbus: Ohio State University Press, 1982).

Hughes, Langston, 'Final Fear,' in *Simple Speaks His Mind* (New York: Simon and Schuster, 1950).

Humm, Maggie (ed.), *Feminisms: A Reader* (New York: Harvester), 1992.

Hurston, Zora Neale, *Their Eyes Were Watching God* (London: Virago Press, 1996).

Hymer, Sharon, 'Narcissistic Friendships,' *Psychoanalytic Review* 71 (1984), pp. 423–39.

Irigaray, Luce, *This Sex Which Is Not One*, translated by Carolyn Burke and Catherine Porter (Ithaca, NY: Cornell University Press, 1985).

Lacan, Jacques, *Écrits*, translated by Alan Sheridan (London: Tavistock, 1977).

Lévi-Strauss, Claude, *The Elementary Structures of Kinship*, 2nd edn, translated by James Hurle Bell et al. (Oxford: Beacon Press, 1969).

Morrison, Toni, *The Bluest Eye*, 1970 (London: Picador-Macmillan, 1990).

Ong, Walter J., *Orality and Literacy: The Technologizing of the Word*, 1982 (London: Routledge, 2002).

Pfaelzer, Jean, 'The Impact of Political Theory on Narrative Structures,' in Kenneth Roemer (ed.), *America as Utopia* (New York: Franklin, 1981), pp. 117–32.

Rimmon-Kenan, Shlomith, *Narrative Fiction: Contemporary Poetics*, New Accents (London: Routledge, 1983).

Shengold, Leonard, *Soul Murder: The Effects of Childhood Abuse and Deprivation* (New Haven: Yale University Press, 1989).

Strombeck, Andrew, 'The Conspiracy of Masculinity in Ishmael Reed,' *African American Review* 40.2 (2006), pp. 299–311.

Williams, Sherley Anne, 'Some Implications of Womanist Theory,' in Gates, *Reading*, pp. 68–75.

Winnicott, D. W., *The Maturational Processes and the Facilitating Environment* (New York: International Universities, 1965).

Winnicott, D. W., *Playing and Reality* (London: Tavistock, 1971).

Woolf, Virginia, *The Pargiters: The Novel-Essay Portion of 'The Years,'* Mitchell Leaska (ed.) (New York: Harvest-Harcourt, Brace, Jovanovich, 1978).

Index

Abbandonato, Linda, 53–4, 135–7
African-American women's writing,
    4–5, 112, 114, 115–22
Africa, representation of in *The Color
    Purple*, 2–3, 11–15, 32–4, 37–40,
    43–4, 49, 55–7, 60, 74, 78–87, 91,
    97, 106, 115, 122
Albert, representation of, 8, 11, 23, 30,
    33, 89, 91, 98–9, 114–15, 126,
    128–32, 138
American South, 11, 53, 74–5, 79–80,
    87, 91, 98, 102, 110, 126, 131–2
Angelou, Maya, 4, 113–14
    I Know Why the Caged Bird Sings,
    113–14
Atwood, Margaret, (*The Handmaid's
    Tale*), 41

Babb, Valerie, 52–6
Baldwin, James, 74
Berlant, Lauren, 76–80, 83–4, 99–101
Bildungsroman, 40, 43–4
Bloom, Harold, 118–19
blues, 1, 12, 25, 28, 30–4, 48, 78, 135
Bracks, Lean'tin, 80–3
Brontë, Charlotte (*Jane Eyre*), 40, 44
Brouwer, Liesbeth, 128
Brown, Tony, 125, 135
Butler-Evans, Elliott, 74, 106, 135
Byerman, Keith, 28–30, 32–4, 74, 97–9

Canby, Vincent, 20
capitalism, 24, 29, 33, 38, 91–103
Celie, 1–2, 6, 8, 10–15, 18, 22–5, 30–8,
    40–4, 48, 50–6, 58, 60, 97–8,
    100–2, 139–40
    as narrator and writer, 48–52, 56–60
    physical appearance of, 70, 108–9
    reader's identification with, 53, 61,
    75, 97, 106, 144
characters in *The Color Purple*,
    conception of, 7–8, 142
Chaucer, Geoffrey, 109–10
Cheung, King-Kok, 50, 110, 129

Christian, Barbara, 19, 134
civil rights movement, 3–4
Cixous, Hélène, 111
class identity, 9, 12, 22, 38, 74, 77,
    91–103
Cohn, Dorrit, 9–10
Collins, Gina Michelle, 110–12
colonialism, 10, 77, 81–8

Davis, Thadious M., 61–2
Digby, Joan, 19, 20
Dix, Carl, 79, 90–1, 125
Du Bois, W. E. B., 64, 78, 80, 83, 87, 93,
    132–3

Early, Gerald L., 12–13
Ellis, Deborah, 109–10
Ellison, Ralph, 57, 75
Elsley, Judy, 64–6, 104, 116
ending of *The Color Purple*, 12–13, 30,
    33–4, 42, 46, 62, 64, 89, 91, 94–6,
    102, 120, 133, 138
epistolary tradition, 27, 30, 37–46, 50–1
'Everyday Use', 4

fairy tale, 9, 28, 30–2, 43, 86, 140
feminism, Walker on, 4, 105
feminist criticism on *The Color Purple*, 15,
    64–6, 92–3, 104–22
Fifer, Elizabeth, 3, 5–6
film of *The Color Purple*, 6, 19–24, 76,
    123–7, 143–4
folk tale, 28, 30, 32–3, 141
free indirect discourse, 56–60
French, Marilyn, (*The Women's Room*),
    130
Freud, Sigmund, 68–70, 113–14, 118,
    136–7
Froula, Christine, 112–15

Gates, Henry Louis, Jr, 37, 43, 49, 54,
    56–60, 104, 116–17
gender politics in *The Color Purple*,
    123–40

generic identity of *The Color Purple*, 27–47
Graham, Maryemma, 11–12, 61, 82, 90, 95, 129, 135

Hall, James, C., 118
Hamilton, Cynthia, 92–4, 96–7
Harpo, representation of, 30, 78–9, 99, 114–15, 128–9, 131–3
Harris, Trudier, 13–16, 21, 48, 50, 71, 108–9, 133–43
Hawthorne, Nathaniel, 70
'To Hell With Dying', 3
Henderson, Mae G., 42–3
Hernton, Calvin C., 37–9, 41–2, 127–8
historical novel, *The Color Purple* as, 7, 12–13, 28, 30, 33–4, 39, 42, 51, 79–84, 94–5, 114–15
Hite, Molly, 5, 34–7, 121–2
Hoogland, Renée C., 138–41
hooks, bell, 1, 15, 27, 39–42, 50–1, 74, 96–7, 111, 130, 137–8
Hughes, Langston, 3
Humm, Maggie, 104
Hurston, Zora Neale, 3, 15, 34–5, 56–60, 75, 107, 116–22
    Dust Tracks on a Road, 120
    Mules and Men, 117
    Jonah's Gourd Vine, 118, 120–1
    Their Eyes Were Watching God, 34–5, 56–60, 107, 117–22
Hymer, Sharon, 68

identity, corporeal, 62–73, 100, 137
    fragmentation of, 61–6, 68–72
incest in *The Color Purple*, 21, 71–2, 130, 136, 138, 143
Irigaray, Luce, 65–6

Jacobs, Harriet, 38
Jenkins, Candice M., 130–3
Joannou, Maroula, 28, 50, 97, 106, 109
Jones, Anita, 21, 125, 135
Jones, Quincy, 19, 24–5

Kael, Pauline, 19, 20, 123
Kaplan, Carla, 107–8
Kaplan, Cora, 74–5
Katz, Tamar, 15, 40
Kauffman, Linda S., 40–2, 51–2

King, Lovalerie, 106–7, 145
Kingston, Maxine Hong (*The Woman Warrior: Memories of a Girlhood Among Ghosts*), 49–50, 110

Lacan, Jacques, 61, 66–9
Lauret, Maria, 5, 27, 43–4, 51, 54, 67
Leder, Priscilla, 116
Lessing, Doris (*The Golden Notebook*), 41
Light, Alison, 75–6, 104
literacy in *The Color Purple*, 37, 42, 49–56, 60, 119, 145
Lorde, Audre, 134

Marvin, Thomas F., 31–2, 34
Marx, Karl, 90
Mary Agnes, representation of, 30, 32, 77–8, 87, 111
McMullen, Wayne C., 22–4
Meridian, 4, 126
Meyjes, Menno, 19
Morrison, Toni, 45, 80, 94, 96, 104
    Beloved, 5
    The Bluest Eye, 94–5
musical of *The Color Purple*, 6, 24–6, 143–4

National Book Award, 1, 4
Naylor, Gloria, 127, 134
Nettie, representation of, 10–11, 13, 16, 31, 36, 38–9, 44–6, 52–6, 71–3, 77, 80, 82–7, 91, 94–5, 100, 118, 121, 136

O'Connor, Flannery, 3
Oedipus Complex, 68–9, 72–3, 120, 136–7
orality in *The Color Purple*, 32, 40, 43, 49–60, 119

plot of *The Color Purple*, 1–2, 9, 16–17, 36, 40, 42, 46, 73, 139, 145
Possessing the Secret of Joy, 5
Powers, Peter Kerry, 101–2
Proudfit, Charles L., 70–3
Pryse, Marjorie, 40, 116
psychoanalytic criticism, 66–73
Pulitzer Prize, 1, 13

quilting, 4, 7, 32, 65–6, 104, 115–16

racial politics in *The Color Purple*, 74–88
Raynaud, Claudine, 44, 145
realist novel, *The Color Purple* as, 4, 9, 11,
  16, 28–9, 31, 44, 121, 140
Reed, Ishmael, 57, 124
Richardson, Samuel, 17, 40–1
  Clarissa, 40
  Pamela, 17, 40
Rimmon-Kenan, Shlomith, 57
Romance, *The Color Purple* as, 34–7
Ross, Daniel W., 66–70
Rukeyser, Muriel, 3

Sadoff, Dianne F., 118–21
*The Same River Twice: Honoring the
  Difficult*, 19, 24, 125, 142–3
Sapphire (*Push*), 145
Scholl, Diane Gabrielsen, 34, 40
'In Search of our Mothers' Gardens'
  (essay), 54, 110
*In Search of our Mothers' Gardens:
  Womanist Prose*, 4, 105, 115
Selzer, Linda, 82–8
sentimental novel, 27, 40, 43, 75
sexuality, heterosexual, 2, 44, 118,
  120–1, 136–7, 140
  lesbian, 19, 24–5, 44, 63, 130, 140
Shakespeare, William, 35–6
Shange, Ntozake, 134
Shengold, Leonard, 71
Shug Avery, representation of, 8, 21,
  30–1, 33–4, 63, 67–70, 72, 79–80,
  95, 107, 112, 117, 124, 129, 134–40
silence, 15, 39, 41–2, 49–50, 63–4, 73–4,
  80, 108–10, 113–14, 117
slave narrative, *The Color Purple* as, 27,
  37–42, 49, 51, 127–8, 141
slavery, 37–42, 76, 81, 98, 102, 106,
  127–8
Smith, Barbara, 135
Smith, Dinitia, 10–11, 79
Sofia, representation of, 1, 11–12, 16,
  25, 32–4, 39–40, 63–6, 77, 79, 85,
  87, 89, 98, 108, 111–12, 115–16,
  131

Solomon, Martha, 22–4
Spielberg, Steven, 6, 19–20, 24–5
Stade, George, 129
Steinem, Gloria, 5, 9–10, 13–15, 48, 81,
  108, 125, 142
Story, Ralph D., 123–5
Strauss, Claude-Lévi, 136

Tavormina, Teresa, 116
The Temple of My Familiar, 5
theological discourses in *The Color Purple*,
  18, 29, 31–4, 36, 84, 101–2, 118,
  139, 141, 148, n. 48
The Third Life of Grange Copeland, 4
Toomer, Jean, (*Cane*), 4
Towers, Robert, 9–10, 48, 121
Truth, Sojourner, 8

Uncle Tom's Cabin (Harriet Beecher
  Stowe), 17, 75
Utopian dimension of *The Color Purple*,
  12–13, 28–30, 39, 84, 89, 97–9,
  101, 107, 133, 141

Walker, Alice
  life of, 2–6, 142–3
  on authorial status, 7–8, 142
  on conception and writing of *The Color
    Purple*, 7–8, 116
  on film of *The Color Purple*, 24
  on reception of *The Color Purple*, 5, 13,
    125, 143
Walker, Melissa, 79–80, 94–6
Wall, Wendy, 62–4
Walsh, Margaret, 30–1
Watkins, Mel, 11, 123–4, 132–3
Weisenburger, Steven C., 16–19
Wesley, Richard, 126–7
Williams, Carolyn, 44–6
Williams, Sherley Anne, 105, 129
Willis, Susan, 96–7
Winfrey, Oprah, 25
womanism, 4–5, 7, 28–9, 105–7, 129,
  145
Woolf, Virginia, 113–15, 119
Wright, Richard, 75, 131

Bryn Mawr Greek Commentaries

Aristophanes'
Clouds

Laura S. Barnard

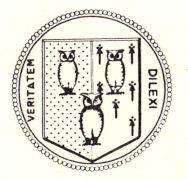

VERITATEM DILEXI